The Hermeneutics of Election

The Significance of the Doctrine in Barth's Church Dogmatics

Douglas R. Sharp

UNIVERSITY
PRESS OF
AMERICA

Lanham • New York • London

Copyright © 1990 by
University Press of America®, Inc.
4720 Boston Way
Lanham, Maryland 20706

3 Henrietta Street
London WC2E 8LU England

Library of Congress Cataloging-in-Publication Data

Sharp, Douglas R., 1949-
The hermeneutics of election : the significance of the doctrine
in Barth's Church dogmatics / Douglas R. Sharp.
p.   cm.
Includes bibliographical references.
1. Election (Theology)–History of doctrines–20th century.
2. Barth, Karl, 1886-1968. Kirchliche Dogmatik.
I. Title.
BT809.S42   1990   234—dc20   90–41775 CIP

ISBN 0–8191–7944–2 (alk. paper)
ISBN 0–8191–7945–0 (pbk.:alk. paper)

The paper used in this publication meets the minimum requirements of
American National Standard for Information Sciences—Permanence
of Paper for Printed Library Materials, ANSI Z39.48–1984.

For Linda,

whose life and love

and self-giving

are indeed a medium

of God's self-giving

Table of Contents

Preface

As with many erstwhile ideas and projects, this particular study had its origins in the most innocent of circumstances. I was engaged in teaching and administration in Berkeley California when I took up a disciplined study of Karl Barth's theology. In some respects, it was strange that I had been so long in coming to Barth, and I confess that it was his view of Scripture that initially piqued my interest. At the time, I was pursuing a study of the historical and theological development of the doctrine of Scripture, intending to write my doctoral dissertation on that topic. However, I had first to complete my comprehensive examinations, and Barth was one of the two major contemporary theologians whose work was to be the subject of one of these. With Barth's view of Scripture as my point of access, I began the torturous movement through the world of the *Church Dogmatics*. The more I progressed, the more I discovered how radical Barth's theological proposals actually were. I found myself becoming increasingly more preoccupied with both the foundations and rubrics of his theology, and the copious literature his theological work had engendered. Furthermore, it seemed to me there was something at work in the development of Barth's dogmatics that had been slighted or depreciated by his interpreters, and through an unexpected turn of circumstances, I chose to formalize my curiosity by committing my dissertation research to this area of inquiry. The present study constitutes a revision of that dissertation.

This is not an introduction to Barth's theology. On the contrary, the analysis and interpretation offered here presupposes a fairly high degree of familiarity with Barth's writings in general and the *Church Dogmatics* in particular, as well as the growing corpus of secondary literature to which this work is designed to contribute. Persons who desire to be exposed to Barth's theology are ill advised to use this study as the principal mechanism for their first encounter with the ideational world of his theology. Such inquirers should begin straightaway with Barth himself, no matter how intimidating and demanding such a study may appear and continue to be. On the other hand, it is hoped that those for whom the second or subsequent coming to Barth is mediated by this study will find here a mode of inquest and exhibition which lends both greater accessibility to Barth's writings and a different framework from within which to engage and evaluate his constructive theological proposals.

It is necessary that something be said regarding the appearance of quotations here from the English translation of Barth's work. In the dissertation, Barth was quoted in the original German in order to allow the structure and nuance of his argument as well as his peculiarly unique vocabulary to be exhibited in all their ingenious vitality. However, in order to make this study available to persons who do not read German, I thought it was necessary that his original words appear in translation. Initially I intended to provide my own translations for the simple reason that, in my judgment, the English *Church Dogmatics* suffers in quality from the fact that something of that argument and vocabulary is indeed lost in translation. This is understandable, given the fact that over the course of the fifteen years during which the English translations of the *Church Dogmatics* appeared, a total of eighteen different translators had a hand in the work. Even under the close editorial supervision of G.W. Bromiley and T.F. Torrance, the uniformity of translation remained a laudable but elusive goal. Nevertheless, we all are certainly indebted to them and to the translators for making such an enormous piece of scholarship accessible to the English speaking world. In spite of its weaknesses, I have chosen to use their translation for yet another simple reason: I wish to encourage the non-German readers of this study to examine Barth's work for themselves, and for those serious students of his theology, to scrutinize the larger contexts from within which the various quotations are gleaned. Had I provided my own translations, I fear that, because mine would have been quite different in many places, such readers would have greater difficulty in both locating the passages in question within the *Church Dogmatics* and discerning my sense of the relation between the quotation and its larger context.

A result of this decision is the unfortunate appearance of quotations marked by the use of exclusive language with reference to God, the discrete persons of the trinity and humankind. Barth frequently emphasizes a point in these areas with the use of possessive and reflexive nouns, pronouns and adjectives, all of which appear in the English translation with masculine forms. A similar fate overtakes Barth's use of such otherwise inclusive words as *Mensch* and *Alle*. While the translators' selection of inauspicious English alternatives for German terms obviously dates the existing translation (and even Barth's own work to some extent), it is hoped that the appearance of these English quotations here will not inordinately offend our present sensibilities regarding the necessity for inclusive language. In the text of the present study, every effort has been made to use words and expressions that evoke an inclusive awareness of both deity and humanity.

Throughout the course of this study, the footnotes will refer the reader to germane disscussions in both the Barth corpus and the secondary literature. In the interests of space considerations, all works are cited in these notes with abbreviated titles. Readers should consult the *List of Abbreviations* for full title and author's name, and the bibliography for complete publication data.

It is customary in a work such as this for an author to offer the disclaimer that, while many others have been instrumental in forging and refining the ideas given expression in the work, still the notions contained therein remain the sole responsibility of the author. This is certainly true here, but it is somewhat difficult to offer such a disclaimer for several reasons. First, those who have been most helpful to me have exercised this role through their own published works. Many of these have taken Barth's theology, or some fragment or dimension thereof, as their principle object of investigation, and the appearance of their works in the bibliography here is tantamount to the acknowledgement of my debt to them. However, more often than not, I found myself on the opposite side of the position being advanced in the discussion, and thus their instrumentality tended to take on a rather dialectical form. Second, many others have engaged theological issues and questions with me over the years, both in conversation and in writing, quite apart from those roused by the study of Barth. Though their influence is less noticeable in the pages that follow, and their published works not included in the bibliography, still these persons are no less significant in their contribution to the formation of my theological sensibilities, values and movements. Their instrumentality is quite expansive, exceeding the boundaries demarcating the study of a solitary 20th Century theologian. The debt I owe to these, and therefore my acknowledgement to them, only grows with each passing year. Third, there are many students whose interest in Barth was founded, amazingly enough, in the distress I inflicted upon them by requiring that they read Barth in some of my classes in theology and ministry. Thankfully, none of these has yet to emerge as a Barthian, and perhaps for that very reason the students' insights and questions which sometimes lay overgrown with confusion and blameless intransigence have contributed immeasurably to my own thinking once the cluttered landscape had been cleared. Their instrumentality always provokes a fresh reading, unshrouded by the *a posteriori* judgments so characteristic of academic scholars and interpreters, among whom I am so often fearful to classify myself.

Nevertheless, because of the particular role he played in the origin and development of this study, there is one individual whom I feel compelled to single out for special acknowledgement, and this one is Benjamin A. Reist of San Francisco Theological Seminary and the Graduate Theological Union. It was the "No" of his understandable disinterest in my original dissertation topic, and the "Yes" of his concise response to my innocuous question of "what if...?" that prompted me to immerse myself in the Barth corpus (in the original German, no less) for the next several years. But it was also his patience, understanding and support across the miles that redeemed the project after several personal crises, a relocation to the Chicago area and a false start had all but drained what little energy and enthusiasm remained in me. His veracity and candor challenged and motivated me to do what seemed impossible, and so it is to him that I confess a profound sense of gratitude, and of him that I acknowledge an inestimable contribution.

In the beginning, and in the end, but especially all the way through, the labor of this study as well as my sometimes failing creativity and stamina were buttressed by the confidence, belief and love of my wife Linda, to whom this book is dedicated with enduring affection and respect. She alone is chief among those who shared the agony and ecstacy of this work, and she accomplished this without typing a single word of the manuscript and while completing a rigorous undergraduate degree at the University of Chicago. Without her, this work would never have been completed. She, too, suffered the distress and grief of dislocation from our many friends and family in the Bay Area, but through it all she has shown herself to be a person of great strength and character, more resilient and tenacious than others whose accomplishments have been widely celebrated.

There are many others who have been instrumental in making possible the publication of this study, and these too must be acknowledged. I am particularly grateful to President Ian M. Chapman and the trustees of Northern Baptist Theological Seminary for a sabbatical leave that provided the otherwise unavailable time for the revisions of the original dissertation as well as several other writing projects. I am especially indebted to those at Northern who were generously willing to discharge my administrative responsibilities during my absence, even while modems and telephones rendered me anything but inaccessible. Among these, Bobbie Kincaid, Irene Taylor, Miriam Mendez, Pat Slowik, Eric Ohlmann and David Nichols must be singled out especially for having gone beyond the call of duty.

Finally, special word of appreciation must also be extended to my teaching assistant, Karen Wells, without whom the burden of preparing the manuscript and submitting it to the publisher in a timely fashion would have been too much to bear. In her own right, Karen is a specialist in medieval history, Shakespeare, modern fiction, college basketball and professional baseball. These loves of her life have endeared her not only to me, but also to my colleagues on the faculty and staff as well as the generations of students whose paths have intersected the life and mission of Northern while Karen has pursued her Master of Divinity degree. She has known suffering and anguish beyond what she should otherwise have to bear, but through it all she has endured with a resolve that would shame stronger persons. The hours we have spent discussing the social, political, economic and ecclesiastical effects of the idiosyncracies of the Elizabethans and Victorians have been some of the most profitable hours

Preface

I have spent in theological education. But no less stimulating have been the hours occupied with prognostications concerning the NCAA Final Four and the likelihood that the Chicago Cubs will finish the season somewhere out of the cellar. To Karen, I owe a debt of gratitude that may or may not be repayable; only the passage of time and the course of our future paths will tell.

Introduction

A. The Main Contention

The present investigation is an attempt to demonstrate the contention that it is the doctrine of election that constitutes the structural as well as hermeneutical key to the *Church Dogmatics*. One may well observe that in Barth's exposition of the doctrine in *C.D. II,2* there are substantive suggestions which anticipate the direction of his doctrinal construction in the subsequent volumes. However, after engaging Barth's doctrine of election, it is a strategic mistake to leave the doctrine behind as one presses on to interact with the other, seeming more important doctrines (i.e., creation in Vol. III and reconciliation in Vol. IV). This investigation is oriented by the fact that it can be shown that Barth's view of election supports and determines to a considerable extent the structure and content of his dogmatics as a whole. This is to say that the themes, emphases and method of analysis and construction that come to expression in the doctrine of election are in no small part the determining factors in the construction of the *Church Dogmatics*, and that without these factors the infrastructure and dogmatic development of the work would fall apart.

Our contention that the doctrine of election is the hermeneutical key to Barth's dogmatics emerges from the fact that election is preeminently *the decisive noetic category* in his thinking and, therefore, in his doctrinal construction. It is God's act of election, executed in eternity and in time, that constitutes the origin, substance and purpose of God's self-revelation and self-impartation to God's creatures, and as such it constitutes the means of our knowledge of God. In Barth's construction, it is election which is the prior category whose terms interpret, delimit and determine the reality and therefore our understanding of revelation, God, christology, creation, humanity, reconciliation and redemption. In short, Barth redefines election as the revelation of God in Jesus Christ as the incarnate Word; the noetic category of election determines the characteristic confluence of "revelation," "Word of God," "incarnation" and "knowledge of God" in the concrete event which is Jesus Christ. In Barth's construction, election is identical with the revelation of God in its concrete form, and revelation is identical with election in its concrete content. Because the election of Jesus Christ is the event of incarnation, and because election is the means of the knowledge of God, election can be seen as the act of God at the center of the knowledge of God, and therefore at the center of the dogmatic exposition of that knowledge. Election thereby is constituted as the noetic key and the controlling element in the arrangement and exposition of the knowledge of God.

The relation between epistemology and election on the one hand, and christology and election on the other, is centrally important to the understanding of Barth's doctrine. The general context in which Barth develops the doctrine is unquestionably epistemological. The fundamental element which determines this is the fact that Barth thinks of God in the act of election as equivalent to God in the act of self-revelation. Now it is well known that in Barth's view, Jesus Christ constitutes the focus and reality of both God's revelation and election, and it is therefore legitimate to speak of the christological determination of revelation and election in Barth's theology. But the issue which remains has to do with the noetic significance of the correlation of christology and election, and the extent to which this determines the construction of the doctrine of election. The reason why Jesus Christ plays such an expansive role in the doctrine of election is not simply that of Barth's tendency to orient and fix the form and content of dogmatic matters in terms of christology, and to develop these matters and their direction in strict relation to christological concerns. While every substantive component of the doctrine of election appears to have its point of departure in the person and work of Jesus Christ, it is not simply a matter of Barth's making a methodological decision to undertake the exposition of election from the point of view and in terms of christology. Rather the reason has to do with the fact that the self-revelation of God which effects the knowledge of God and which comes to expression in dogmatics has its origin, basis and goal in God's eternal act of election which is executed concretely in the incarnation of the Word in Jesus Christ, and that the form and content of the knowledge of God is determined by this eternal act of election and accomplished in time in the temporal execution of this act in and through the revelation of Jesus Christ. Election is thus the *a priori*, the *prius* of the execution of God's self-revelation, and therefore of the reality of Jesus Christ. Consequently, the christological determination of the doctrine of election in particular is not an influence brought to bear upon the idea of election. Rather it is a determination which has its origin in election and which takes a peculiarly christological form. In Barth's construction, it is election which precedes christology, giving to christology its characteristic form and content, determination and qualification. In a clear sense, the dogmatic movement is from election to christology, and this movement takes place because the significance of election lies primarily in its noetic function.

In this investigation, we will contend that in its scope, structure and content, the doctrine of election has the epistemological and dogmatic function of describing and interpreting the manner in which the being and activity of God are known so that something can be said about the God who is in fact known. Because of this function, the doctrine can be shown to be the hermeneutical principle which informs the construction of Barth's theology and which must therefore be reckoned with in any sustained attempt to interpret the *Church Dogmatics*.

B. The Distinctiveness of the Investigation

Many of Barth's critics and interpreters have noted the importance of the doctrine of election and its significance for Barth's theology as a whole. Some of these have even identified election as the key to his theology,[1] while others have argued for some other idea or emphasis as the fulcrum of his dogmatic construction.[2] It can safely be said that there is not a consensus of opinion as to the dominant constructive motif in Barth's theology, with the possible exception of the almost universal observation that his theology is christologically determined with Jesus Christ as the Word of God at its center.[3] Nevertheless, it should be noted that these commentators have not critically examined the connection between the biblical-dogmatic hermeneutic informing the doctrine on the one hand, and the determination of the content and structure of the *Church Dogmatics* by the noetic function of election on the other. This observation is particularly noteworthy in light of the fact that Barth claims that his dogmatics is constructed on the basis of the biblical witness to Jesus Christ. But given the decisive role that election plays in his theology, Barth needs to be examined not only about his dogmatics as a whole, but also about the extent to which he has constructed his doctrine of election in particular on a consistent basis of biblical exegesis. Barth's construction revolves around three poles, namely the dogmatic exposition itself, the critical engagement of the history of theology and philosophy,

---

[1]See e.g., Amberg, *Christol.*, p. 133; Balthasar, *Theo. KB*, pp. 155-56, 164; Berkouwer, *Triumph*, p. 99; Come, *Preach.*, pp. 77, 136-38; Gloege, *Prädest.*, p. 194; Hausmann, *KB Doct.*, p. 45; Jenson, *Alpha*, pp. 17-18, 141-45; Jüngel, *Trinity*, p. 41; Park, *Man*, p. 1; and Woyke, *Doctrine*, pp. 95, 253.

[2]See e.g., Bloesch, *Victor*, pp. 9-22; Bouillard, *Knowledge*, p. 97; Camfield, *Ref.*, pp. 26-28; Casalis, *Portrait*, pp. 17-19, 112; Hartwell, *Theology*, pp. 15-17, 20-22; Klooster, *Signif.*, pp. 27-28; Küng, *Just.*, pp. 3-10; McLean, *Humanity*, pp. 14, 38; Mueller, *K. Barth*, pp. 50, 141; Polman, *Barth*, p. 33; Sykes, *Studies*, p. 2; Thompson, *Perspec.*, p. 10; Toon, *One*, pp. 79, 84; and Van Til, *Christian.*, pp. vii, 13-29.

[3]For works which are (or which contain) general, but useful surveys of Barth's theology, see Bolich, *KB & Evang.*; Bromiley, *Intro.*; Camfield, *Ref.*; Come, *Preach.*; Hartwell, *Theology*; Mackintosh, *Types*; Mueller, *K. Barth*; Torrance, *Early*; and Weber, *Report*.

and the exegesis of the biblical material. Barth's contention is that, while all three poles are important, it is the exegetical work that is the most important for dogmatic reflection and construction. It is therefore somewhat surprising that the relationship between exegesis and dogmatics in Barth's doctrine of election has not been more fully explored. The present investigation will attempt to correct this.

Among those who focus on the doctrine of election in their study of Barth, there is lacking a critique of the components of the doctrine of election which are generated and defined on the basis of his exegesis.[4] The substantive works on Barth's theology recognize the christological influence on the *Church Dogmatics* and the correlation of christology and election, but they are concerned more with the examination of a particular feature or perspective and its development in the *Church Dogmatics* than with the doctrine of election itself as a determinative key.[5] The deficiency of the Barth literature at this point is the failure to expose the correlation between Barth's hermeneutic and the content of the doctrine of election, and in the light of this correlation, to demonstrate the influence of this doctrine on the whole work. The present investigation will endeavor to expose this connection and the corresponding structural influence of the doctrine of election.

C. The Course of the Investigation

The intent of this study is to trace Barth's doctrine of election through the *Church Dogmatics* in order to show that election must be understood to be the essential key to the whole of Barth's theology. The investigation is divided into four parts, and will unfold in the following way:

In Part I, attention will be focused on the constructive dogmatic context out of which the doctrine of election programmatically emerges. This is the place where the material and formal matters of Barth's methodology and the structure of the *Church Dogmatics* will be examined

---

[4]E.g., see the discussions on Barth's views of double predestination, supralapsarianism, and his corrective to the *decretum absolutum* in Hausmann, *KB Doct.*; Park, *Man*; and Woyke, *Doctrine*. No attempt is made in these studies to address the question of the correlation between Barth's exegesis and his reconstruction of the doctrine. Three shorter studies make suggestions in this area, but do not carry them further than a preliminary indication (Buess, *Zur Präd.*; Gloege, *Prädest.*; and Sparn, *Revision*).

[5]E.g., Balthasar and the concept and function of "analogy" (*Theo KB*); Berkouwer and "triumphant grace" (*Triumph*); Bloesch and objectivism (*Victor*); Bouillard and the ontology of faith (*KB*); Jenson and the relation of God and history (*Alpha*); Küng and the determinative influence of "justification" (*Just.*); Thompson and christological determinism (*Perspec.*); and Van Til and Christ as *Geschichte* (*Christian.*).

as the environment in which the doctrine is drafted. In particular, Chapter One will be concerned with Barth's rationale for locating the doctrine within the doctrine of God. This exemplifies an innovation by which Barth departs from the possibilities represented by previous, more traditional constructions, and the decision to locate the doctrine here is anything but arbitrary. We will attempt to show that the logic behind this location has to do primarily with the knowledge of God and the extent to which this determines dogmatic methodology and construction. The question which will concern us here is not so much the appearance of election in the doctrine of God, but rather the extent to which the epistemological and dogmatic context of the doctrine of election is mandated for Barth by the ontic and noetic structure of the knowledge of God. More particularly, we will seek to show that the matter of location for Barth is irrevocably decided by the noetic function of election as the means of the actual knowledge of God which lies at the base of dogmatics.

The scope and structure of the doctrine of election itself will engage our attention in Part II. In Chapter Two, we will inquire into the epistemological formulation of the doctrine and set up the basic construct which will allow us to illustrate the implications of Barth's view of election for the whole of the *Church Dogmatics*. Toward this end, we will examine the nature and extent of the christological determination of election in terms of the function of election as the means of the knowledge of God. This will establish a basis for examining the extent to which the noetic function of election calls for Barth's polemical reconstruction of the doctrine which is expressed in his criticism and redefinition of the *decretum absolutum*, supra- and infralapsarianism, and double predestination. Then, in Chapter Three, we will penetrate the construct of election further by examining its extension to, and determination of, the understanding of the community and the individual. Here our attention will focus on the noetic correlation between christological determination on the one hand, and the content of the constructions of the election of the community and the individual on the other. Here we will perceive that the essential core of the extension of election is precisely the function of the community and the individual as participants in God's continuing self-disclosure. In Chapter Four, we will move into an examination of the implications of Barth's doctrine of election for cognate dogmatic matters. Here attention will be fixed on the introductory section on theological ethics in the doctrine of God. This we will examine from the point of view of the human participation in the actualization of the knowledge of God. Furthermore, in this chapter we will address the question of Barth's tendency toward universalism as an implication of the christological determination of the doctrine, and pay particular attention to the ways in which Barth understood and avoided universalism with a view toward determining whether he suggests a meaningful solution to the problem. We will also offer a preliminary description of the distinctive christology which both has its origins in election and determines the later christological construction in *C.D. IV*.

Because Barth affirms his commitment to basing dogmatics on biblical exegesis, it will be necessary to examine the exegetical support of the doctrine of election in particular. This we will do in Part III. Here we will examine the extraordinary biblical hermeneutic of election that stands in many respects as the epitome of Barth's peculiarly unique contribution to biblical hermeneutics. It is Barth's contention that the only legitimate basis for the doctrine is the biblical witness to the electing God in Jesus Christ, and it is this orientation that signals Barth's departure from the traditional formulations of the doctrine. In Chapter Five, we will investigate the nature of Barth's hermeneutic agenda for dogmatic construction and examine in particular the exegesis that supports the foundation on which the doctrine is developed. This chapter will concentrate on the biblical support for the contention that Jesus Christ is himself the electing God and the elect human. Chapter Six will examine the extension of Barth's electional hermeneutic into the construction of the election of the community and the election of the individual. Here we will find a suggestive and innovative employment of the election hermeneutic in the engagement of the biblical text. In both chapters, we will be concerned about the extent to which the development of the doctrine and the consistent use of Barth's exegetical principles are capable of establishing whether the hermeneutic supports the doctrine as it is formulated. We will take our orientation in this regard from the relation of the concepts of "elected" and "rejected." In this inquiry, we will attempt to identify the broader contribution of Barth to hermeneutics in terms of his hermeneutic of election and its tendency toward typological exegesis.

In Part IV, we reach in many respects the pinnacle of the election hermeneutic in Barth's theology. In Chapter Seven, we will show that the doctrine of election as we have come to understand it is the construct which gives significant form and content to Barth's dogmatics. In this regard, we will take up the basic construct of the doctrine developed in Part II and trace its significance and determination through the remainder of the *Church Dogmatics*. In this concluding chapter, we will proceed by identifying and investigating the form and content of those sections of *C.D. III-IV* where the dogmatic construction clearly presupposes and requires the content, emphases and structure of the prior formulation of the doctrine of election in *C.D. II:2*. In this way, it will be shown that Barth's doctrine of election constitutes the hermeneutical key to his theology, without which its internal development and infrastructure would fall away.

Part I

The Dogmatic Context

Chapter One

The Location
of the Doctrine

The specific location of the doctrine of election in Barth's *Church Dogmatics* is not without significance. Quite the contrary. However novel it may appear, the doctrine of election can in theory be located anywhere along the sweep of dogmatic construction, depending on the particular orientation one may take in regard to its importance in, and implication for, theological construction. It may stand alone, in isolation, unrelated to the larger themes of theology; or it may be subsumed under some grander doctrinal category, where it plays a supportive, but nonetheless limited and relative role in theological reflection; or it may stand beside, in formative proximity to the vital centers of theology, exercising a function peculiarly unique and perhaps even out of proportion to what is commonly perceived to be its dogmatic relevance. If the doctrine of election is included in the construction of a dogmatics, it will always and forever have to defend itself against the inclination to narrowly affirm or excessively deny its fundamental importance to Christian faith. It will always and forever have to be developed within, or at least in relation to, a constructively theological environment. Given this doctrine's proclivity to obfuscation and banishment, it is all the more significant that Barth not only takes the doctrine seriously, but makes it the epistemological and therefore constructive foundation on which the whole of his dogmatic theology is formulated. In order to establish the foundation for the present investigation, we will consider in the present chapter the particular rationale promoted by Barth for locating the doctrine of election within the doctrine of God. Without question, Barth's construction represents an innovation which moves far beyond the dogmatic constellations portrayed in more traditional constructions. There is a certain logic behind Barth's decision for this location, and it is not possible to grasp either the significance of his view of election or its determination of the whole of his theology unless this logic is perceived at the outset. So it is that we must attend the methodological and constructive prolegomena to the doctrine, and in this exercise seek to arrive at an understanding of the logic of, or the basis for, the preeminent role played by the doctrine of election. What we will observe here in this prelude is the noticeable fact that election, methodologically and programmatically, has to do primarily with the knowledge of God. The question with which we shall be occupied in this chapter is the extent to which the epistemological and dogmatic context of the doctrine of election is authorized for Barth precisely by the ontic and noetic structure of the knowledge of God. What we can expect to discern in these matters is the fact that the location of the doctrine of election is settled for Barth by the function which election exercises in constituting the means of the actual knowledge of God.

A. Context: An Ontic and Noetic Rationale

It is necessary that we begin the investigation of Barth's doctrine of election with a consideration of both its immediate and larger context. The fact that the doctrine is located within, and developed in relation to, the doctrine of God directly suggests that the doctrine of election is speaking first and foremost about who God is and what God does. The appearance of the doctrine of election in the development of the doctrine of God is intended by Barth to suggest that it is not possible to know and speak about God without knowing and affirming at the same time that this One is the electing God. Election is in fact the distinctive act by which God is *who* God is. There is thus an interrelationship between the doctrine of God and the doctrine of election which requires that they be treated in intimate proximity to one another. For Barth, the doctrine of God has dogmatic priority over the doctrine of election, and as such it points to the ontic priority of the Subject of the doctrine of God. But the doctrine of election is a component of the doctrine of God because, as we will seek to show, it is precisely election which constitutes the basis for the fact that God is *who* God is, and is known by us to be this God and not another. This is to say that for Barth, the *content* of the doctrine of God has ontic priority, while the *content* of the doctrine of election has noetic priority. The arrangement of the entire doctrine of God betrays methodological considerations which we will shortly examine, but at this point our preliminary contention has to do with the fact that the location of the doctrine of election within the doctrine of God is intended to make clear the idea that the Subject of the doctrine of God is known only because of this Subject's act of election, and therefore any discussion of the Subject God in a doctrine of God must account for the fact that this Subject always was, is and will be the electing God. From God's perspective, God is first and foremost complete in Godself, with God's own ontic reality, apart from any disclosure of the divine self. It is this that constitutes the ontic priority of God which is to be maintained in the dogmatic reflection upon God. But in Barth's view, election is the divine act which has priority over all the other acts of God, and is indeed the primal self-determining and self-expressing act which constitutes the very

10

presupposition of these other acts. In Barth's construction of the doctrine, it is apparent that one is able to reflect dogmatically upon God (the ontic reality) only because God has given the divine self concretely in order that God might be known (the noetic reality), and this concrete self-giving is not only revelation, but more importantly, as we will seek to demonstrate, it is fundamentally election. Thus from our perspective, election as God's act has noetic priority, so much so for Barth that election must be treated dogmatically as a component to the doctrine of God.

In brief, this represents Barth's rationale for the inclusion of election in the doctrine of God, and we will have occasion to examine this more thoroughly as we proceed through this chapter. But this rationale itself begs the question of the context of the doctrine of God, and it would therefore be inappropriate to jump straight away into an examination of the doctrine of God as the context for the development of the doctrine of election without first giving our attention to this larger context. The fact of the matter is that the doctrine of God does not stand alone; it too has a context, the influence of which can be perceived in the structure of the doctrine as it reflects Barth's methodology and the dogmatic scheme employed in the construction of the doctrine of God and the doctrine of election. Therefore, in order to grasp the significance of the appearance of the doctrine of election within the *doctrine* of God, we must consider the structure of the *knowledge* of God articulated in the Anselm study and show how this structure determines and gives shape to the methodology employed in the dogmatic scheme, which in turn provides the larger context for the doctrine of God in the *C.D.* Only then will we be in a position to comprehend the rationale for constructing the doctrine of election from within the doctrine of God.[1]

B. The Ontic/Noetic Structure of the Knowledge of God

It is a fundamental axiom for Barth that the consideration of the actuality of the knowledge of God must precede the consideration of the possibility of such knowledge. In terms of the ontic and noetic base and structure of the doctrine of God, this axiom has its origin in Barth's study of Anselm.[2] Our concern at this point is with the way in which the study

---

[1]For the most part, the literature on Barth's doctrine of election is noticeably silent with respect to a formative discussion of the larger significance of the context of the doctrine within the doctrine of God. A small yet insightful exception to this can be found in Gunton, *Doct.*, where it is acknowledged that Barth's treatment of election in the context of the doctrine of God "forms a bridge between the Prolegomena and the later volumes" (p. 391). See also Sparn, *Revision*, pp. 45-48.

[2]See Barth, *Anselm*, p. 11; *C.D. II,1*:4; and Busch, *Life*, p. 209-11. For critical discussions of the Anselm study and its influence on Barth's theological method, see

of Anselm stimulated Barth's attempts to work out the structure of the knowledge of God in terms of the relation between its ontic and noetic aspects, and how it is that this structure came to be expressed later in the doctrine of God in *C.D. II,1.*

In his interpretation of Anselm, Barth is concerned with the meaning of *intellectus fidei,* and he understands Anselm's point of departure to consist in the presupposition of faith. By listening to Anselm, Barth came to believe that it was not legitimate to begin with human possibilities and capabilities for knowledge and understanding for the reason that this would limit and perhaps even do away with the object of faith. Rather knowledge and understanding resulted from faith which contains within itself a compulsion which drives it toward knowledge.[3] *Intelligere* thus presupposes *credere,* and what Barth is suggesting here is that faith as the intentional decision to believe (*credo*) is the preliminary and necessary step to the *intelligere* which faith seeks. This *intelligere* which issues in *intellectus fidei* and which faith is driven to seek is related to *credere* in such a way that the awareness in *credere* is joined to the assent of *intelligere,* and together they move toward *intellectus fidei.* Barth describes their distinction and relationship in this way:

> In recognizing and assenting to truth *intelligere* and *credere* come together and the *intelligere* is itself and remains a *credere* while the *credere* in and by itself,... is also an embryonic *intelligere.* But *intelligere* means still more than that: to read and ponder what has been already said--that is to say, in the appropriation of truth, actually to traverse that intervening distance (between recognition and assent) and so therefore to understand the truth as truth.[4]

It is in connection with this relationship between *credere* and *intelligere* that Barth takes up the ontic and noetic structure of the knowledge of God, and his principle concern here is with Anselm's concept of *ratio.* The *intelligere* which is sought by faith lends itself to demonstration, and what is demonstrated is the *ratio* of faith.[5] This *ratio* is not intended to prove faith, or function as the foundation or requirement for faith. Rather this demonstration is a result of the *intelligere* which faith is driven from within itself to seek. What Barth is contending for here is the idea that the demonstration of the *ratio* of faith

---

Balthasar, *Theo. KB,* pp. 127-47; Bouillard, *KB,* vol. I, pp. 134-48 and vol II, pp. 147-70; Charlesworth, *Proslog.,* pp. 40-46; Hartwell, *Theology,* pp. 42-48; Parker, *Karl Barth,* pp. 69-82; Prenter, *Glauben,* pp. 176-92; and Torrance, *Early,* pp. 180-98.
[3]Barth, *Anselm,* pp. 16-19, 39-40, 171.
[4]Ibid., p. 40; see also pp. 24-25.
[5]Ibid., pp. 14-16.

follows upon the *intelligere* which is sought by faith, and it is this *ratio* that points to the ontic and noetic structure of *intelligere* as the knowledge of God. The *ratio* itself is not the proof, ground or end desired by faith. Rather, as *credere* issues in *intelligere*, *ratio* is the ontic and noetic structure of faith itself.

Barth is concerned about the structure of the knowledge of God, not because there are questions concerning the possibility of such knowledge, but because there is the actuality of the knowledge in faith, and because something is given to be known in the *credo* of faith which drives toward *intelligere*. The principle concern is to *demonstrate* faith, not in the sense of proving faith, or setting up its basis, or establishing its ends, but in the sense of *showing* its actuality in terms of the structure of the knowledge of faith. With Anselm, Barth distinguishes three forms of *ratio*.[6] First, there is noetic *ratio* which is the knowing *ratio* peculiar to the knower and which has to do with the rationality of the knower. This noetic *ratio* is the human side of knowledge, the subjective *ratio*. Second, there is ontic *ratio* which is that which belongs to the known object and which renders it accessible as knowable to the knower. This is objective *ratio*. In making the distinction between these first two forms of *ratio*, Barth is positioning himself inside faith and addressing the structure of the actual knowledge of God. In the first form, he is concerned with the subject *of faith*, with the noetic *ratio* of the one who believes, or the *fides qua creditur*; in the second form, he is concerned with the object *of faith*, with the ontic *ratio* of that which is believed, or the *fides quae creditur*. This correlation of the noetic *ratio* and the ontic *ratio* points toward the third form which is of particular concern to Barth, namely the *ratio veritatis* or the *ratio Dei*. Of this form, Barth says:

> Strictly understood the *ratio veritatis* is identical with the *ratio summae naturae*, that is with the divine Word consubstantial with the Father. It is the *ratio* of God. It is not because it is *ratio* that it has truth but because God, Truth, has it.... The following holds good only of all those other *rationes* with which the *ratio Dei* is not identical but which as the *ratio* of his creation participate in the *ratio Dei*: Truth is not bound to it but it is bound to Truth.[7]

The *ratio Dei* thus stands as the *a priori* of the ontic and noetic *rationes*. Through the agency of the Word, God creates these *rationes* and bestows upon them an actual correspondence to the truth which enables

---

[6]See Barth's interpretation of Anselm's views on *ratio* in ibid., pp. 44-59. So far as our present purpose is concerned, this section represents the heart of Barth's treatment of Anselm.

[7]Ibid., pp. 45-46.

them to participate in the *ratio Dei*. The truth of the ontic and noetic *rationes* is thus conferred by the Truth, God. Whether the truth of the ontic *ratio* conforms to the *ratio Dei* is something which is decided and determined in the creation of the object by the Word.[8] However, the truth of the noetic *ratio* is the truth of the knowing subject, and it stands in relation to the ontic *ratio* of the object of faith; its truth is dependent upon the ontic *ratio*, and it must ever and again become truth: "The way in which the right use of the human *ratio* is determined primarily by its object is therefore, as it were, only the operation by means of which Truth, that is God himself, makes this decision."[9]

By virtue of their creation by the Word, the ontic and noetic *rationes* resemble, are bound to and depend upon the *ratio Dei*. With respect to the ontic *ratio* of the object of faith, the truth actually inheres in a standing way by virtue of its creation. But with respect to the noetic *ratio* of the knowing subject, this occurs only as God chooses again and again to confer the truth upon the subject. When this decision is made, the noetic *ratio* recognizes the *ratio veritatis* in the ontic *ratio*; the *ratio Dei* becomes the *ratio fidei* in the knowing subject.

The point here is that in the *ratio fidei*, there is effected a conformity of the noetic *ratio* to the ontic *ratio* under the creative *ratio Dei*, and it is this conformity which is of decisive significance for Barth when it comes to the actual knowledge of God. It is this conformity which exposes the structure of the knowledge of God in ontic and noetic terms. It is the *ratio* common to both the ontic and the noetic that makes it possible for them to resemble and conform to one another and to the *ratio Dei* in the act of knowing.[10]

In the act of knowledge, the ontic always precedes the noetic, and behind the noetic *ratio* of the knowing subject stands the ontic *ratio* of the known object, both of which are bound to the *ratio Dei*, the Word and Truth which is God.[11] "Ratio" is the structure of the relationship among the three forms, and "truth" is the conformity of one to the other as this results from God's decision to allow the *ratio Dei* to be reflected in that relationship. The quest for knowledge consists in the drive within faith to go back across the way already traversed in the movement of conformity from the object of faith to the knowledge of faith, from the ontic *ratio* to the knowing of the noetic *ratio*. This quest consists in the reflection upon the object of faith in order that the object may be demonstrated, and in this way, known in faith as it is believed in faith. In the movement of traversing back across this way, or this structure, one "achieves true

---

[8]Ibid., pp. 46-47.
[9]Ibid., p. 46.
[10]Ibid., p. 47.
[11]Barth demonstrates this order in a sequence of tightly-knit propositions which are concerned with the way Anselm correlated *ratio* and *necessitas* (ibid., pp. 47-53).

noetic *ratio*, a real comprehension of the ontic *ratio* of the object of faith; he attains to the *intellectus fidei*."[12]

The actuality of the knowledge of God begins with the *credo* of the believer which is a volitional response to God's self-revelation, an act of confession in which the object of faith is acknowledged and affirmed. Because faith is bound to its object, it is driven to know and understand its object, and the *intellectus fidei* which results bears the structure of the confluence of the ontic and noetic *rationes* and the *ratio Dei*. True knowledge of God can consist only in the meditation on the object of faith, and in this meditation, the task given to faith is "actually to traverse that intervening distance (between recognition and assent) and so therefore to understand the truth as truth."[13]

From this brief look at Barth's study of Anselm, we can identify the following elements as vital components to Barth's view of the structure of the knowledge of God. (1) It is the very essence of faith to seek understanding, and the relation of faith and knowledge is one in which faith is the presupposition of understanding; knowledge assumes and requires faith, and the *credo* must precede the *intellectum*. (2) Faith is a decision in which one says "*credo*" in response to the decision of God to make Godself known. As the response to hearing God's self-revelation, faith is rational in so far as it corresponds to its object, the Word of God. For faith to move toward understanding, it must exercise the noetic *ratio* in reflection upon the ontic *ratio*, and in this way penetrate further into the reality of the object. (3) This movement is possible only in so far as the knowing subject adheres strictly to the object. In the quest for understanding, faith is noetically and ontically constrained only by its object, being bound to it and to follow after it. (4) Theology can only be understood as the exercise of faith in following after its object. As *fides quaerens intellectum*, theology stands on the *credo* which has its origin in the Word, enabling that penetration into the reality of its object, reflecting on the actuality of its object as it is given to be known, and describing the possibility of the knowledge of its object as this can be seen only in the light of the actuality of the knowledge. Theology, therefore, assumes the actuality of the knowledge of God, for its task is not only the quest for deeper, more explicit knowledge, but also the reflection upon that object which is given to faith to know.

C. The Dogmatic Scheme

With these elements in Barth's view before us, we need now to

---

[12]Ibid., p. 55. See also p. 53.
[13]Ibid., p. 40.

give our attention to the manner in which these methodological values found their way into his constructive theology, and thereby take a further step toward setting the context of the doctrine of election. For Barth's theological program, the Anselm study marks the radical change of course taken between the appearance of *Die christliche Dogmatik im Entwurf* in 1927 and the publication of the *Church Dogmatics I,1* in 1932. Our immediate concern will therefore be with the dogmatic scheme to the extent that it is itself an important element in establishing the context of the doctrine of God. It is this scheme which to a great extent provides the structure for the *Church Dogmatics*, and as such it magnifies the important methodological aspects of the task and center of dogmatics.[14] The question of the location of the doctrine of election is a decisive, methodological question which helps bring into focus the nature of dogmatics as carried out by Barth.

For Barth, dogmatics is concerned with the content and truth of the Church's peculiar talk about God, and the question as to whether that talk conforms to the reality of Jesus Christ as the basis, goal and content of the Church's talk.[15] Dogmatics neither finds nor creates the standard by which this conformity is to be assessed. Rather the standard or criterion is given by God in God's self-revelation in Jesus Christ, and as a human and critical task examining this conformity, dogmatics can only be undertaken in response to this revelation, and therefore from within the reality of faith. In Barth's view, this means that dogmatics is concerned to be accountable and obedient in the determination of the faith given by God, just as the Church's peculiar talk about God is true talk to the extent that it is accountable and obedient talk in faith.[16] The Church's peculiar talk, about which dogmatics is concerned, is that talk which is directed toward others with the claim and expectation that the Word of God will be heard and served in and through this human talk.[17]

In Barth's view, it is the task of dogmatics to inquire into the conformity which may obtain between the Church's peculiar talk about God and Jesus Christ who, as the Word of God, constitutes the basis, goal and content of the Church's proclamation. In this respect, Barth understands the term "dogma" to refer to the correlation of Jesus Christ, Scripture and proclamation, and as such it designates the conformity of

---

[14]For useful discussions of Barth's dogmatic scheme and the nature of its christological determination, see Amberg, *Christol.*, pp. 13-96; Bouillard, *KB*, vol. I, pp. 221-42, vol. II, pp. 114-23, vol. III, pp. 41-91; Bouillard, *Knowledge*, pp. 7-127; Casalis, *Portrait*, pp. 104-116; Come, *Preach.*, pp. 133-49; Hartwell, *Theology*, pp. 20-37; Mueller, *K. Barth*, pp. 49-93; Sykes, *Studies*, pp. 17-55; Thompson, *Perspec.*, pp. 1-20; and Torrance, *Early*, pp. 79, 106-107, 193-95.

[15]Barth, *C.D. I,1*:3-4.

[16]*C.D. I,1*:3-4, 12-13, 17, 18.

[17]*C.D. I,1*:47, 52, 67, 71-72.

the Church's talk to the Bible and the revelation of the Word of God attested in the Bible.[18] Dogma is the true content of the Church's proclamation in so far as it is true as measured by Scripture and Jesus Christ. In Barth's view, proclamation is true when it conforms to the Word of God, when what is said about its object is in fact true of its object:

> One may thus define dogma as Church proclamation to the degree that it really agrees with the Bible as the Word of God. To know dogma and to have dogma is to know and have the Word of God itself in a specific and specifically demonstrable form and manifestation of Church proclamation, for dogma is Church proclamation that is really in agreement with the Word of God.[19]

It is certain that the task of dogmatics for Barth lies wholly in the inquiry into the degree to which the Church's proclamation conforms in obedience to Jesus Christ as given in revelation attested in Scripture.[20] No less certain is the fact that the criterion by which this conformity is indicated is Jesus Christ, himself the revelation, the Word of God. It is precisely at this point of conformity and criterion that the christological determination of dogmatics becomes explicit:

> A church dogmatics must, of course, be christologically determined as a whole and in all its parts, as surely as the revealed Word of God, attested by Holy Scripture and proclaimed by the Church, is its one and only criterion, and as surely as this revealed Word is identical with Jesus Christ. If dogmatics cannot regard itself and cause itself to be regarded as fundamentally Christology, it has assuredly succumbed to some alien sway and is already on the verge of losing its character as church dogmatics.[21]

The christological determination of dogmatics means for Barth

---

[18] *C.D.* I,1:265, 268.

[19] *C.D.* I,1:268. See also p. 265. It is apparent that we are dealing here with Barth's three-fold form of the Word of God. Because our immediate concern is with articulating the overall thrust of the dogmatic task as Barth perceives it, we will not go further into the exposition of proclamation, Scripture and revelation.

[20] *C.D.* I,1:274-75.

[21] *C.D.* I,2:123. With this jump from *C.D.* I,1 to *C.D.* I,2, we do not intend to overlook the seven years which transpired between their respective publication. Some significant literature which impinges upon our study appeared from Barth's pen in these years, and we shall turn to this in the next section below. However, it is important at this junction that we have before us the entire dogmatic scheme as it is articulated in *C.D. I,1-2.*

that the method by which dogmatics is undertaken is also decisively determined by christology. The reason for this is that it is the object of dogmatics that determines the method employed in dogmatic construction.[22] Jesus Christ as the Word of God is the object in dogmatics which determines its method; he alone is the basis, foundation and center of dogmatics for the reason that he alone is the reality of God's self-revelation.[23] This determination of method reflects the fact that dogmatics is preoccupied with both rendering an account of the truth and content of God's self-revelation as well as assessing the conformity of the Church's talk to that same revelation. In Barth's view, this means nothing less than a substantive and methodological preoccupation with following after Jesus Christ:

> God is active in His Word; therefore dogmatics must remain bound to His Word, and can undertake only to give an account of that which is revealed in the Word of God as the past, present and future activity of God, of that which is an event in the Word, with all the force of what occurred yesterday, occurs to-day and will occur to-morrow. And God's Word is His Son Jesus Christ. Therefore in the most comprehensive sense of the term dogmatics can and must be understood as Christology.[24]

Barth's contention here simply means that the task of dogmatics is to elucidate the actuality of the Word of God to its outermost reaches as it is manifest in Jesus Christ. Furthermore, this means that the conception and exposition of the various doctrines in the dogmatic scheme must reflect at every point the preeminence of the object and center, the basis, goal and content of dogmatics.[25] For Barth, to say that dogmatics is fundamentally christology is not to reduce or subsume dogmatics to christology, but rather to open up and expand the christological focus of the Word of God in and through which God reveals the divine self and accomplishes the divine work. In terms of dogmatic construction, what Barth is after here is the "fundamental principle of interpretation by means of which the whole could be understood, surveyed and ordered."[26] The center of dogmatics is thus to

---

[22]C.D. I,2:866.
[23]C.D. I,2:866-72. See also C.D. I,1:304, 411-12. For an indication of the manner in which Barth develops the inter-relation between "revelation," "Word of God," "Son of God" and "Jesus Christ," see the propositions at C.D. I,1:295, 348, 384, 399, 448 and C.D. I,2:1.
[24]C.D. I,2:883.
[25]C.D. I,2:869.
[26]C.D. I,2:872.

be the Word of God *per se* as noetically manifest in the revelation of God as it has occurred in Jesus Christ. And though it is true that reconciliation is identical with this revelation,[27] the Word of God or Jesus Christ as the center of dogmatics is not to be limited to, or understood only in terms of, this work of reconciliation. The Word of God as the center of dogmatics includes but is more than reconciliation, and Barth rejects a systematic theology which is constructed with a view of reconciliation alone as its center and principle.[28]

Still less can a doctrine of God, or doctrine of creation, or doctrine of redemption function as the controlling principle under which all else is ordered, controlled, reduced and subordinated.[29] For Barth, the reason why none of these doctrines can be the center and ordering principle of dogmatics is that none in themselves either contain or exhaust the true content of the Word of God. What connects these doctrines and holds them together in all their distinctiveness in the dogmatic scheme is the fact that they all have their common origin and end in the Word of God. Taken all together, these doctrines constitute the center of dogmatics in that their one, irreducible center is the Word of God which is reflected in all its moments in each of these in a distinct way, and which determines their structure and content as this is generated out of the knowledge of the Word of God given in and through Jesus Christ. With respect to the distinct doctrines of God, Creation, Reconciliation and Redemption, Barth says:

> At all four points, the Word of God itself provides
> the basis of our knowledge, and similarly the coherence of
> the lines which we have to draw from these four points
> (with a hint, but only a hint, at infinity). At the centre, in
> the Word of God itself as the original point from which

---

[27]See *C.D. I,1*:409 and *C.D. I,2*:871.

[28]See particularly *C.D. I,2*:870-72. Eleven years later, Barth wrote in the Foreword to the english re-publication of his *Dogmatics in Outline* (trans. G.T. Thomson. Harper Torchbook ed., New York: Harper & Row, 1959): "A 'system' is an edifice of thought, constructed on certain fundamental conceptions which are selected in accordance with a certain philosophy by a method which corresponds to these conceptions. Theology cannot be carried on in confinement or under the pressure of such a construction. The subject of theology is the history of the communion of God with man and of man with God.... The subject of theology is,... the 'Word of God.' Theology is a science and a teaching which *feels itself responsible* to the living command of this specific subject and to nothing else in heaven or on earth, in the choice of its methods, its questions and answers, its concepts and language, its goals and limitations. Theology is a free science because it is based on and determined by the kingly freedom of the Word of God; for that reason it can never be 'Systematic Theology'" (p. 5). For opposing views on Barth and "system," cf. Klooster, *Signif.*, p. 27 on the one side; and Hartwell, *Theology*, pp. 20-22; Come, *Preach.*, p. 82 on the other.

[29]See the discussion at *C.D. I,2*:873-77.

19

they diverge, they are one.... It is in this way, in differentiation, that the Word and the existence of God are revealed to us, that God grounds the knowledge of Himself, even the knowledge of Himself in His unity. This distinction and independence of the four *Loci* arises from the fact of the self-revelation of the one and triune God.[30]

Dogmatics is fundamentally christology because Jesus Christ is the Word of God in and through which the reality and work of God are made known in the moments of creation, reconciliation and redemption. What Barth is contending here is the idea that no particular aspect of the work of God can be the center of dogmatics. But because Jesus Christ is the Word of God and therefore the reality of God's self-revelation, he is the center and ordering principle which determines the content and structure of dogmatics, and this means that christology (and therefore the christological determination) is expanded to embrace the means by which the particular knowledge of God and God's work in each of these doctrinal areas is attained. In the light of this center, dogmatic construction will coordinate these doctrines on the basis of their common origin in the Word of God and as they follow in revelation from the work of God. In this correlation of doctrine and revelation, Barth contends that "we hold to the way in which the process of revelation has actually taken place...."[31]

What these observations suggest is that it is precisely the matter of conformity of the Church's talk to the Word of God that gives rise to the christological determination of dogmatics. On the whole and in part, dogmatics must take the Word of God as its methodological center and criterion, and this means taking the Word of God in its capacity as revelation concretely expressed in Jesus Christ. The context of all doctrines is therefore the dogmatic scheme which emerges from, and is determined by, the Word of God. Just as the Word of God constitutes the center of dogmatics, so the doctrine of the Word of God constitutes the circumference of the dogmatic task. The particular work of God which is executed in the Word of God and which thus forms the basis for dogmatic reflection is precisely the work of revelation, and therefore the doctrine of the Word appears first in the dogmatic scheme. The controlling center of dogmatics must be dealt with first because it marks the way and reality of the knowledge of God in all the areas of dogmatics. In this sense, the doctrine of the Word of God is *prolegomena* to the *loci*, but it is also itself dogmatics.[32] In short, if the Word of God

---

[30]*C.D. I,2*:877.
[31]*C.D. I,2*:878.
[32]See the discussion at *C.D. I,1*:25, 42.

is the way of knowledge, and if *prolegomena* is the dogmatic clarification and indication of that way, then the whole of dogmatic construction altogether depends on the Word of God as its center and criterion as well as its content.[33] It is therefore the doctrine of the Word of God which sets the all-embracing context in which the *loci* are to be constructed.

Having concluded this brief survey, we are now in a position to see how the methodological values discovered in the Anselm study have found their way into the dogmatic scheme of the *Church Dogmatics*. (1) The concern for the structure of the knowledge of God in the Anselm study has become the concern for a methodology which demonstrates the center and order of dogmatics as this is given in the knowledge itself. The indication of the way of knowledge must consist in an exposition of the structure and content of the knowledge. Because faith precedes knowledge and knowledge presupposes faith, dogmatics is said to be a work of faith and a reflection upon what is said and known in faith as well as a traversing back upon the way of faith to its object. (2) The contention in the Anselm study that the object of faith determines the knowledge of faith, and that the noetic *ratio* of the knowing subject is dependent on and determined by the ontic *ratio* of the known object has become in the dogmatic scheme the contention that the object of faith, the Word of God, provides the criterion by which the knowledge of faith is to be assessed. (3) The idea that true knowledge is achieved to the extent that the noetic *ratio* conforms to the ontic *ratio* as this is decided by the *ratio Dei* is operative in the dogmatic scheme at the point where "dogma" is understood to be the conformity of the Church's talk to the Word of God, and where "dogmatics" is understood to be the critical examination of dogma in terms of the extent of this conformity.

What we have here is a transition in which the perceived *structure* of the actual knowledge of God in faith comes to be the determination of the *methodology* which governs the dogmatic task of demonstrating the way and content of the knowledge of God. In short, as God in self-revelation, the Word of God constitutes the structure, content and means of the knowledge of God. In Barth's view here, this is known only to the extent that the knowledge of God is actual, and this is demonstrated in dogmatics only to the extent that the dogmatic scheme is constrained by the Word of God. On the one hand, the structure, content and means are given ontically in the reality of Jesus Christ as the object of faith, and noetically in the actual knowledge of Jesus Christ as the Word of God. The noetic is bound to, determined by and follows after the ontic. On the other hand, the dogmatic scheme, as it seeks to show the way of the knowledge of God in terms of its structure, content and means, takes the

---

[33]*C.D.* I,1:43.

21

The Hermeneutics of Election

Word of God as its ordering principle, center and criterion in correspondence to structure, content and means. In this way it is bound by and follows after the Word of God, and in this correspondence is to be found the basis for the christological determination of dogmatics. The question that remains, however, has to do with whether there is a more fundamental sense in which the Word of God as the center and controlling principle reflects the employment of a particular aspect of the *work* of God.

D. Interlude: The Influence of Maury

Before going directly to the doctrine of God in *C.D. II,1*, we need to pause to consider the influence of Pierre Maury on Barth's early thinking on election. This was a significant development in that it suggested to Barth how he might finally deal with the doctrine of election in a way which departed considerably from the classical formulations. What Maury did for Barth was to demonstrate dogmatically not only the possibility of linking christology and election in a new way, but also the importance of grounding election in christological thinking.[34]

Woyke has pointed out the polemical role that election played in Barth's early thinking in opposition to the prevailing theology of the Nineteenth Century, especially in the 1919 and 1921 editions of *The Epistle to the Romans*.[35] Evidence of Barth's engagement with the doctrine is also present in several occasional pieces that appeared during those years.[36] After the publication of *Die christliche Dogmatik* in 1927 and the Anselm study in 1931, Barth was more deeply concerned to

---

[34]Though Barth's encounter with Maury's ideas occurs three years before the publication of *C.D. I,2* and six years before the publication of *C.D. II,2*, the christological foundation for the doctrine of election articulated by Maury is taken up by Barth in the construction of his own doctrine. It is the fact that this impetus from Maury transpires before Barth takes up the construction of the doctrine of God in *C.D. II,1*, and the fact that this impetus helped focus the relation between election, revelation and the knowledge of God, that require us to consider it here in the form of an interlude.

[35]See Woyke, *Doctrine*, pp. 34-102. We will not take the time to repeat or summarize Woyke's analysis of Barth's thinking on election up to *C.D. II,2*, except to note this comment of Woyke's on the first edition of *Der Römerbrief*: "Although there is here no systematic treatment, [Barth] already establishes most of the positions which are to be the structure of the complete theory which he is to develop later. In his later writings he amplifies, restates, revises and systematizes what he has here asserted, but he does not fundamentally change his approach" (p. 59. See also pp. 64, 69, 76). It is remarkable that in his otherwise insightful study of the development of Barth's doctrine of election, there is no mention of the influence of Maury whatsoever.

[36]See e.g. "Biblical Questions, Insights and Vistas" (1920); "The Word of God and the Task of the Ministry" (1922); "The Problem of Ethics Today" (1923); and "The Doctrinal Task of the Reformed Churches" (1923), all of which were reprinted in 1924 in Barth, *Word*.

construct his theology on an entirely christological foundation, and to rethink and restate everything he had said before by concentrating on the reality of God's revelation in Jesus Christ. He found it necessary at this time to carry on and extend the "Reformation line" and to consider again the relation between christology and election.[37] Yet even before the Anselm study, Barth had contended that election had to be a central idea in theology, that election and christology stand in strict relation to one another, and that each is to be interpreted by means of the other.[38] Nevertheless, his constructive efforts during this time were directed toward working out a view of the revelation of God and the knowledge of God which was distinctively christological at its foundation and in its content.[39] The emphasis upon the Word of God and the christological determination of the understanding of the revelation and knowledge of God came to full expression with the publication of the *Church Dogmatics I,1* in 1932.[40]

In the late spring of 1936, Barth attended the *Congrès international de théologie calviniste* in Geneva and heard a lecture on the subject of election given by his friend Pierre Maury.[41] In his lecture, Maury laid out the basic profile for an understanding of election that was distinctly christological in its foundation and orientation. From this profile, we can identify four components whose influence on Barth's thinking were to be decisive.

(1) To hold that predestination is an inscrutable mystery does not relieve us from struggling to understand it. There is nothing to be gained by either focusing discussion on an imperceptible event or abandoning discussion in the face of a secret decree. Rather we must speak of election from a biblical perspective as believers, and this means we must speak from within the reality of faith, for election is manifest only to faith. Maury contended that the real problem of election is not the multitude of our questions, theories and objections, but whether we

---

[37]See Busch, *Life*, pp. 209-211.

[38]See Barth, *Fate*, p. 58-60.

[39]See Busch, *Life*, pp. 205-216; Weber, *Report*, pp. 19-40; and Torrance, *Early*, pp. 48-198.

[40]The christological determination of the revelation and knowledge of God can also be seen in the identification of incarnation and revelation developed in Barth, *Credo*, published in 1935. Election as such is not discussed in these lectures, but the principle components of the doctrine as it would be constructed are present on the periphery.

[41]Maury's lecture, "Election et Foi" was published in the April-May 1936 issue of *Foi et Vie*, and published in German translation as "Erwählung und Glaube" in *Theologische Studien* Heft 8, 1940. All citations are from the German translation, and hereafter will be noted as *Erwähl*. On the Barth-Maury connection, see Busch, *Life*, pp. 277-78. Barth's own testimony to the significance of Maury's view of election can be found in *C.D. II,2*:154-55, 191, and in his Foreword to Maury, *Pred. & Other*, pp. 15-18.

believe in faith.[42]

(2) Abstraction and speculation in thinking about election is therefore to be avoided, and the only protection against such idle thinking is the one concrete reality where election in all its scope is manifest, namely the concrete reality of Jesus Christ. To speak truly of election is to speak of him and to keep ourselves in his reality, for it is only in his reality that the otherwise hidden mystery of God is revealed to us. Maury argued that outside of Jesus Christ, there is no election and thus there can be no knowledge of election: "Outside Christ we know neither the electing God, nor God's elect One, nor the act of election."[43] Election is known to be a concrete reality because in Jesus Christ it is revealed to be such: "Election has the reality of the historical and real life of Jesus Christ who has lived for us, died and rose again for us."[44]

(3) God's eternal decree of election is neither more nor less than God's will to save, and we can know this because Jesus Christ himself is identical with this eternal decree. Apart from his eternal and temporal reality, there is no other decree of election. He himself is the origin, cause and goal of the divine election of grace: "'That we may be like him', that we might reflect his image, that we may become the children of God through him, this is what the eternal decision is about."[45]

(4) Election is to be understood unquestionably as double predestination. It is both condemnation and salvation, rejection and acceptance. But one can only speak of condemnation and rejection as a decision of God by regarding the crucifixion on Golgotha. There God's wrath and judgment against godlessness and disobedience are executed, and there the negative side of election is carried out upon God's own Son on behalf of all others. For Maury, this execution of condemnation and judgment on Jesus Christ means for us that "election finally is always positive election, always election to salvation when it is election in Christ, that it was election to condemnation only for him on Good Friday."[46] Election is thus to be designated as double predestination not because it divides persons into two separate categories, but because it has a twofold content, one directed toward God's divine self in the person of God's Son, and the other directed toward us. Such a division of humanity into two categories will occur at the last day, but until then all stand under the cross and there is no one whom the cross cannot save. "According to the New Testament, the old human and the new human are not two separate peoples, two humanities. Each of us bears signs of the divine election and

---

[42]Maury, *Erwähl.*, pp. 4-6.
[43]Ibid., p. 7. Translation mine. See also p. 10.
[44]Ibid., p. 10. Translation mine. See also p. 9.
[45]Ibid., p. 9. Translation mine. See also pp. 8-11.
[46]Ibid., p. 13. Translation mine.

signs of the rejection."[47]

Maury's lecture made a deep impression on Barth. In his Foreword to the publication of Maury's 1954 lectures on predestination given in the United States, Barth said that Maury's address

> ... ought to be considered as one of the best contributions made towards the understanding of the problem.... One can certainly say that it was he who contributed decisively to giving my thoughts on this point their fundamental direction. Until I read his study, I had met no one who had dealt with the question so freshly and daringly.[48]

Barth had immediate occasion to articulate his now well-founded view of election because he was scheduled to give a series of lectures on predestination in the fall of 1936 to the Reformed communities in Eastern Europe. This was to be his first formal effort at articulating his own view of election, and the influence of Maury in these lectures is clearly discernible. It is necessary to conclude this interlude with a glance at the contours of Barth's own doctrine of election as he worked them out in the lectures titled "Gottes Gnadenwahl,"[49] for this enables us to anticipate the major development in *C.D. II,2.* Also, this constructive effort of 1936 clearly indicates both the central role election was coming to play in his thought and the ways in which his views were a departure from the classical formulations of the doctrine.

In the first lecture, Barth argued that the real theme of Romans 9-11 was not the idea of God's harsh word of an immutable decree or a twofold predestination in the traditional sense. Rather it was the merciful and gracious will of God to save. Predestination signifies that divine grace is required even to receive grace, and that there is no higher will of God than this will of God's grace. It means that there is no higher determination of the human being than his/her determination by grace to receive grace. A doctrine of predestination, therefore, cannot be anything other than the answer to the question of how we receive grace, and the interpretation of the work of this grace by which alone we may be saved.[50]

In the second lecture, Barth contended for a christological foundation by arguing that election is a truth of revelation and that knowledge of election is the knowledge of faith. Such knowledge is grounded in neither human rationality nor human experience. Rather it

---

[47] Ibid., p. 19. Translation mine. See also pp. 11-19.
[48] Maury, *Pred. & Other*, p. 16.
[49] See Barth, *G.G.*
[50] Ibid., pp. 4-10.

is knowledge grounded in and obtained by the revelation of God concretely in Jesus Christ, and therefore it can only be understood and interpreted christologically. Over against the traditional formulations that saw Jesus Christ only as the means of election in the execution of an eternal decree, Barth argued that he must be seen as the very ground and substance of election in whom alone we can recognize both the reality of election and the reality of rejection. All that can be said about predestination is to be said first and foremost about Jesus Christ. What election is and what it signifies can only be grasped by going back to the incarnation where God joined Godself to humanity, and to the resurrection where election is revealed as the final word and completion of the incarnation. Barth rejected the traditional idea of an eternal decree prior to or apart from the concrete reality of the life, death and resurrection of Jesus Christ.[51]

In the third lecture, Barth built upon the christological foundation by affirming that election is indeed double predestination, but not in the sense of the traditional doctrine. He rejected the fastidious equilibrium between election and rejection, suggesting that an architectonic symmetry between the two is in fact an inferior view. He castigated the traditional doctrine because it excluded rejection from a christological context. Because Jesus Christ is also the bearer of the divine No, it is not possible to speak meaningfully and truly about rejection apart from the knowledge of Jesus Christ. It is Golgotha that tells us that the Son of God who took humanity upon the divine self is indeed the rejected Son of Man in our place. In him alone is the wrath and judgment of God revealed and executed, and for this reason our rejection is borne away and any equilibrium between election and rejection is abolished. We know about rejection, therefore, only in our knowledge of our election in Jesus Christ, only in our knowledge that in him it has been nullified.[52]

In the final lecture, Barth further addressed the problem of two groups by arguing that it is not only impossible to determine who is and who is not elected, but also that we have no right or authority even to posit two such separate classes. All that is given here and now is the promise of God's gracious election, and the threat of rejection from which we are freed by the promise of election. Our election is fulfilled when we say Yes to our election in Jesus christ and to the cancelation of our rejection in him. At this point, Barth sought a middle ground between the absolute certainty of our election and the absolute uncertainty of our election by saying that we can have only a relative certainty which can in no way be grounded in ourselves. Rather the certainty of our election rests in the certainty of Jesus Christ as the object

---

[51]Ibid., pp. 11-17.
[52]Ibid., pp. 18-25.

of our faith, and this certainty can only take the form of our own definite decision of obedience in faith as our response to God's election. It is this decision in faith which corresponds to the divine prior decision and repeats the decree of election in Jesus Christ.[53]

The connection and mutual influence of election and christology now had a firm dogmatic foundation in Barth's thinking, and he began intentionally to work with christological themes in terms of election, and election themes in terms of christology in anticipation of the treatment of election which would appear in the *Church Dogmatics*.[54] In principle, a reading of "Gottes Gnadenwahl" gives us a basic outline of the dogmatic rationale for locating the doctrine of election in the doctrine of God: because Jesus Christ as the incarnate Son of God is the revelation on the basis of which we can know and therefore speak of who God is and what God does, because the knowledge of God is christologically grounded and determined, because in and through this revelation of God Jesus Christ is shown to be both the elect and the rejected human, and because election has to do with the concrete decree of God's gracious and merciful will to save, it is not otherwise appropriate in faith to construct a doctrine in which God is the Subject without expositing both the content of the knowledge of this particular God as well as the way in which this particular knowledge is obtained. A doctrine of God must traverse back along the way of knowledge in order both to know truly and to assess the degree of conformity between the noetic and the ontic *rationes*. With this rationale before us, we can now turn directly to the doctrine of God in *C.D. II,1* and inquire more fully into its construction.

E. The Ontic/Noetic Structure of the Doctrine of God

In our view, it is the fact that the doctrine of God is intended to correspond to the structure of the knowledge of God that constitutes the fundamental reason why Barth locates election in the doctrine of God. The organization of the doctrine is determined by the dogmatic scheme, and the scheme is determined by the reality and structure of the knowledge of God. Barth's dogmatic scheme indicates that the doctrine of God is to take up the exposition of the knowledge of God's being as

---

[53]Ibid., pp. 26-32. In addition to the four lectures, the publication of *G.G.* contained Barth's answers to twenty-four questions on the subject of predestination addressed to him by his listeners (pp. 33-56). Almost all of these questions and answers constitute further clarification of Barth's views, but they do not really add anything to the lectures themselves.

[54]See e.g. Barth, *Know.*, pp. 55-91, especially pp. 70-78, which constitute the Gifford Lectures given in 1937; and Barth, *Sov.*, pp. 11-27, the publication of which took place at about the same time (1939) that Barth began writing his Basel lectures on the doctrine of election in the context of the doctrine of God (see Busch, *Life*, pp. 301-302).

it is given in God's work. This signifies the ontic structure of the doctrine to the extent that it points to the object of knowledge. However, this knowledge is actualized as it is mediated in and through the Word of God, and this means that it is through God's work of revelation that the being of God is accessed. This signifies the noetic structure of the doctrine to the extent that it points to the knowing activity taking place in the knower. In dogmatics as in faith, the movement is from the work to the being, from the noetic to the ontic, and the ontic and noetic bases of the doctrine are brought together in the all-embracing reality of the Word of God:

> In the doctrine of God we shall have to examine and expound the whole content of the Word, the whole work and activity of God in His Son Jesus Christ, from the standpoint of an investigation of the characteristic being and attributes of God as Subject. Our theme, then, will be the deity and sovereignty of God--not, of course, in abstraction from His activity, but the being of God Himself in the light of His activity.[55]

As Godself in divine revelation, the Word of God constitutes the ontic basis. As God's work of self-revelation, the Word of God constitutes the noetic basis. It is because the Word of God is Godself in the activity of self-revelation that the ontic and noetic bases of the knowledge of God are joined together concretely in Jesus Christ, and therefore joined together as the noetic and ontic bases of the doctrine. Thus the ontic and noetic structure of the *doctrine* of God is intended to reflect the ontic and noetic structure the *knowledge* of God.

But more fundamentally, it is the noetic structure of the knowledge of God, and therefore the noetic structure of the doctrine of God, that dictates that election must be dealt with here. The doctrine of God can be seen to take up the peculiar being and activity of God by way of the structure, content, means and implications of the knowledge of God. Methodologically this is possible only because the being and activity of God in the Word is identical with God's self-revelation in Jesus Christ which actualizes the knowledge of God. The inquiry into the Subject of the doctrine of God is ordered, centered and controlled by the Word of God. The giving of the knowledge of God's being and activity in and

---

[55]*C.D. I,2*:881. This statement represents the programmatic function and scope of the doctrine of God in the *C.D.* For discussions on the ontic and noetic elements in the structure of the *C.D.* in general and the doctrine of God in particular, see Berkouwer, *Triumph*, pp. 192-94; Camfield, *Ref.*, pp. 47-66; Hartwell, *Theology*, pp. 72-79; Jüngel, *Trinity*, pp. 42-49; McLean, *Humanity*, pp. 14-19; Park, *Man*, pp. 8-14; Rosato, *Spirit*, pp. 39-43, 52-65, 160-69; and Sykes, *Studies*, pp. 102-108.

through the Word is itself a work of God, namely the work of revelation, and to a great extent it is this work with which the doctrine of God is principally concerned. This work is ordered by the Word to the extent that the structure of knowledge is determined by conformity to the object; it is centered by the Word to the extent that the content of knowledge is God's being and activity; and it is controlled by the Word to the extent that the means by which knowledge is actualized is itself determined by God. This indicates that the structure, content and means of the knowledge of God is itself the work of God in and through the Word of God, Jesus Christ. Stated more explicitly, Jesus Christ as the Word of God constitutes the ontic and noetic *structure, content* and *means* of the knowledge of God, and therefore as such he constitutes the ontic and noetic *ordering principle, center* and *criterion* of dogmatics in so far as dogmatics is intended to scrutinize and explicate the knowledge of God.

Barth has constructed the doctrine of God in such a way that the ontic follows upon the noetic, and in this way, the development of the doctrine of God reflects the way of the knowledge of God in light of the fact that the dogmatic method is constrained by the knowledge of God to follow after that knowledge in exposition. Thus the four chapters of the doctrine can be seen to correspond respectively to the structure, content, means and implications of the knowledge of God. This contention becomes evident from a look at each of these chapters.

Chapter V: "The Knowledge of God".[56] It is clear that Barth's primary concern is to ground the doctrine epistemologically by dealing first with the noetic structure of the knowledge of God. Because the knowledge of God is the work of God which points us to the being of God, Barth begins with the actuality, possibility and limits of knowledge, and thereby sets up the noetic *structure* of the knowledge of God, and therefore the noetic *structure* of the doctrine of God.

Chapter VI: "The Reality of God".[57] By placing the discussion of the "knowledge" of God before that of the "reality" of God, Barth indicates that the knowledge of God leads us back to the object of that knowledge, namely the being of God in God's act. Thus it is the noetic that provides the access to the ontic; it is out of the consideration of the structure of the knowledge of God that there emerges the exposition of the content of this knowledge. Here the concern is primarily ontic as Barth deals with the peculiar being of God as the one who is knowable and known in and through God's act, and he thereby sets up the ontic content of the knowledge of God and of the doctrine of God.

---

[56]See *C.D. II,1*:3-254.
[57]See *C.D. II,1*:257-677.

Chapter VII: "The Election of God".[58] Barth now moves to a central consideration of God's act. It is the act of knowledge that accesses the being of God, and from this act it is possible to consider more specifically the divine act which effects the knowledge of God. As this act, election constitutes the means of the knowledge of God. If it is true that dogmatics follows after the way of the knowledge of God, if it is true that God is known only in and through the work of self-revelation in the Word, and if it is true that the knowledge of God is itself a work of God, then the means of this revelation and knowledge is of decisive importance for dogmatics. But more particularly, if the act of God's self-revelation is the incarnation of the Word of God,[59] and if the incarnation is itself the act of election, then election is not only the act of revelation which as the means of the knowledge of God points to the being of God, but it also necessarily belongs to the doctrine of God as the primal act which effects the knowledge of God that lies at the base of the doctrine of God. Election is the divine act by means of which God makes Godself known concretely in the incarnation of the Word in Jesus Christ, and this means that election is the work of God by which we access the being of God in the actual knowledge of God. Thus Barth's discussion of election can be viewed as the dogmatic consideration of the *means* of the knowledge of God wherein God establishes the union of the noetic and ontic in which both the knowledge and doctrine of God are grounded.

Chapter VIII: "The Command of God".[60] Finally, having charted the structure, content and means of the knowledge of God, Barth now undertakes a constructive exposition of what this knowledge means for the one in whom it is effected. His concern here is to articulate the divine command which accompanies God's self-revelation and which requires and enables the actualization of the knowledge of God. He therefore gives attention to the implications of the knowledge for the knower in the life of faith, and thereby describes the human acknowledgement and response which constitutes the completion and fulfillment of the knowledge.

What remains for us now is to identify the vital components of the knowledge of God which will call for and be expressed in the doctrine of election as a part of the doctrine of God. We need to see what it is noetically about the doctrine of God that will illuminate our contention that election for Barth constitutes the means of the knowledge of God, and therefore the noetic and ontic basis for dogmatics. As constitutive of the structure of the knowledge of God, these components point toward the being and activity of God as this is manifest in the determination and

---

[58]See *C.D. II,2*:3-506.
[59]See *C.D. I,1*:88-124; 295-489; *C.D. I,2*:1-202; and *C.D. II,1*:3-254.
[60]See *C.D. II,2*:509-781.

actualization of knowledge. The ontic content follows out of the noetic structure because God is wholly present in the act and determination of the knowledge which is bounded by God alone as its origin, basis and goal.[61] In brief, these components point toward the content, means and implications of the knowledge of God. In Barth's view, it is God alone who constitutes the human being as a knower of God, and it will become apparent that two fundamental axioms are operative throughout the discussion, namely the precedence of God's act and the determination of the knowledge of God by God alone.[62]

1. Objective knowledge. The knowledge of God is knowledge of an object *in intellectu* because God is an object *in re* given to the knower.[63] Knowledge of God is therefore an objective knowledge because the revelation of God is the act in which God makes the divine self objective. The goal of this act is a knowledge which corresponds to the object, or better, the Subject of this act. God is known to the extent that in this knowledge, God is recognized as the one "whom we must fear above all things because we may love Him above all things; who remains a mystery to us because He Himself has made Himself so clear and certain to us."[64] The objectivity of the triune God, and thus the objectivity of the knowledge of God, consists in the fact that God speaks and gives the divine self in the Word.[65]

2. Mediated knowledge. The object of the knowledge of God is rendered present to the knower through a medium in such a way that the object is to be distinguished from the knower, and this medium is the concrete reality of the Word of God. God's self-knowledge is objectively immediate, and the knowledge given to the knower is God's self-knowledge mediated to him/her through the agency of the Word.[66] God is an object not merely in the sense of being external to the knower. God is an object in that God takes upon Godself an objectivity which renders this self indirectly present to the knower in a concrete medium that is different from the divine self and part of creaturely reality.[67] This indirect and mediated objectivity, this object in and through which God is revealed, has its original and primary expression in the incarnation of the Word of God in Jesus Christ.[68]

---

[61]See especially *C.D. II,1*:179-272.
[62]See *C.D. II,1*:63-178.
[63]*C.D. II,1*:3, 14.
[64]*C.D. II,1*:3. This is part of the opening proposition to this section of Chapter V. See *C.D. II,1*:32-44, 272-97 for its development, particularly with regard to what it suggests concerning the being of God in his act.
[65]See *C.D. II,1*:44-49, 65, 67-68 and *C.D. I,1*:295-383.
[66]See *C.D. II,1*:9-10, 16, 151, 173.
[67]See *C.D. II,1*:17, 49-50, 225-31.
[68]See *C.D. II,1*:52, 53-54, 252. Also *C.D. I,2*:3-44 where Jesus Christ is described as

3. Faith knowledge. Faith as knowledge is understood here as the orientation of the knower to the object of knowledge, and the relationship between the knower and the known. As such, faith has its origin in God who creates and establishes it in the act of becoming its object. The difference between the knowledge of God and the knowledge of any other object lies in the fact that God is uniquely different from any other object, that the knower stands in a decisively different relationship to the object of this knowledge, and that it is wholly this object of knowledge that effects its actualization. In sum, faith is God's determination of the knowledge of God to the extent that it is faith alone which perceives, acknowledges and conceives God in this mediated objectivity.[69]

4. Bound by its object. Even in mediated objectivity, God is and remains the only object of faith, and it is precisely in this bondage of knowledge to its object that the reality of the knowledge of God is determined.[70] This bondage consists in the fact that the act of God's revelation casts the knower in the direction of the being of God; the content of knowledge that is bound to the Word of God is the very existence of the one who gives the divine self to be known.[71] Knowledge of God, therefore, is true knowledge only to the extent that the content of the knowledge of faith is constrained in its establishment and determination by its object.

5. Encounter with God. The knowledge of God has its temporal origin in the event in which the knower comes into contact with God's mediated objectivity in the creaturely reality external to God, and is thereby made accessible to God as the object of his/her knowledge.[72] The significance of this encounter lies in the fact that the initiative rests entirely with God, and the knower can only follow after.[73] In this event, God is known as the one who can and does effect encounter, and thus preeminently as a Subject.[74]

6. Given in grace. The *prius* of God as the object of knowledge points to the sovereign freedom of the object over against the knower. As an object, God is not given to the knower in such a way that the knower

---

the objective reality and possibility of revelation.

[69]See *C.D. II,1*:12-15, 55, 199. For substantive discussions on Barth's concept of *analogia fidei*, see Balthasar, *Theo. KB*, pp. 73-150; Berkouwer, *Triumph*, pp. 179-94; Brown, *Kierk.*, pp. 129-46; Camfield, *Ref.*, pp. 37-45; Casalis, *Portrait*, pp. 14-17; Come, *Preach.*, pp. 142-49; Hartwell, *Theology*, pp. 56-58; Prenter, *Glauben*, pp. 185-89; Van Til, *Christian.*, pp. 45-51; and Wingren, *Conflict*, pp. 23-44.

[70]See *C.D. II,1*:7-12.

[71]See *C.D. II,1*:39, 43-44.

[72]See *C.D. II,1*:12-17.

[73]See *C.D. II,1*:32.

[74]See *C.D. II,1*:57-58.

can control the object. The position of the knower is prescribed as a subsequence which can only follow the precedence of God's creative and free initiative, and it is this divine freedom in which God gives the divine self in objectivity that constitutes the grace in the knowledge of God. This means that faith does not have the freedom or privilege to choose what objects in creaturely reality can and will become God's objectivity. This is entirely God's choosing, and God must always and again give the divine self because God will not be held by the knower. The posture of grace is not determined by the knower, but given by God in and with the knowledge of Godself. The fact that God takes on objectivity and the fact that there is effected a real human act of knowing both signify grace as God's positioning of the divine self for accessibility to humanity, and God's positioning humanity for accessibility to God.[75]

7. *Obedience.* God's making the divine self known to faith means that the knower can respond only in a subsequent act to God's prior act of self-revelation, and the only form this response can take is that of obedience. This act of response is a human act which is to be characterized as a deliberate volitional act which intentionally follows as subsequence to the act of God as precedence.[76] Nevertheless, this response is not determined soley by the knower. Rather it is a human act precisely to the extent that it is enabled by God to correspond to God's own act; it consists in a decision which follows after and corresponds to the divine decision which makes it possible. Obedience is the divine determination of faith, and it is this human decision of obedience, supported and made possible by the prior decision of God's grace, that makes knowledge of God actual. In this obedience, God not only actualizes knowledge of the divine self in the knower, but God also brings it about that, through this very human act of knowing, the knower genuinely corresponds to and participates in the divine being and activity of God.[77]

Barth's chapter on the reality of God can be viewed as the place in the dogmatic scheme where he connects the content or object of the knowledge of God to the structure of that knowledge, and together these anticipate the discussion of the concrete form of the means of the knowledge. The crucial significance of this chapter can be seen to lie in the identity of God's being and act, and the fact that because God has made the divine self known, nothing at all can be said of God except that it emerges from, and is constrained by, the act which creates and determines the knowledge.[78] It is because the being of God is accessed

---

[75] See *C.D. II,1*:21-22, 27, 31, 68-74, 128-178, 212-13.
[76] See *C.D. II,1*:26, 128-30.
[77] See *C.D. II,1*:12, 27, 29-30, 156, 204, 209-52.
[78] See *C.D. II,1*:261-63, 267-72.

through the structure of the knowledge of God which is determined by God in the act of self-revelation that the being of God has concretion and objectivity. God is the Subject of this act, and God's being is present in this act. And the particularity of this act, its content and the knowledge which it effects, is the particularity of the divinity and humanity of Jesus Christ in whom the knowledge of God finds its original, proper and true substance and reality:

> This does not have only the general meaning that we must know Him in order to know God. It has the particular meaning that we must know Him as the first and proper Subject of the knowledge of God.... In Him who is true God and true man it is true that in His true revelation God gives to man a part in the truth of His knowing, and therefore gives to man's knowing similarity with His own and therefore truth. On the basis of the grace of the incarnation, on the basis of the acceptance and assumption of man into unity of being with God as it has taken place in Jesus Christ, all this has become truth in this man, in the humanity of Jesus Christ. The eternal Father knows the eternal Son, and the eternal Son knows the eternal Father. But the eternal Son is not only the eternal God. In the unity fulfilled by the grace of the incarnation, He is also this man Jesus of Nazareth. It is not our knowledge of God, but the knowledge which is and will be present in this man Jesus, that we have described in our description of its reality, its possibility, and now finally its limits.... When we appeal to God's grace, we appeal to the grace of the incarnation and to this man as the One in whom, because He is the eternal Son of God, knowledge of God was, is and will be present originally and properly; but again through whom, because He is the eternal Son of God, there is promised to us our own divine sonship, and therefore our fellowship in His knowledge of God.[79]

On the basis of this act of revelation, God is not only known, but the knowledge of God is given its determination in its noetic and ontic structure, content, means and implications by the Word of God.

---

[79]*C.D. II,1*:252. See also p. 286.

The Location of the Doctrine

F. Barth's Material/Formal Rationale

We are now in a position to make the statement that it is the location of the doctrine of election within the doctrine of God that in large measure constitutes the significance of its polemical reconstruction at Barth's hands. Furthermore, we are now in a position to anticipate our discussion of the doctrine of election by identifying more clearly the rationale which both legitimates this location and gives to the doctrine its distinctive contour and emphasis.[80]

There is a material and a formal dimension to the rationale which determines that election can only be dealt with in the context of the doctrine of God, and both are suggested by the fact that Barth distinguishes, but does not separate, the being and activity of God. The context of the doctrine of God is the dogmatic scheme which is itself determined by the ontic and noetic structure, content and means of the actual knowledge of God. We have observed that Barth's methodological contention is that an examination of the structure, content, means and implications of the knowledge of God takes us to the structure, content, means and implications of God's being-in-act. Thus, we can express the material and formal rationale as the identity of God's being and act reflected in the actual knowledge of God as this is created and determined solely by God's being-in-act.

The material dimension of the rationale consists in the fact that the doctrine of God takes up the examination of God's being as it is reflected in the knowledge of God. The subject of the doctrine is the peculiar being and attributes of God, God's divinity and sovereignty. As a subject, the being of God is known only in the act of self-revelation, and this act tells us that God is not apart from this act. Because God is this act, and is known only in this act, this act must be a part of the doctrine of God whose purpose it is to exposit the knowledge of the being of this subject. In the doctrine of God, the being of God is revealed being, out-going being, being demonstrated in act and reflected in knowledge. It is this act which Barth understands as election, which as such has to do with the specific being and activity of God in God's outgoing toward an other.[81] The being of God is none other than the being of the electing God. The material dimension of the rationale is to be uppermost in our mind when Barth states:

---

[80]For helpful, but not penetrating discussions of the location of the doctrine of election in *C.D. II,2*, see Amberg, *Christol.*, pp. 136-38; Berkouwer, *Triumph*, pp. 89-90; Bouillard, *KB*, vol. II, pp. 125-29; Buess, *Zur Präd.*, pp. 6-8; Gloege, *Prädest.*, pp. 201-3; Gunton, *Doct.*, pp. 381-92; Hartwell, *Theology*, pp. 18-19; Hausmann, *KB Doct.*, pp. 8-10; Jensen, *Alpha*, pp. 141-45; Jüngel, *Trinity*, pp. 68-82; Park, *Man*, p. 8; and Woyke, *Doctrine*, pp. 33, 112-14.
[81]See *C.D. I,2*:881, *C.D. II,2*:5-11, 49-53.

> ... God ... in Himself, in the primal and basic
> decision in which He wills to be and actually is God, in
> the mystery of what takes place from and to all eternity
> within Himself, within His triune being ... is none other
> than the One who in His Son or Word elects Himself, and
> in and with Himself elects His people. In so far as God
> not only is love, but loves, in the act of love which
> determines His whole being God elects. And in so far as
> this act of love is an election, it is at the same time and as
> such the act of His freedom. There can be no subsequent
> knowledge of God, whether from His revelation or from
> His work as disclosed in that revelation, which is not as
> such knowledge of this election.[82]

It is this material dimension of the rationale that constitutes the basis for Barth's rejection of all other arrangements of the doctrine in the history of dogmatics. In these other arrangements, Barth sees that election is regarded as one aspect of God's relationship to the world, or one divine work which is nevertheless preceded by other works, or a subsumed component of a particular work.[83] In the final analysis, however, all of Barth's objections can be reduced to the fact that in these arrangements there is an unacceptable separation of God's being and activity, so that we are left with a God whose being is not knowledgeably accessible to us, and whose actions therefore can never really be understood. But he can advance this criticism and innovatively relocate the doctrine of election only because he understands revelation to posit the identity of God's being and act in reality and in knowledge, and because he is determined on this basis to understand revelation as identical with election (i.e., we can distinguish, but not separate, the material of the being of God from the act of God).

The formal dimension of the rationale consists in the fact that the doctrine of God takes up the examination of this divine act of self-

---

[82]*C.D. II,*2:76-77. See also pp. 90-93 where for this same reason Barth contends that his location of the doctrine of election makes it possible for it to take up and discharge its "necessary function" in dogmatics.

[83]See *C.D. II,*2:77-91. Barth's perceptive analysis of the recent history of theological construction is perhaps no more insightful than it is here in his review and critique of the role and place of election in doctrinal formulation. He offers a fair, but not unbiased description of the manifold ways election has been incorporated into theological schemes. One comes away from this passage with the impression that the question as to where election should be dealt with (if at all) in theological construction has never been answered to the satisfaction of the majority of theologians. Its continued absence from some contemporary theological constructions as well as the preaching of the church has been duly noted and mourned, and efforts are being made to correct this (see eg. Basinger, *Pred. & FW*; Berkouwer, *Div. Elec.*; Daane, *Freedom*; and Jewett, *El. & Pr.*).

revelation which expresses God's being. There is no knowledge of God apart from this work which creates and determines knowledge. This is to say that in Barth's view, the structure, content, means and implications of the knowledge of God correspond to and are determined by the structure, content, means and implications of the act of revelation in which God is and has the divine being. The concrete form which this act of self-revelation takes is the incarnation of the Word of God in the human Jesus of Nazareth, and this is understood by Barth to be the divine act of election. For this reason, the knowledge of God the Subject takes its form from the act of election which takes place at the very center of divine self-revelation.[84] The act of God which effects and determines the knowledge of God is none other than the electing act of God in the form of Jesus Christ. The formal dimension of the rationale is suggested when Barth states:

> As we have to do with Jesus Christ, we have to do with the electing God. For election is obviously the first and basic and decisive thing which we have always to say concerning this revelation, this activity, this presence of God in the world, and therefore concerning the eternal decree and the eternal self-determination of God which bursts through and is manifested at this point. Already this self-determination, as a confirmation of the free love of God, is itself the election or choice of God. It is God's choice that He wills to be God in this determination and not otherwise.... He is so in Jesus Christ, in His only-begotten Son, and therefore from all eternity in Himself.[85]

It is this formal dimension of the rationale that constitutes the basis for Barth's rejection of other sources and foundations for the doctrine of election. In these, Barth perceives the doctrine to be grounded either in previous theological construction which functions as the norm; or in an orientation determined by the practical function of the doctrine in Christian life; or in an empirical explanation in anthropological, individual and deterministic terms as to why some believe and others do not; or in the idea of abstract, irresistible power logically deduced from the general idea of a necessary and sovereign being who determines all things.[86] However, in the final analysis the

---

[84] See *C.D. II,2*:25-27, 34, 51-60, 88-91.

[85] *C.D. II,2*:54.

[86] See *C.D. II,2*:35-51. Here again we find Barth engaged in a penetrating exposé of the dangers which beset the theological construction of the doctrine of election when the attempt is made to build it upon one of many possible ecclesiastical, pastoral, sociological and philosophical foundations. His criticism of Calvin and Aquinas in this regard is

whole of Barth's protest can be summed up in the fact that in these other foundations, the supposed knowledge of election is grounded in and oriented by something other than the concrete self-revelation of God in Jesus Christ, and therefore they are grounded not in the actual knowledge of God, but ultimately in a capricious and arbitrary act of an unknown and unknowable God. But Barth can propose his disapproval only because he understands the knowledge of God at the base of the doctrine of election to be true to the extent that it is effected and determined only by the act of God's self-revelation, and because he is determined on this basis to understand election as identical with God's self-revelation in Jesus Christ (i.e., we can distinguish, but not separate, the form of the act of God from the being of God).

In short, the material dimension of the rationale is *the being of God* in the act of revelation, and thus the being of God the Subject which lies at the base of and is expressed in our knowledge of God. The formal dimension is the being of God *in the act of revelation*, and thus the act of God the Subject which lies at the base of our knowledge. Barth's criticism and suggestion regarding both the location and the basis of the doctrine reflect the fact that the act of divine self-revelation effects both the conformity of the noetic/material (content of our knowledge) to the ontic/material (being of God), and the conformity of the noetic/formal (form of our knowledge) to the ontic/formal (act of God). In Barth's view, as we noetically traverse back across the knowledge of God to the ontic, we discover that God's being in the act of self-revelation is identical with election, and the conformity between the noetic and the ontic, both materially and formally, is in fact achieved by way of election as the means of the knowledge of God.

This identity of God's being and act makes the distinction between the ontic and the noetic to be tenuous at best. The fact is that for Barth, this identity means that the ontic and noetic coincide, and above all in the doctrine of election they are one in the same. By the time Barth gets from the Anselm study to *C.D. II,2*, election has become the decisive noetic category in his thinking, and as such it informs the dogmatic exposition from that point on in terms of both its structure and content. As we now turn directly to the doctrine of election, we will see more clearly how it is that the significance of Barth's doctrine lies primarily in the noetic function of election in dogmatic construction.

---

particularly noteworthy.

Part II

The Noetic Structure of Election

Chapter Two

The Epistemology
of Election

Having discerned the elemental ground and rationality for the appearance of the doctrine of election in the doctrine of God, we can now examine more directly the epistemological scope and structure of Barth's doctrine. Our task in the present chapter will be to pursue the epistemological formulation of the doctrine and establish the basic construct which will allow us in later chapters to elucidate the methodological and constructive implications of Barth's view of election for the *Church Dogmatics*. This task will move us down two paths. First, we will bring our analytical inquiry to bear upon the nature and extent of what otherwise appears to be the christological determination of election in Barth's construction. In this regard, we intend to uncover and explicate the function exercised by election as the means of the knowledge of God. This in turn will constitute the direction for our passage down the second path, namely an examination of the extent to which the noetic function of election requires the polemical reconstruction of the doctrine which comes to be expressed in Barth's view of the concrete decree and his subsequent criticism and redefinition of the *decretum absolutum*, double predestination and supra- and infralapsarianism.

A. Election as the Means of the Knowledge of God

Our approach to Barth's doctrine of election is oriented by the fact that this doctrine addresses in a singular way one particular element in the actuality of the knowledge of God executed in revelation/incarnation, namely the *means* by which this knowledge is achieved.[1] In the doctrine of God, it is the work of effecting the

---

[1]This orientation exhibits Barth's methodological axiom that dogmatic reflection must be bound to and follow after its object, and that the place to begin dogmatic reflection is the actuality of the knowledge of God. We have noted that a significant component to this axiom is the fact that movement in the knowledge of God, and therefore in dogmatics, is from work to being because God's being can be known only to the extent that it is present in God's work. This obviously makes revelation central

knowledge of God that is central to the construction, and this work is the Word of God who as such constitutes the structure, content, means and implications of the knowledge of God, joined together ontically and noetically in Jesus Christ. The task before us in this section is to demonstrate that for Barth, the Word of God as God's self-revelation which creates and determines the knowledge of God, and which thus provides the center, ordering principle and criterion of dogmatics, is precisely nothing other than the act of election.

When we say that in Barth's theology, election constitutes the means of the knowledge of God, we intend to suggest that election is the instrumentality or the medium of the knowledge of God. It is to say that the knowledge of God, from its possibility and basis to its goal, is actualized *by means of* election, and that the relationship which obtains between the knowledge of God and election is that in which a concrete event (election) actually issues in the knowledge of the One who is the prime actor in the event, and whose intention it is that such knowledge be tied exclusively to that event. It is to say that in Barth's view, the act of election is the concrete form in and through which God's self-revelation is executed, the substantial medium in and through which the divine self-giving overcomes the abyss between God and the knower. That this is the case will become evident as we identify the constructive ontic/noetic elements that support Barth's doctrine of election, and which require the precedence of election for the fulfillment of the knowledge of God.

1. The Identity of Election, Revelation and Incarnation. In his exposition of the doctrine of the Word of God in *C.D. I,1-2*, Barth established the identity of the act of revelation and the act of incarnation by constructing a triadic scheme in which the media of the threefold form of the Word of God intersect with the three modes of God's being and activity. The exposition of the total reality of revelation is undertaken in terms of the doctrine of the trinity so that this whole reality can be

---

to the construction of any dogma. The issue here, however, is the *origin and determination of revelation/incarnation itself*, and any analysis of the presence and function of this issue in Barth's theology must, in the light of his axiom, take this origin and determination seriously; it must deal with revelation/incarnation *in the context of election*. For the most part, the discussions of Barth's view of election only glance at revelation and incarnation, while the discussions of his view of revelation and incarnation virtually ignore the fundamental influence and determination of these by election. Cf. Balthasar, *Theo. KB*, pp.75, 101-6, 152-62; Berkouwer, *Triumph*, pp. 90-103; Bloesch, *Victor*, pp. 44-52, 110; Bouillard, *KB*, vol. II, pp. 114-64; Camfield, *Ref.*, pp. 47-50, 71-86; Deegan, *Determ.*, pp. 126-35; Gloege, *Prädest.*, pp. 206-17; Hartwell, *Theology*, pp. 67-82; Hausmann, *KB Doct.*, pp. 35, 77-82; Jenson, *Alpha*, pp. 48-51, 68-73, 85, 91, 125-39; Jüngel, *Trinity*, pp. 18-23, 45, 52-53, 74; Klooster, *Signif.*, pp. 31-71; Küng, *Just.*, pp. 35-39; Mackintosh, *Types*, pp. 278-85; McLean, *Humanity*, pp. 55-60; Mueller, *K. Barth*, pp. 55-70; Park, *Man*, pp. 31-39, 116-17; Sykes, *Studies*, pp. 105-7, 122-28, 150-80; Thompson, *Perspec.*, pp. 15-24, 36-39, 93-110; Van Til, *Christian.*, pp. 19-29, 54, 90; Wingren, *Conflict*, pp. 28-44; and Woyke, *Doctrine*, pp. 33, 51-59, 94-97, 153-54, 207, 254.

understood to be comprised of three aspects which correspond to a particular function of God in self-revelation. This total reality is described as *Revealer, Revelation* and *Revealedness,*[2] or *Unveiling, Veiling* and *Impartation,*[3] or *Being, Speech* and *Action.*[4] This triad reflects the distinctions of the three modes of the being of the one God in self-revelation. The first of the terms has to do with *who* God is in this revelation (subject), and corresponds to the mode of being as Father; the second has to do with what God *does* in this revelation (act/event), and corresponds to the mode of being as Son; the third has to do with what God *effects* in this revelation (goal), and corresponds to the mode of being as the Holy Spirit. For Barth, the doctrine of the trinity answers and interprets the question of this subject, act and effect of revelation because of the noetic correspondence between the reality of revelation and the being of God: "If we really want to understand revelation in terms of its subject, i.e., God, then the first thing we have to realise is that this subject, God, the Revealer, is identical with His act in revelation and also identical with its effect."[5]

The truth of God's self-revelation depends on the identity of God's being-in-revelation and God's being-in-Godself.[6] As the doctrine of the trinity interprets the *Actor* (or Subject/Revealer) in divine self-revelation, so the doctrine of the incarnation interprets the *Action* (or object/revelation) by means of which God takes on objective reality in space and time in order to be known. In the doctrine of the incarnation, we have to do with God in the mode of being as the Son of God or Word of God who becomes flesh in Jesus of Nazareth. Here God takes on the objective form of that which God is not, and thereby distinguishes Godself from Godself.[7] As the action of revelation, incarnation is the primary form or medium of the Word of God which ontically and noetically connects the threefold form of the Word of God to the actual knowledge of God.

In similar fashion, the doctrine of the Holy Spirit interprets the *Acting* (or actualization/revealedness) in self-revelation by means of which God takes on subjective reality and effects the goal of the divine

---

[2] See *C.D. I,1*:295.

[3] See *C.D. I,1*:332.

[4] See *C.D. I,1*:383.

[5] *C.D. I,1*:296. See also pp. 295-304, 308-12, 333, 345-50, 363, 375, 380. Barth's view of the identity of God's being and act in revelation as the basis for the doctrine of the trinity is carefully analyzed with great perception in Jüngel, *Trinity.* Also, see Moltmann, *Kingdom,* pp. 139-44; and Toon, *One,* pp. 78-94.

[6] See e.g. *C.D. I,1*:371, and the proposition statements and subsequent expositions that begin at pp. 384, 399 and 448.

[7] See *C.D. I,1*:111-20, 132-86, 314, *C.D. I,2*:1-44, 239-40. Also, cf. Brunner, *Enc.,* pp. 139-48; Mackintosh, *Types,* pp. 275-98; Thompson, *Perspec.,* pp. 20-46; and Wingren, *Conflict,* pp. 28-32.

self-revelation in the knower by bringing it to its intended fulfillment. Here the Holy Spirit constitutes the reality of revealedness in terms of the actual reception of and belief in God's self-revelation. This acting of God in the knower completes the total reality of revelation.[8]

Thus, in the context of the threefold form of the Word of God as the media of God's self-revelation, Barth establishes the noetic link between the knower and the known by demonstrating how the *Actor, Action* and *Acting* of the divine self-revelation constitute the ontic link between the being and action of God. The triune God *is* God's self-revelation in its totality, and its reality and truth depend upon the fact that "God's being *ad extra* corresponds to his being *ad intra* in which it has its basis and prototype."[9]

It is apparent in Barth's triadic construct that the term "Word of God" refers both to God's second mode of being and to the action of revelation of the triune God. This term signifies the noetic link between the threefold form of the Word of God on the one hand and the triunity of the being and activity of God on the other. It does this by virtue of the being of God (Son) becoming the focal event of revelation (Jesus Christ) to which Scripture and proclamation give witness. From the point of view of the *being* of God, the becoming is the incarnation of the Son, and on one side is the Father/Revealer and on the other is the Spirit/Revealedness. And from the point of view of the *activity* of God, the becoming is the incarnation of the Word, and on one side is Scripture and on the other is proclamation. In other words, the noetic link between the three modes of being of the one God and the threefold form of the Word of God is *the act* in which the Son of God takes on concrete form by becoming Jesus of Nazareth.[10]

For Barth, the identity of God's being and act is established in the fact that God's revelation takes the form of incarnation in which the divine being is united with the human being. This means that the content of the incarnation is the two natures of the one Jesus Christ. Incarnation is divine self-revelation precisely because *God is here in the form of a human being*; it is understood to be the reality in which God's existence becomes human existence. Between God and humanity, there is an infinite chasm, but in the incarnation (and therefore in revelation) the two come together, meet and are united in oneness. In the act of revelation

---

[8]See *C.D. I,2*:203-79. For an exceptionally fine analysis of Barth's pneumatology in this regard, see Rosato, *Spirit*, especially pp. 44-107.

[9]Jüngel, *Trinity*, p. 23.

[10]In Barth's view, the relation between the threefold form of the Word of God and the three modes of God's being/act in the reality of God's self-revelation is one of *analogy*. His rejection of any other *vestigium trinitatis* except that of the threefold form assumed by the Word of God is maintained only on the basis of the identity of God's being and act in this self-revelation (see *C.D. I,1*:121, 304-5, 347). See also Barth, *Know.*, pp. 55-91; *Sov.*, pp. 11-21; and *Credo*, pp. 19-27, 63-72.

in the concrete form of the incarnation, God and humanity are a unity. As the *form* of revelation, incarnation points to God's *act* of assuming objectivity in the *humanity* of Jesus Christ (the Word became *flesh*); as the *content* of revelation, incarnation points to God's *being* in the *deity* of Jesus Christ (the *Word* became flesh). Without this particular concrete act and being, there would be no revelation, and thus no knowledge of God.[11]

The connection between revelation/incarnation and election which shaped Barth's early thinking[12] is developed with far greater substance and precision in the formulation of the doctrine of election in *C.D. II,2.* Here, election as the fundamental motif determines the continuing development of his view of revelation and incarnation. The construction of the doctrine clearly reflects another triad (*Elector, Election* and *Electing*) in which there is a continuation of the dogmatic discussion of the ontic and noetic being and activity of the triune God. In this regard, Barth contends:

> As we have to do with Jesus Christ, we have to do with the electing God. For election is obviously the first and basic and decisive thing which we have always to say concerning this revelation, this activity, this presence of God in the world, and therefore concerning the eternal decree and the eternal self-determination of God which bursts through and is manifested at this point. Already this self-determination, as a confirmation of the free love of God, is itself the election or choice of God. It is God's choice that He wills to be God in this determination and not otherwise.... It is in the utter particularity of His activity, and therefore of His volition, and to that extent of His self-determined being, that He is the electing God. He is so at that one point upon which Scripture concentrates our attention and thoughts.... He is so in Jesus Christ, in His only-begotten Son, and therefore from all eternity in Himself.[13]

Barth's doctrine of election is noetically grounded in revelation because the knowledge of God is grounded ontically and noetically in

---

[11]On the incarnation as the form and content of revelation see especially *C.D. I,1*:315-16, *C.D. I,2*:25-35, 43-44, 122-202. See also Barth, *Credo*, pp. 40, 63-66; *Know.*, pp. 36-48; *Sov.*, p. 15; Cf. Barth, *Hum.*, pp. 49-52, where Barth argues that God does not exclude humanity in the divine being, but that God's deity includes and encloses humanity in itself. It is in fact in the humanity of Jesus Christ that the enclosed humanity of God is revealed.
[12]See e.g. Barth, *G.G.*, pp. 11-15; and *Know.*, pp. 55-79.
[13]*C.D. II,2*:54. On the correlation of revelation/incarnation and election, cf. Balthasar, *Theo. KB*, pp. 156-64; Gloege, *Prädest.*, pp. 193-217, 233-55; Sykes, *Studies*, pp. 147-93; Woyke, *Doctrine*, pp. 31-34, 94-101, 215-228; and Thompson, *Perspec.*, pp. 20-46.

Jesus Christ as God's being in the act of self-revelation:

> Election is that which takes place at the very centre of the divine self-revelation.... It is the name of Jesus Christ which, according to the divine self-revelation, forms the focus at which the two decisive beams of the truth forced upon us converge and unite: on the one hand the electing God and on the other elected man. It is to this name, then, that all Christian teaching of this truth must look, from this name that it must derive, and to this name that it must strive.[14]

Thus the doctrine of election continues the interpretation of revelation because the ontic and noetic reality of election consists in the act of self-revelation executed in the incarnation in Jesus Christ. As the self-revealing God, God is also the electing God. This means for Barth that revelation, incarnation and election as God's action cannot be separated. The meeting and being together of God and humanity in Jesus Christ is (ontically) incarnation and (noetically) revelation, and together these constitute the reality of election. Indeed, it is precisely because of election that Jesus Christ is the revelation of God in incarnation; he alone, therefore, can be the manifest form and content of God's election.[15] It is only because God's revelation and incarnation in Jesus Christ is at the same time the execution of election that Barth can contend that the electing God and elect human are known. The reality of God's election is known because the Subject and the object of election are one, concretely and manifestly in Jesus Christ as very God and very human.[16]

From Barth's perspective, election is properly understood only when it is viewed in relation to the concrete particularity of God's self-revealing action in Jesus Christ. The action of revelation in the form of incarnation is the action of election: God the Word making Godself known (revelation) by becoming a human being in Jesus Christ (incarnation), in order to execute the relationship, fellowship and unity of God and humanity (election). There can be knowledge of this election only because it is itself revelation given concretely in Jesus Christ.

We can articulate the relation between revelation, incarnation and election in Barth's construction by distinguishing between revelation *of* election and revelation *as* election. The first, revelation *of* election,

---

[14]*C.D.* II,2:59. See also pp. 53-54, 94-95, 118, 161-65. In brief, this constitutes the fundamental expression of the need to orient the doctrine of election to christology, or to ground the doctrine in christology (see *C.D.* II,2:34-76, § 32, subsection 2, "The Foundation of the Doctrine").

[15]See *C.D.* II,2:105, 118-20, 155-58, 161-67, 175-77.

[16]See *C.D.* II,2:146-54, 178-79.

suggests that revelation has election as its *content*, and as such, revelation *makes known* the primal and basic *act* of God, and therein the being of God as determined in and by this act. Here, revelation is the act of making election known as God's act in which God determines the divine self to be this God and only this God by entering into an external relation; revelation makes known the *God*-who-elects. Thus revelation *of* election has to do with the matter of *knowledge*, or knowing through revelation that God is none other than the One whose election constitutes the basic determination of the divine being.

The second, revelation *as* election, suggests that revelation has election as its *form*, and as such revelation is the *entering into* the external relation and thus the actualization of election. Here revelation is the act of executing the relation in which God has determined Godself to be this God and only this God; revelation accomplishes the *election*-of-God. Thus revelation *as* election has to do with the matter of *executing the act*, or actualizing through revelation the relation with the God who is none other than the One whose being is determined in this relation.

2. Election as Eternal Act. Election is an eternal act of the eternal God, an act executed in, from and conditioned by eternity, and only for this reason is it the primal act which constitutes the beginning of all things. As an essential perfection of God's being,[17] eternity denotes the fact that the being and activity of God subsist in pure simultaneity: "Eternity is God in the sense in which in Himself and in all things God is simultaneous, i.e., beginning and middle as well as end, without separation, distance or contradiction."[18] The past, present and future that characterize time are simply the form God's being takes in this relation to that which is outside God, and eternity is not characterized by the discrete temporal opposition of these moments. Rather eternity is itself the unconditioned oneness of beginning, succession and end without opposition or contradiction. As such, eternity is the prototype of created time which is included in and accompanied by eternity.

The eternal being and activity of God is to be distinguished in relation to time in three ways: (1) God's pre-temporality (or the pre-time of eternity) indicates the precedence of eternity in which God decides and determines everything that will come to be in time; (2) God's supra-temporality (or the co-time of eternity) indicates the togetherness and inter-penetration of eternity and time, and the fact that the eternal God enters into time so that temporality becomes a form of eternity; and (3) post-temporality (or the after-time of eternity) indicates the subsequence of eternity after all things in time no longer exist because they will have achieved their goal and completion.

---

[17]See *C.D. II,1*:608-40.
[18]*C.D. II,1*:608.

In its relation to time, and as God's eternal being and act, election bears the marks of pre-, supra- and post-temporality. In Barth's view, election is to be understood "as eternal, preceding time and all the contents of time. We also think of it as divine, a disposing of time and its contents which is based on the omnipotence of God and characterised by His constancy," and therefore "as the beginning of all things" outside God which have their origin in the divine being of God.[19] Election is the eternal, living act of the eternal, living God, and as such it is the pre-temporal or primal act which contains and originates all things, accompanies and infuses all things, and brings all things to their fulfillment. It is the eternal act in which God wills God's own living and acting in relation to that which is outside God.

In Barth's construction, revelation in the form of incarnation constitutes the concrete execution of this eternal act in time. The act of election in the concrete form of revelation/incarnation is the transition from eternity to time in which the internal being and activity of God overflows and moves outward toward the reality distinct from Godself.[20] Revelation is thus understood to be the temporal execution of the eternal election to the extent that the eternal God enters time by taking objective form in the incarnation of the Son. The time of revelation is concretely executed and fulfilled in the incarnation,[21] but it is the being and act of God in election that constitute the origin and basis of this temporal execution. In this respect, election signifies the fact that in and from eternity, God chose to take temporality upon the divine self and become objective in the human Jesus of Nazareth precisely in order to be knowable and known, and thus to execute spatially and temporally the meeting and being together of God and humanity. The eternal origin, succession and end of God's divine activity, God's reality as the Elector, Election and Electing, are executed temporally in the event of Jesus Christ:

> ... at the beginning of all God's ways and works, in the eternal decree of God, there stands the relationship between Himself and the creature which became event and revelation in Jesus Christ.... For what took place in Jesus Christ--and we shall have to take this further step if

---

[19] *C.D. II,2*:155. See also pp. 175, 180-81, 184.

[20] See especially *C.D. II,2*:51-54, 160-1, 184-94. Outside the *C.D.*, see Barth, *Know.*, pp. 70-74; *Outline*, pp. 28, 69; *Evang.*, pp. 70-71. For insightful discussions of Barth's view on revelation as transition from eternity to time, see Gloege, *Prädest.*, pp. 233-34, 240-41; Hartwell, *Theology*, pp. 30-37; Jenson, *Alpha*, pp. 74-92; Park, *Man*, pp. 51, 62, 177; Thompson, *Perspec.*, pp. 98-101.

[21] See § 14, "The Time of Revelation" in *C.D. I,2*:45-121, especially subsection 1, "God's Time and Our Time" (45-70), for the substantive exposition of Barth's view of the eternal basis and temporal execution of revelation/incarnation.

we are to see and confess in God's revelation God's eternal decree--was not merely a temporal event, but the eternal will of God temporally actualised and revealed in that event.[22]

Barth's notion of God's beginning in the sphere of eternity refers to God's activity by emphasizing that it has its origin, source or starting point in God's being and nowhere else. It is Barth's contention that the divine act of election constitutes the beginning not only of God's self-revelation, but also of all God's actions and dealings with Godself and with the reality outside Godself. Election denotes "the beginning of all things, i.e., the beginning which has no beginning except in God's eternal being in Himself; the beginning which in respect of God's relationship with the reality which is distinct from Himself is preceded by no other beginning;..."[23] Election is thus the particular and original divine act in eternity that determines the being and activity of God, and it indicates the basis and origin of revelation in the form of incarnation. On the basis of a definite attitude, God made a definite decision to enter into an external relationship with an other, and has given concrete expression to this by the movement out of the divine self toward this other. The origin of this work is the free love of God to be for an other, and the goal of this work is the actualization of the relationship with an other. This work is essential to God in that God has no reality apart from this attitude, decision, relationship and movement; it is the activity which gives particular determination and expression to God's eternal being.[24] Because God is not God apart from this work, God can be known only in and through this work. This work takes the concrete form of incarnation, and it is solely on the basis of the identity of God's being and act in election that Jesus Christ is the incarnate Word and the self-revelation of God. As very God and very human, Jesus Christ concretely manifests the primal act in which God determines the divine self and all things outside the divine self,[25] and God therefore takes us to the point in God's eternity where the source of God's activity is to be found.

3. *God's Triune Being in the Act of Election.* Barth's doctrine of revelation is based on the fact that the act of revelation is determined by the revealing Subject, and that the Subject is knowable and known because this subject is identical with the act of self-revelation. In Barth's construction, the origin of this act is itself the act of God's eternal

---

[22]*C.D. II,2*:178-79.

[23]*C.D. II,2*:155. For discussions germane to election as God's eternal beginning, see also pp. 95-102, 116, 175-81.

[24]See *C.D. II,2*:5-11, 25-26, 91.

[25]This construction thoroughly dominates the exposition in §33, but see especially *C.D. II,2*:94-100, 115-17, 120-22, 140-42, 145-48, 152-62, 169, 175-81.

election. The Subject of the doctrine of election is the one God who has being in the act of concrete decision, and it is only in this decision that God intends to be and is God. It is therefore this act above all others which determines that the triune God is and acts as the One who loves in freedom:

> ... God ... in Himself, in the primal and basic decision in which He wills to be and actually is God, in the mystery of what takes place from and to all eternity within Himself, within His triune being ... is none other than the One who in His Son or Word elects Himself, and in and with Himself elects His people. In so far as God not only is love, but loves, in the act of love which determines His whole being God elects. And in so far as this act of love is an election, it is at the same time and as such the act of His freedom. There can be no subsequent knowledge of God, whether from His revelation or from His work as disclosed in that revelation, which is not as such knowledge of this election.[26]

The decision to be and to act as the electing God is originally an intra-divine decision which involves each of the three modes of the divine being. The Father chooses to give the Son and become a human being in order to establish the covenant with humanity, and the Son in obedience to the Father chooses self-giving in order to become a human being so that the covenant might become a reality. The Holy Spirit chooses to maintain, confirm and demonstrate the intra-divine fellowship and unity of God in the fulfillment of this covenant with humanity.[27] In the whole of this divine decision, God is the active subject. But the true significance of this lies in the fact that this is the primal act in which God determines who God is to be and what God is to do, and thus it is the triad of *Elector, Election* and *Electing* that stands as the basis and origin of the other triad of *Revealer, Revelation* and *Revealing* which constitutes the origin, basis and goal of the knowledge of God.

    4. Election as Grace. In Barth's view of election, grace is God's

---

[26] *C.D. II,2*:76-77. See also *C.D. II,1*:257-321; *C.D. II,2*:9-14, 24-34, 79, 91. Hendry notes Barth's insistence on the "coincidence" of God's being and activity, and indicates that election is the "copula" between them (*Review*, p. 396). In a similar vein, R.H. Roberts argues that Barth's doctrine of election is conditioned by what he calls "God's ontology of act" (Sykes, *Studies*, p. 121). See also Buess, *Zur Präd.*, pp. 121-22; Camfield, *Ref.*, pp. 30-37; Jüngel, *Trinity*, pp. 61-83; Woyke, *Doctrine*, pp. 150-77.

[27] Though Barth urges that each of the three modes of the divine being is active and has a unique function in the decision of election and its temporal execution, his exposition clearly focuses on the roles of the Father and the Son. See *C.D. II,2*:101-2, 105-6, 110, 115, 158, 169.

undeserved self-giving and overflowing to an other, and the enabled reception of God by an other. Grace is thus a particular determination in the expression of the identity of God's being and act. In seeking to demonstrate that God has the divine being in this act, Barth speaks in terms of the identity of the Lover and the loving in the act in which God wills and creates fellowship with an other as an overflowing of God's own intra-divine fellowship. God does not need an other outside Godself in order to exercise this divine love, and God is unconditionally free in both God's inward and outward loving.[28] As a perfection of the divine loving, grace is the inward being and attitude of God toward an other which gives love its particularly unique character, expressed in God's desire for fellowship with an other who has no merit to compel or effect this fellowship except that which is itself given in and through God's love.[29] Grace is also the activity of giving in which the being of God is the gift, and because there is no cause which necessitates this self-giving other than God, this overflowing is absolutely and unconditionally free grace. As the divine act of loving in which God determines God's being, and as the unmerited overflowing of God toward the other, grace finds its supreme reality and expression in the incarnation, which represents God in the movement outward as well as the attitude in which this movement has its origin. The grace which signifies the Giver, gift and giving is originally and concretely the union and fellowship of God and humanity in Jesus Christ.[30]

In Barth's view, the doctrine of election is necessary for the interpretation of grace as the giving and receiving of God because only the act of election reflects the being of God in its self-determination for giving and fellowship. Election adds nothing to grace; rather it accentuates who God really is in Godself and in God's act:

> Election should serve at once to emphasise and explain what we have already said in the word grace. God in His love elects another to fellowship with Himself. First and foremost this means that God makes a self-election in favour of this other. He ordains that He should not be entirely self-sufficient as He might be. He determines for Himself that overflowing, that movement, that condescension. He constitutes Himself as benefit or favour. And in so doing He elects another as the object of His love. He draws it upwards to Himself, so as never again to be without it, but to be who He is in covenant

---

[28]See *C.D. II,1*, "The Being of God as the One Who Loves," especially pp. 272-85; *G.G.*, pp. 6-10; *Know.*, pp. 38, 48, 71-75.
[29]See *C.D. II,1*:351-58.
[30]*C.D. II,1*:354. See also *Know.*, p. 38; *Message*, pp. 28-31, 38-39.

with it.[31]

The grace of election chooses and decides for movement, condescension and fellowship as the outward manifestation of the inward love of God. This gracious choice is the being and act of God, the primal and fundamental act which precedes absolutely all other choices and decisions. The fact that God is under no compulsion to be and do this underscores the freedom of God; the fact that God is and does this underscores the love of God. All election is therefore grace to the extent that in God's being as love God freely chooses to give Godself to an other. As the particular form and execution of grace, election manifests the primal being and activity of God as the One who loves in freedom.

5. *The Gospel in nuce.* Barth's view of election as the gospel *in nuce* connects the identity of election and revelation/incarnation with the other two forms of the Word of God (Scripture and proclamation). In his view, election is brought into a position where it constitutes the gospel so thoroughly that gospel and election in effect become identical.[32] The gospel is understood to have election as its basis, substance and goal, and what the gospel announces and proclaims is the good news that God's election means only joy, salvation and life.

The gospel does not have its beginning in time, but in God's eternity, in the pre-temporal life of the triune God before created time. This is the being and activity about which election and therefore the gospel speak. God's primal act of election precedes the announcement of election in history, but this divine decision reaches us in, with and through this announcement. It is thus a manifestation of election. Such a gospel, therefore, can contain no neutrality or mixture of good and evil. Rather as the medium for the gracious expression of God's being in the act of self-revelation, it contains only the love and mercy which characterizes God's being-in-act:

> ... God has decided for this loftiest and most radical movement towards His creation, ordaining and constituting Himself its Friend and Benefactor. It is in this way, in the form of this election, that God has made His decision. And the tidings of the divine decision in this

---

[31] *C.D. II,*2:10. See also pp. 19-20.
[32] See *C.D. II,*2:3-34 for Barth's discussion of the relation between election and gospel. Barth's contention that "the doctrine of the election of grace must be understood quite definitely and unequivocally as Gospel," that election is "the sum of the Gospel" and "the whole of the Gospel, the Gospel *in nuce*" (p. 13-14), places him in the company of James Arminius, who stated that predestination "is the sum and the matter of the gospel; nay it is the gospel itself,..." See James Arminius, *The Writings of James Arminius*, trans. James Nichols, vol. I (Grand Rapids: Baker Book House, 1956), p. 248. See also pp. 217-18, 232-34.

form are glad tidings.... In this form and this form alone the tidings of the divine decision made in Jesus Christ are glad tidings directed to all men, directed indeed to the whole world.[33]

In Barth's construction, the concept of election represents the substance of the gospel because it reflects the primal being and act of God the Subject in God's eternal and temporal movement out of Godself toward an other. The gospel as good news is nothing other than the announcement of this eternal act; through the proclamation of the gospel, it is manifest to the hearers that God has determined to be God only in this way.[34]

6. *Election as Knowledge of God.* In Barth's construction, everything that can be said about the knowledge of God has its basis in God's act of election which is itself the act of self-revelation in which knowledge of God is actualized. The knowledge of God with which the doctrine of election is concerned is the knowledge of the One who determines the divine self to be a certain kind of God, i.e., God's being as Elector. The activity with which the doctrine is concerned is the activity of God in which God actualizes this knowledge in a particular way, i.e., God's activity as election. The doctrine explicates the manner in which God elects, and it does so by explicating the manner in which God reveals Godself; the divine self-revelation is the being and act of God in the human Jesus Christ, and it is precisely this that constitutes the reality of election. "If we would know who God is,... and in what respect He is the electing God, then we must look away from all others, and excluding all side-glances or secondary thoughts, we must look only upon and to the name of Jesus Christ...";[35] the *being* of the One who is revealed in Jesus

---

[33] *C.D.* II,2:26.

[34] Barth's interpretation of the gospel in terms of election is a significant departure from the prevailing views of election. His view of the relation between election and gospel is a corrective to what he saw to be a gospel informed more by a dualism of shadow and light, condemnation and salvation, terror and joy, death and life, Yes and No, than by the gracious and loving being and act of God in the divine self-giving to an other. In his view, there is no biblical warrant or support for either a gospel or an election which contains anything but the unmitigated announcement of God's favor, grace, mercy and love for the other. Any other gospel or election can only be advanced and defended on non-biblical and speculative grounds (see *C.D.* II,2:12-18). Nevertheless, this reconceived relation between gospel and election depends entirely on the premise that election is identical with revelation, and that proclamation is one form of the Word of God (see *C.D.* I,1:88-99, *C.D.* I,2:743-58; *Word*, pp. 97-135, 183-217; *Message*, pp. 28-44; *Sov.*, pp. 11-27). In light of the fact that Barth's discussion of gospel and election signals the radical nature of his reconstruction of the doctrine, it is odd that some of Barth's interpreters have ignored, discounted or misunderstood his position here. See e.g. Berkouwer, *Triumph*, pp. 91-95; Buess, *Zur Präd.*, pp. 23-23; Camfield, *Ref.*, p. 74; Hartwell, *Theology*, pp. 104-6, 157; Hauspann, *KB Doct.*, pp. 2-3; Hendry, *Review*, pp. 396-97; Jenson, *Alpha*, pp. 142-45.

[35] *C.D.* II,2:54.

Christ is the *Elector*. "If we would know what election is, what it is to be elected by God, then we must look away from all others, and excluding all side-glances or secondary thoughts we must look only upon the name of Jesus Christ...";[36] the *activity* of the One who is revealed in Jesus Christ is *election*. The revelation of God which effects the knowledge of God has its origin in, and is wholly determined by, God's primal self-determining act of election executed concretely in the incarnation. It is for this reason that the doctrine of election constitutes the central element in Barth's theology.

The triad of Revealer, Revelation and Revealing can be shown to have its basis in, and its structure determined by, the triad of Elector, Election and Electing in the fact that Barth's construction of the doctrine of election reflects the structural components of the knowledge of God. This is particularly true of both the *objective* and *mediated* character of the knowledge of God. On the one hand, we have the total reality of God's self-revelation described as Revealer, Revelation and Revealing, and in terms of Barth's concept of revelation this means that the being of God takes on human form in order to be known by humanity. God's self-revelation is executed objectively in the incarnation of the Son in the human Jesus of Nazareth in whom God is an object of knowledge. God's self-revelation is executed subjectively in the illumination of the Holy Spirit who effects knowledge. The Subject God (Revealer) has objective being in and through the medium of God's act (Revelation) and is therefore knowable and known (Revealing).

On the other hand, this total reality can be described as Elector, Election and Electing, or Chooser, Choice and Choosing. God becomes human in Jesus Christ, and in terms of Barth's concept of election this means that God elects to become human and unite the divine self with humanity in a relation of fellowship. It can therefore be said that God's election is executed objectively in the incarnation of the Son in the human Jesus of Nazareth with whom God unites the divine self in a relation of fellowship; it is executed subjectively in the effecting of this election in the actual relation of God with humanity. Without the activity of electing, there is no relation, for it is electing that constitutes the subjective reality of God's eternal election. The Subject God (Elector) has objective being in and through the medium of God's act (Election) and is therefore able to relate and actually be in relationship (Electing).

In short, what we find in Barth is this: God elects to be Revealer, the One who is known in relationship (being); this election is executed in revelation, taking objectivity upon the divine self in order to be knowable and relatable (activity in Godself toward an other); God's electing is executed in revealing, effecting subjectivity in order actually to be known

---

[36]*C.D. II*,2:58-59.

54

and in relation (activity with an other). The center and basis of the execution of this total reality is in each case the second term, namely election or revelation, for both signify the identity of God's being and action in Jesus Christ.

The other structural components of the knowledge of God also find their basic expression in terms of election. *Faith* as a noetic relation of the knower to the known, created and established by God's act of becoming its object, is the goal of God's activity of election, and as such it is actualized only in relation to the election executed in Jesus Christ.[37] The knowledge of the electing God and the divine election is true because it is *bound to its object*, i.e., given in its particular form by the divine object who is such as an expression of the primal decision of election. Looking only to the objectivity of God in this electing act for the truth regarding who God is, knowledge is constrained by election.[38] The temporal event in which God *encounters* humanity, in which the divine Subject meets the human subject in order to be and have fellowship with him/her, has its origin in the attitude and eternal decision of God in which God determines Godself to be God objectively in this relationship. Election is executed in the event in which God and humanity are together, knowing and being known by each other.[39] *Grace* is the attitude that characterizes the being and activity of God as freedom and undeserved love for an other. It is in grace that God positions the divine self and humanity for mutual accessibility, and as such it signifies the precedence and initiative of God. It is the being and act of God in election that gives grace its particular determination and fulfillment in the knowledge of God, and apart from election there is no knowledge of the God who freely loves and moves toward an other.[40] There is knowledge of God only because God in this self-revelation has taken the initiative in the decision of election, and because the knower is enabled by the divine decision to respond in an *obedience* whose form and content is determined to correspond to the divine act of election. Except that God elects, and the human responds to this election with obedience, there can be no knowledge of God.[41]

Given these constructive elements and the obvious ontic and noetic precedence of the primal decision of election as the origin and basis of revelation and incarnation, we can make the conclusive

---

[37]See *C.D. II,2*:83, 111, 161, 177, 186. See also *G.G.*, pp. 9-11, 26-32; *Know.*, pp. 25-28, 104-7.
[38]See *C.D. II,2*:51-60, 94-103, 111. See also *G.G.*, p. 30; *Sov.*, pp. 20-21.
[39]See *C.D. II,2*:5-8, 52-54, 103-27, 145-48, 175-88.
[40]See *C.D. II,2*:9-10, 18-19, 27, 62, 91, 101, 118, 121-26, 176, 193-94. See also *Outline*, pp. 15-18.
[41]See *C.D. II,2*:30-31, 177-81. See also *Word*, pp. 58-60; *G.G.*, pp. 29-32; *Sov.*, pp. 19-23; *Know.*, pp. 103-15; and *Outline*, pp. 15-17, 28-29.

observation that it is precisely the divine action of election constitutes the means of the knowledge of God in Barth's theology.

B. Polemic: The Christological Determination of Election

Barth's radical reconstruction of the doctrine of election has its foundation in the identity of election and revelation/incarnation (i.e., in the noetic function of election), and the polemic of the doctrine emerges from the fact that election constitutes the means of the knowledge of God. What may be called the christological determination of the doctrine has its origin in the noetic function of election. For Barth, the fact that election is originally executed and fulfilled in Jesus Christ means that Jesus Christ is the point of departure for the development of the doctrine. But the intra-divine basis for God's self-revelation is the eternal election executed in the incarnation of the Word in Jesus Christ, and it is this choice which is manifest in the divine-human nature of Jesus Christ. The origin of the person and work of Jesus Christ is thus election. The result is that christology is grounded in election, and without his view of election as the primal and self-determining decision of God to reveal the divine self to and be with an other in the concrete form of this union with humanity in Jesus Christ, Barth's christology could not be developed as it is.[42] Dogmatically, subsequently and noetically, the movement is from the objective reality of Jesus Christ as the concrete revelation and execution of election in his unity as God and humanity (object) back to the electing God in God's primal being and act of decision on which everything is based (Subject). Viewed dogmatically, christology is the basis, context and hermeneutic for election. However, this is possible in dogmatic construction only because actually, originally and ontically, the movement is from God's being and primal act of decision (Subject) to the execution and revelation of the decision in the reality of Jesus Christ

---

[42]Barth's christology is articulated in three locations in the *C.D.*: (1) the doctrine of the Word of God in *C.D.* I,2 where the focal point is the incarnation as objective reality and possibility of revelation; (2) the doctrine of election in *C.D.* II,2, where the subject is the being and act of God; and (3) the doctrine of reconciliation in *C.D.* IV:1-3, where christology proper is dealt with. The christological character of Barth's theology is widely noted, and his commentators use a variety of terms, all prefixed with the adjective "christological," to describe the function of Jesus Christ in the construction of his theology as a whole (e.g. orientation, definition, basis, understanding, foundation, interpretation, grounding, approach, formulation, circumscription, concentration, and of course the ubiquitous term christocentric). For discussions of Barth's view of christological election, see Amberg, *Christol.*, pp. 133-38; Balthasar, *Theo. KB*, 25-32, 151-70; Berkouwer, *Triumph*, pp. 89-122; Buess, *Zur Präd.*; Gloege, *Prädest.*; Hausmann, *KB Doct.*; Park, *Man*, pp. 8-59; Klooster, *Signif.*, pp. 39-74; Küng, *Just.*, pp. 9-34; Woyke, *Doctrine*, pp. 103-214, 255-75. For general discussions of Barth's christological emphasis in dogmatics, see e.g. Thompson, *Perspec.*; Hartwell, *Theology*; and Mueller, *K. Barth*.

as fully God and fully human (object). Thus in reality, election is the constitutive basis, context and hermeneutic for christology. It is this twofold movement which contextualizes and qualifies Barth's christological determination, and substantiates his polemical reconstruction of the doctrine. In this section, we will examine Barth's reconstruction in the light of the identity of election and revelation/incarnation, and show that his revision has its origins and determination not in christology, but rather in the noetic function of election which constitutes the basis for his christology in particular and his dogmatics in general. In this way we will expose the priority of election and the roots of what can be called Barth's electional christology.

1. The Origin and Determination of Election. In Barth's view, the eternal living God has never been other than the electing God, and has never acted otherwise than in the confirmation and expression of God's being as the electing God. There is no other God above or beyond the God whose being and activity are originally and finally determined by election. For Barth, this is the God who is the Subject of the doctrine of election, the God whose being and activity are known only in and through election. First and foremost, election is an ontic determination of God, and only on that basis is it subsequently a determination of everything else outside of God. Election does not stand alongside other divine acts. Indeed, there are no other divine acts except those which have their own origin and determination in the act of election.

The fundamental orientation of Barth's reconstruction lies in this view of God in which election as an ontic and noetic category refers primarily not to humanity as the object of election as in the traditional formulations, but preeminently to the being of the triune God as God exists in this self-constitutive act. For Barth, election has its origin in God's decision to choose what kind of God to be, and as such this decision is the ontic *prius* which eternally and temporally precedes and determines all that is constituted by this decision. Election is divine self-determination in the sense that God's being, will and action are wholly determined by Godself; election is the "concrete determination and limitation of his being" which is at the same time "the primal decision which is identical with the basis of the election, and therefore of the eternal divine being in the determination and limitation in which it is the divine being;..."[43] Apart from this volitional act of self-definition, God is not and acts not, and this self-determination is itself election:

> Already this self-determination, as a confirmation of the free love of God, is itself the election or choice of God. It is God's choice that He wills to be God in this

---

[43]*C.D. II*,2:50. See also pp. 6, 52-53, 79, 91-93, 157-58, 168-69, 186.

determination and not otherwise.... It is in the utter particularity of His activity, and therefore of His volition, and to that extent of His self-determined being, that He is the electing God.[44]

The intra-divine decision in which God determines God's being is at the same time an extra-divine decision in that God determines the divine self to be and to be with and for an other outside the divine self.[45] The outward directing of election has its origin and determination in God's choice of Godself to be and act as a being-for-an-other. This is to say that implicit in God's self-determining choice is the choice and determination of an other, and therefore the other must be posited precisely in the divine self-determination, and as such be an object along with God.[46] In this fashion, God's self-determination requires an other and a relation between God and the other, so that this self-determination can indeed precede, determine and give rise to all God's other activity.[47] In Barth's construction, the particularity of this divine self-determination is the constitutive factor in the identity of God's being and act in that God is God in the act of self-giving to an other. God defines and fixes the divine being in a specific character, and this constitutes God's intra- and extra-divine activity which confirms and expresses God's being as the gracious and self-giving One who is free to love and who in this freedom actually loves.[48] In Barth's scheme, this eternal divine decision is identical with the decree of election, and God is known to be this particular God and to act in this particular way because election is at the same time identical with revelation/incarnation.

2. The Rejection of the Decretum Absolutum. Barth's wholesale repudiation of the Calvinist doctrine of the *decretum absolutum* as the origin of election constitutes perhaps in a singular way his most critical reaction to the traditional formulations of the doctrine,[49] and this repudiation can be seen to have its basis in the noetic function of election *vis-a-vis* its identity with revelation/incarnation. The same components

---

[44]*C.D. II,*2:54.
[45]See *C.D. II,*2:6-8, 51-53, 76, 91, 101-2, 115-16, 156-57, 177-78. See also *Know.*, pp. 70-74, 132-33; *Credo,* pp. 62-72; *Outline,* pp. 88-89.
[46]See *C.D. II,*2:161-65.
[47]See *C.D. II,*2:5-11, 51-54, 88-93, 162.
[48]See especially *C.D. II,*2:9-11, 94-95, 124, 163, 167-68, and *C.D. I,*2:377-78.
[49]For assessments of Barth's rejection of the *decretum absolutum* and its constitution as the prime signal for his dogmatic revision, see e.g. Berkouwer, *Div. Elec.*, pp. 156-56; Buess, *Zur Präd.*, pp. 7-13, 25-28, 33-40; Camfield, *Ref.*, pp. 84-85; Gloege, *Prädest.*, 205-17, 233-43; Hartwell, *Theology,* pp. 96-112; Hausmann, *KB Doct.*, pp. 11-35; Polman, *Barth*, pp. 36-40; Sparn, *Revision,* pp. 53-58; Thompson, *Perspec.*, pp. 98-109. For other critical discussions on the idea of *decretum* in election, cf. Brunner, *Chr. Doc.*, 303-20; Daane, *Freedom*; Muller, *Decree*; Reid, *Office*; Riddell, *Decrees*; and Weber, *Found.*, pp. 420-63.

that substantiate this rejection also establish the fact that election functions as the origin and foundation of christology in his dogmatics.

The reasons for Barth's dismissal of the idea of *decretum absolutum* as the point of reference for the doctrine of election in its various traditional forms can be summarized as follows: (1) the idea of a *decretum absolutum* ultimately means that there is an unknown electing God beyond the God who reveals the divine self in Jesus Christ, and this necessarily means that there is finally a separation between election and revelation; (2) the idea can be maintained and defended only by way of a speculative beginning *in abstracto* and an excessive emphasis on the absolutism of God's sovereign freedom and will which is expressed in other ways before and beside electing, and thus by way of ignoring the concrete identity of God's being and act in self-revelation; (3) *decretum absolutum* requires the distinction between God's general will and God's salvific will, between the decree of election and God's other decrees (especially the decree of salvation) which are understood to precede or follow the decree of election, but which may or may not necessarily relate to election *per se*, the result being that the knowledge of election is sought somewhere else than in Jesus Christ; (4) the absolute and unconditional nature of the *decretum absolutum* necessitates the establishment of an inflexible and unalterable system of determinism to which everything must conform and which everything can only fulfill, including God; and (5) the construction of a doctrine of election around the *decretum absolutum* reflects the fact that something anthropologically oriented is ultimately the measure and indicator of the fulfillment of either election or rejection (e.g., the individual's belief or unbelief, obedience or disobedience). But Barth is not only critical of the resolve of the Reformed proponents to hold to and develop the notion of *decretum absolutum*; he is also critical of their opponents who also rejected the idea of *decretum absolutum* on christological grounds (i.e., the role played by Jesus Christ in election), but did not go far enough in the construction of their own polemic by identifying the single and primal decree of election with God's self-revelation in Jesus Christ.[50]

There are two foci to Barth's rejection of the *decretum absolutum*, and together these constitute the substance of the apparent christological determination of the doctrine in its reconstructed form. These foci are Jesus Christ as the concrete decree of election, and Jesus Christ as the Subject/Object of election, and an examination of these two vital

---

[50]Barth's critical discussion of the history and influence of the *decretum absolutum* in the Reformed doctrine of election and the attempts by its Arminian and Lutheran opponents to extricate the doctrine from its overwhelmingly negative consequences are to be found scattered throughout chapter 7. By far the most important discussions appear in the historical excursuses at *C.D. II,2*:60-76, 106-15, 118-20, 127-45, 158-61, 181-84, 192-94, 329-33, but see also the expositions at pp. 24-34, 44-55, 99-106, 166-75. Cf. also Barth, *G.G.*, pp. 17, 23-25, 44-45; *Know.*, 77-79.

components to Barth's polemical reconstruction will advance our contention that election is the origin and basis of revelation and christology.

According to Barth, Jesus Christ is identical with the decree of election because his reality consists entirely in the fact that he is the execution and revelation of the primal self-determining decision of God to be and to be with and for an other in mutual relatedness. As Barth states:

> ... then as the beginning of all things with God we find the decree that He Himself in person, in the person of His eternal Son, should give Himself to the son of man, the lost son of man, indeed that He Himself in the person of the eternal Son should *be* the lost Son of Man. In the beginning with God, i.e., in the resolve of God which precedes the existence, the possibility and the reality of all His creatures, the very first thing is the decree whose realisation means and is Jesus Christ.[51]

In the concrete decree, we have to do with the being and activity of the electing God, concretely conjoined in the ontic and noetic reality of Jesus Christ. The identity of election and revelation/incarnation is what makes it possible to know the electing God and the fact that God's decree is concrete and particular rather than ambiguous and obscure. The concreteness of the decree in its execution and revelation consists in the actual union of this particular God and this particular human being as the basis for God's relationship to the reality external to God. As Barth states:

> [This decree] is the eternal will of God. The will of God is Jesus Christ, and this will is known to us in the revelation of Jesus Christ. If we acknowledge this, if we seriously accept Jesus Christ as the content of this will, then we cannot seek any other will of God, either in heaven or earth, either in time or eternity.... The Son of God determined to give Himself from all eternity. With the Father and the Holy Spirit He chose to unite Himself with the lost Son of Man. This Son of Man was from all eternity the object of the election of Father, Son and Holy Spirit. And the reality of this eternal being together of God and man is a concrete decree. It has as its content one name and one person. This decree is Jesus Christ,

---

[51]*C.D. II*,2:157. See also pp. 5-7, 51-52, 76, 91, 94-145, 178. Also, see Barth, *Know.*, pp. 70-74; and *Outline*, pp. 88.

and for this very reason it cannot be a *decretum absolutum*.[52]

The linkage between God's inner being and activity and God's external being and activity is thus the decree of election in the concrete form of Jesus Christ. God not only wills to be with and for an other; God wills primarily *to be* the other, and the transition from "in Godself" to "outside Godself" is precisely what God decrees. The decree of election is thus the actualization of the divine self-determination: "This self-determination is identical with the decree of His movement towards man.... The reality and revelation of this movement is Jesus Christ Himself."[53] It is his reality as the concrete decree in which God executes this self-determination to be human and thereby be with and for humanity that Jesus Christ is also the revelation of God. The character, form and content of God's self-determining will is identical to the character, form and content of its revelation. The decree has to do with the being together of God and humanity, and it is therefore in his capacity as the God-human that Jesus Christ is the revelation. But the fact that Jesus Christ is the God-human is nothing less than the substance of God's particular, concrete decree, and the concreteness of this decree depends on the identity of God's being and act and the union of God and humanity in the individual Jesus Christ.[54]

Barth contends that the basis of the doctrine of election lies in the fact that the Subject and object of election are knowable and known, and in Barth's conception these two are conjoined in an identity: the Subject and object of election are known because they are identical with the Subject and object of revelation/incarnation.[55] The acting Subject in election is the triune God,[56] and there is an election in God's eternal being and activity *ad intra* before there is a being and activity *ad extra*. As the electing Subject, God the Father wills and decrees the covenant in which God and humanity are together, and toward this end God elects Godself as the Son to be and act as the agent and instrument of this decree. As the electing Subject, God the Son co-wills with the Father, and elects in obedience to be the other *ad extra* in giving the divine self

---

[52]*C.D. II,2*:157-58. See also pp. 8, 52-53, 91, 94-95, 115, 175. Also, see Barth, *G.G.*, p. 51; and *Know.*, p. 70, 77.

[53]*C.D. II,2*:91-92. It is this particular form of the identity of God's being and activity which gives substance to the idea that God's life takes the "form of the history, encounter and decision between God and man" (see *C.D. II,2*:175-94).

[54]See e.g. Barth's discussion at *C.D. II,2*:155-58.

[55]For discussions which clearly indicate the conjoining of the Subject and object of election and revelation/incarnation, see especially *C.D. I,2*:122-39, 147-71; and *C.D. II,2*:49-66, 88-90, 103-8, 115-20, 149, 161.

[56]See *C.D. II,2*:101-15, 158.

to be and act as the executor of the covenant and self-revelation of God. As the electing Subject, God the Holy Spirit co-wills with the Father and the Son, and elects in obedience to be and to preserve the unity and relationship of the Father and Son in the execution of the covenant with the other. But this is known only on the basis of the identity of God's being and act, only on the basis of the fact that God's decision (election) to enter into covenant with an other by becoming human (incarnation) is at the same time the act in and through which God makes Godself knowable and known (revelation).

We therefore must look to the act of this Subject in which the being of the electing Subject is fully present in order to know who this Subject is. In Barth's construction, the being and act of the electing God is predicated of Jesus Christ because as the incarnate Son, he is "very God," and this logically means that God the Son is the acting Subject in the human Jesus Christ. His being is the divine being of the Son who participates actively in the determination and execution of election.[57]

The object of election in Barth's view is first and foremost God: in self-determination, God elects Godself in the person of the Son to be and to be with and for an other in mutual relatedness. Thus the primary object of election is the Son of God, but to the extent that this self-election consists in God's becoming human, it can be said that the human being whom God becomes is also the object of this election. *This particular election of self necessarily implies the election of an other.* Thus the Subject and object of election coalesce in a single reality: the God-human Jesus Christ. The fact that Jesus Christ is the object of election has its basis in the fact that he is the electing Subject. Precisely as the God-human, Jesus Christ is the one whom God elected to be. As the elect human, Jesus Christ is "very human" whose reality consists exclusively in his being the other whom God became. In this respect, Barth contends that "the eternal divine decision as such has as its object and content the existence of this one created being, the man Jesus of Nazareth, and the work of this man in His life and death, His humiliation and exaltation, His obedience and merit."[58]

Jesus Christ's election as "very human" is the direct and explicit goal of his own electing as "very God." Because God's election consists in God's own becoming human, the Subject and object of election merge into a single reality with two distinct facets which are to be described as "very God" and "very human." It is precisely as the identity of Subject and

---

[57]See *C.D. II*,2:95-99, 103-7, 112, 175-81. Jesus Christ is also the electing Subject as "very human," but only in subsequence to his electing as "very God": "It is not that He does not also elect as man, i.e., elect God in faith. But this election can only follow His prior election, and that means that it follows the divine electing which is the basic and proper determination of His existence" (p. 103).

[58]*C.D. II*,2:116. See also pp. 103, 107, 110, 161-63, 175-81.

object that Jesus Christ constitutes the beginning with God, the decree of God, and the revelation of God. Because God's eternal election has to do with the being together of God and humanity concretely in Jesus Christ, the "very human" aspect of the object of election has its reality only in relation to the "very God" aspect which is first and foremost the object of election.[59]

In summary, we can note that the name Jesus Christ signifies an inclusive reference to the God and the human who are involved in election and who come together in a fellowship of mutual relatedness. At its primary level, this election is a self-determination of God in which God chooses to be God in relation to an other outside Godself. This election is a self-election *ad intra* in which God is both Subject and object (the Father electing the Son, and the Son electing to be obedient to the Father). At its secondary level, this election is executed *ad extra* in that it has to do with one who is outside and other than God. Here again, the Subject and object are identical (the Son is the other in the human Jesus Christ). By conjoining the ontic Subject and object of election in the God-human Jesus Christ with the noetic identity of God's being and act in the divine self-revelation executed in Jesus Christ, Barth has most effectively dislodged the *decretum absolutum* and its attendant unknown electing God and elect human being from its traditional position as the origin and determination of both the reality and the knowledge of election. But even as the alternative to the *decretum absolutum*, the concrete decree must still account for the divine Yes and No which Barth is unwilling to surrender, and it is his rejection of the *decretum absolutum* that both clears the way and provides the means for the reconceptualization of the twofold nature of the divine decree of election.

3. *Reconstruction of Double Predestination.* Barth's view of double predestination represents the substance of the one concrete decree of election, and as such it materializes and extends his corrective to the *decretum absolutum*. Barth's objections to the traditional view of double predestination had to do with the fact that it was intrinsically associated with the *decretum absolutum*; it required a deterministic dualism in the form of a logical correlation of two exclusive and opposing wills of the one God directed toward a single object, a speculative and human-oriented foundation for the knowledge that is sought elsewhere than in God's self-revelation in Jesus Christ, and ultimately a separation of the Subject and object of election. In Barth's construction, it is only within the context of election as God's self-determination that the idea of double predestination can have any meaning at all.[60] One must therefore begin

---

[59]For discussions that clearly indicate this identity of the Subject and object in the "very God - very human" construction, see especially *C.D.* II,2:99-107, 110, 116-17, 120-21, 126, 153-63.

[60]Many otherwise helpful discussions of Barth's view of double predestination take

not with humanity as the object of a double predestination, but with God as the Subject of double predestination in terms of what God elects for Godself and what this self-election implies for the other; one must begin with God as the conjoined Subject and object of election.

In Barth's view, the eternal will and decree of God in election is primarily God's self-giving to be with and for an other. As such, this will has a twofold object and content: the primary object is God, and the secondary object is the other; the content refers to what God wills for the divine self and what God wills for the other.[61] God chooses Godself and in this self-choice God posits and chooses the other. The particular determination and choice which God makes concerning the divine self is at the same time a determination and choice of the other.

The fundamental component to Barth's reconstruction of double predestination lies in the fact that the twofold predestination inherent in the singular will of God consists in what God elects for Godself and for the other in order that God and the other may be together in mutual relatedness. God chooses humanity's portion and place for Godself in order that humanity might be received into God's portion and place. God's self-determination consists in electing the negative for the divine self, i.e., God's own humiliation and self-surrender to the judgment and rejection which belongs properly to humanity. But inherent in this self-determination is the determination of the other for whom the positive is chosen, i.e., humanity's exaltation and salvation to participation in life and fellowship with God. The No of predestination refers exclusively to God as the primary Subject and object of election, while the Yes refers only to humanity as the secondary subject and object.

This view of double predestination constitutes the substance of Barth's understanding of the incarnation. Jesus Christ is God in self-determination to become human and be with and for humanity in mutual relatedness, and at the same time Jesus Christ is the human being in humanity's determination to be with and for God. Jesus Christ is God rejected and humiliated, and human elected and exalted.[62] In Jesus Christ,

---

their orientation from his view of Jesus Christ as the electing God and the elect human, or from the relation of election and rejection, rather than from the primal decision in which God determines himself. E.g., see Berkouwer, *Triumph*, pp. 89-122; Buess, *Zur Präd.*, pp. 7-13; Camfield, *Ref.*, pp. 71-85; Hartwell, *Theology*, pp. 96-111; Hausmann, *KB Doct.*, pp. 32-60; Klooster, *Signif.*, pp. 44-71; and Woyke, *Doctrine*, pp. 101-76. Others who do take their orientation from the self-determining decision are Jenson, *Alpha*, pp. 34-36, 66-74, 141-45; Jüngel, *Trinity*, pp. 61-108; Park, *Man*, pp. 24-46; and Thompson, *Perspec.*, pp. 20-33, 61-73, 98-106. One study given completely to Barth's doctrine of election does not deal significantly at all with Barth's views of God's self-determination and double predestination (Gloege, *Prädest.*). Cf. also Brunner, *Chr. Doc.*, pp. 321-39; Vogel, *Gemina*, pp. 222-42.

[61]See the discussion at *C.D. II,2*:161-75.

[62]See especially the discussion at *C.D. II,2*:94, 162-63, 173-75. Barth frequently uses the images of humiliation and exaltation even where election is not the subject of

The Epistemology of Election

the actualization of rejection gives way to the actualization of election. This is the ontic exchange and transition which takes place in double predestination, and because of this, the noetic reality in the life and activity of the God-human Jesus Christ gives rise to the knowledge of this double predestination in a way which is itself determined by that reality. As Barth states:

> The order proclaimed in the work of revelation and atonement must be regarded and respected as also the order of the divine predestination. Naturally we must know what it is that God wills to remove from us. But much more we must know what it is that he wills to give to us. And we can know this only in terms of what God has put behind us because He willed to take it from us and has in fact done so. We can know it only in terms of the abyss on whose brink we are held.[63]

The innovation of Barth's polemical reconstruction of the idea of double predestination, and therefore the creative edge of his doing in the *decretum absolutum*, lies in the fact that the negative side of double predestination refers only to the conjoined Subject and object of election, and not to humanity as such. "In so far, then, as predestination does contain a No, it is not a No spoken against man.... Man is not rejected. In God's eternal purpose it is God Himself who is rejected in His Son."[64] Rejection is therefore not excluded from predestination. Indeed, it is required, but it is utilized by Barth to give form and substance to God's self-election. Removed from its reference to humanity as the object of divine predestination, the idea of rejection becomes a category which lends specific definition and qualification to the reality of the union of God and humanity as executed in the incarnation. In Barth's construction, rejection is the peculiar form of Jesus Christ's election, and as such it refers to his being both "very God" and "very human." Rejection does not apply exclusively or even primarily to the human Jesus as the object of election. Rather it applies primarily to the divine Subject and object in that it refers to what God elects for the divine self in the decision to become a human being in Jesus Christ; it refers to the Son of God as the Subject and object of election.[65] But given Barth's conjoining of the

---

discussion, but rather the matter of incarnation. Outside the *C.D.*, see e.g. *Credo*, pp. 73-104; *Know.*, pp. 45-91; *Sov.*, p. 15; *Outline*, pp. 101-28; and *Hum.*, pp. 46-52. This connection of incarnation with double predestination is described by Hendry as Barth's "dialectical interpretation" which "marks his most radical departure from the tradition and at the same time provides the best clue to the pattern of his thought" (*Form*, p. 310).
[63]*C.D. II*,2:174. See also pp. 164-68, 171-72.
[64]*C.D. II*,2:166-67.
[65]See especially *C.D. II*,2:120-25, 163-68, 172. See also Barth, *G.G.*, p. 22; *Know.*, pp.

65

Subject and object in the God-human, election in the form of rejection is applicable to the human Jesus as well. The acting subject in Jesus Christ is God the Son, and therefore rejection is properly ascribed to God. However, this rejection, suffering, humiliation and death is elected for and by God *as a human being.* It is precisely in this union with the *Son of Man* that the *Son of God* undergoes this rejection, and thus it is precisely as the *Son of Man* that this rejection is executed and manifest.[66]

It is the conjoined Subject and object of election in the God-human Jesus Christ that constitutes the focus of the concrete decree and the notion of double predestination. It is only because this twofold decree is executed and manifest in the incarnation that there can be real knowledge of the electing God and the elect human. In Barth's doctrine, it is this identity of the Subject and object in the execution of election in revelation/incarnation, this identity of the ontic and noetic, which unequivocally precludes any legitimacy to a speculative or anthropologically determined view of the electing God and elect human, or to a logical or systematic equilibrium of election and rejection with respect to humanity.

4. Beyond Supra- and Infralapsarianism. The overthrow of the *decretum absolutum* and the reconstruction of double predestination takes Barth's doctrine of election beyond the circle of discussion on the issues and questions that occupied the lapsarian controversy of the 17th Century. In Barth's estimation, the fundamental errors that beset all parties to this controversy and which prevented any clear and sustaining resolution from emerging into a consensus had to do with the presuppositions which oriented the issues and predetermined and limited the options. The issue in the controversy was the order and relationship between the decree of predestination on the one hand and creation and the fall on the other. Did God predestine individuals first, and then create them and permit them to fall, or did God create first, permit the fall, and then predestine? Was the object of predestination *homo creabilis et labilis* or *homo creatus et lapsus*? Barth saw no possibility of resolution to this controversy on its own terms, and chose not to side with or defend one view over against the other for the reason that he could not share the presuppositions common to both sides. Though the lapsarians were to be commended for their attempt to laud the free grace and sovereignty of God, their positions could not be endorsed because they were based on faulty assumptions: (1) the primary object of predestination in any case is individuals as such who are either elected or rejected, and though Jesus Christ plays a role in the execution of the election for those so chosen, he has nothing whatever to do with those who are rejected; (2)

53, 76, 83-84, 132-33.
[66]See *C.D. II,2*:122-26, 164-67. Also *Credo*, pp. 83-94; *G.G.*, pp. 20-22; *Know.*, pp. 83, 132-33; and *Outline*, pp. 101-18.

predestination necessarily implies the predetermination and establishment of a fixed system which actual existence and history can only fulfill, and this includes God and God's activity in history; (3) predestination also implies an unequivocal equilibrium between the divine Yes and No, mercy and judgment, salvation and damnation, and both sides of this system are directed solely toward humanity, constituting together the divine will to self-glorification; (4) the basis and meaning of the act of divine freedom and the good-pleasure which decides between salvation and damnation are completely hidden and unknown, and can only be understood as *decretum absolutum*.[67]

It is Barth's conception of the content and form of the concrete decree of election that constitutes his advance beyond the alternatives offered by the two sides in the lapsarian controversy, and his construction manifestly presupposes the identity of God's being and act as well as the identity of election and revelation/incarnation. The content of this decree is the mutual relatedness and being together of God and the other, and this implies (1) the creation of this other, (2) the movement toward the other and (3) the mutual relationship between the two. The other by itself is not the content, but rather *the other with God in relationship*. In this respect, being together means not only that God enters the life of the other, but also that God gives God's own being to the other who therefore shares and participates in God's own life.[68] This being together is not a merely occasional and casual togetherness, but a determined and intentional being together whose reality is signified actually and concretely in Jesus Christ as the God-human: "The mystery of the elected man Jesus is the divine and human steadfastness which is the end of all God's ways and works and therefore the object and content of the divine predestination."[69] The conjoined Subject and object of election in Jesus Christ constitutes the concrete content of predestination as God's self-giving for the purpose of uniting the divine self with an other.

The particular form which the decree of predestination takes in Barth's construction is also described as the *covenant relation* which

---

[67]For Barth's discussion of the erroneous presuppositions, see *C.D.* II,2:133-35. Though it is not enumerated by Barth here as a presupposition, it is clear that both sides of the controversy presupposed that the primary purpose of the decree was God's self-glorification in terms of God's mercy and justice accomplished in the salvation of some and the damnation of others. Barth's construction indicated that this too is to be rejected. For discussions of Barth's view of lapsarianism and his reconstruction, see Berkouwer, *Triumph*, pp. 255-61; *Div. Elec.*, pp. 254-71; Hausmann, *KB Doct.*, pp. 23-27; Jenson, *Alpha*, pp. 54-64; Jüngel, *Trinity*, pp. 68-71; Klooster, *Signif.*, pp. 42-52; Park, *Man*, pp. 97-98; Polman, *Barth*, pp. 33-34; Woyke, *Doctrine*, pp. 101-36. For general discussions of the controversy and its issues *vis-a-vis* the doctrine of election, see Brunner, *Chr. Doc.*, pp. 303-53; Daane, *Freedom*; DeJong, *Crisis*; Heppe, *Ref. Dog.*, pp. 133-89; and Muller, *Decree*.
[68]See especially *C.D.* II,2:75, 116-27, 155-58, 161-65, 168-69.
[69]*C.D.* II,2:126.

decisively links God's being and action in Godself to that reality which is distinct from God. The determination of this covenant and the sphere of creation in which this relation is concretely executed constitute the formal reality of the decree of predestination which is promulgated as the origin, basis and goal of all things.[70] The decision of God to be a covenant God in relation to a covenant partner outside the divine self has its primal, eternal and temporal reality in the God-human Jesus Christ. As a subject, Jesus Christ is God choosing humanity, and humanity choosing God; as an object, Jesus Christ is God chosen by the divine self and humanity, as well as humanity chosen by God. At every point, the chooser and the chosen have their reality only in relation to the covenant by which their being and action are determined.[71]

We can summarize the polemic of Barth's doctrine by noting eight areas where he has advanced beyond the supra-lapsarian construction and the traditional components of the *decretum absolutum*, a fixed system determined in eternity and fulfilled in time, and the equilibrium between election and rejection.[72] (1) The decree of predestination is indeed the first decree, and everything else is subordinated to it as the means to its fulfillment. However, the content and form of this decree is not God's election of some and God's rejection of others in order to realize God's self-glorification, but rather God's self-determination to be and to be with and for one who is other than Godself. (2) Humanity and the universe are indeed created to serve the goal of this decree. However, the goal is not primarily God's self-glorification in the display of God's righteous mercy and judgment, but rather God's gracious self-impartation and humanity's exaltation as God's partner in covenant fellowship. (3) The primary object of election is indeed the individual. However, this individual is the God-human Jesus Christ, or God in the union with the human Jesus, and this means that the primary object of predestination is the individual who is brought by God into covenant relation. (4) Predestination is indeed determined in and from eternity in a twofold decree. However, human beings as such are not the objects of this decree. Rather God takes the No of divine judgment of sin upon the divine self and extends the Yes of divine favor on God's covenant partner. (5) Creation is indeed a necessary and vital part of the decree of predestination. However, creation is not the means and forum for the distinction between the elected and the rejected,

---

[70]See *C.D. II,2*:5-9, 95, 102, 116, 155-57, 180-81, 191.

[71]See the discussion at *C.D. II,2*:101-6, 115-17, 145-48, 174-81.

[72]Our observations at this point will both recapitulate the discussion of this section in somewhat different terms as well as anticipate our analysis of Barth's expositions of the election of the community and the election of the individual. Some of what is to be said in this summary will in fact require those expositions for the substantiation of Barth's views of the signification of Jesus Christ's electing and election.

between the mercy and judgment of God *vis-a-vis* humanity. Rather creation is essential to the decree in as much as it constitutes the sphere external to God in which the covenant relation is realized. (6) It is indeed necessary that humanity fall into sin. However, the fall is not necessary in order that one can be saved and so attest God's mercy while another will be damned and so attest God's justice. Rather the fall is necessary so that humanity may actually confront and know that which God rejects, and by God's grace and power actually overcome the evil and sin which God repudiates. God does not will that human beings should sin, but that the covenant partner should say No to what God denies as a possibility, and recognize that he/she cannot overcome the greater power of evil and be reunited with God by his/her own efforts. (7) God does indeed will *homo labilis* as the object of predestination. However, this humanity does not fall in order that it may be either elected or rejected in time, and thus fulfill one or the other of its eternally assigned destinies. *Homo labilis* is not one who will be elected or will be rejected, and who then fulfills this as *homo lapsus*. Rather *homo labilis* is only elected, and remains so after its creation and fall. (8) Human beings are indeed predestined to be witnesses to God's glory, to God's mercy and justice. However, they are not predestined in such a way that one as elected attests God's mercy while another as rejected attests God's justice. Rather they attest God's glory by attesting to God's love which chooses the human being as a sinner and overcomes the sin and evil which keep him/her from participating in God's life. As predestined, the individual attests the Yes which God wills and gives to him/her, and at the same time he/she attests the No which God does not will for humanity and which God rejects by taking its merited judgment upon the divine self precisely in order that it should not fall on humanity. This twofold witness to God's glory is not assigned to two human beings, one elect and the other rejected. Rather both are attested by a single individual.

Barth's polemical reconstruction of the doctrine of election requires that the God who elects and the human who is elected are actually known in the fullness of their respective realities. But the knowledge on which this reconstruction is based can be actual only to the extent that revelation is election in its noetic reality. It is only because Jesus Christ is the revelation of God's being and act that the eternal will and decree of God which precedes and disposes time can be known. This is the case, however, only because ontically Jesus Christ is himself the divine will and decree; God's eternal decree of predestination is identical with its revelation in time because God's decision is the concrete existence of the human Jesus of Nazareth. To the extent that the reality of Jesus Christ is constituted by the fact that he is God electing and relating to humanity, and humanity being elected by and relating to God, the origin, execution, meaning and goal of the will and decree of God are concretely manifest and known, rather than hidden and obscure.

Chapter Three

The Extension
of Election

Because it is centered in the ontic and noetic reality of God's self-disclosure in Jesus Christ, the dogmatic construct of election is vital to the understanding of Barth's view of the election of the community and the individual. When we turn to these areas, we can discern a pronounced correlation between the christological determination of election on the one hand, and the form and content of the constructs of the election of the community and the individual on the other. Our task in the present chapter will be to examine this correlation which consists essentially in what can only be called the functional extension of the reality of God's election into the spheres of the community and the individual, rendering them participants in God's continuing self-disclosure. Here we encounter a subtle and intricate series of interpretations of the community and the individual as objects of election. The notions explicated creatively in these areas not only interpose a medium between Jesus Christ and the individual, but call for the override of traditional opinions regarding the nature and condition of the individual in terms of election and rejection.

A. The Election of the Community

In his discussion of the election of the community, Barth extends the reality of Jesus Christ's election into a new sphere. Indeed, the community as such has no reality apart from its relation to and extension of the election of Jesus Christ, and what we encounter in this discussion is a distinctly theological view of the origin and function of the community *vis-a-vis* the election and revelation/incarnation executed in Jesus Christ. Barth's view of the community has its basis in the noetic function of election, and his exposition consists in an interpretation of the manner in which the community manifests and extends the concrete reality of election accomplished in Jesus Christ.

The dominant motif which informs Barth's discussion is the idea of one elect community which exists in two distinct yet mutually related forms. Barth posits a relation of continuity between Jesus Christ and the one community, and this relation is manifest in the mutuality and

70

continuity of the respective functions of the two forms in relation to Jesus Christ and to each other. The most important element in this motif is the fact that the existence of the community is a concrete manifestation and expression not of election itself, but of the election of Jesus Christ. The community is a revelation not of its own election, but of Jesus Christ's election: "The election of grace, as the election of Jesus Christ, is simultaneously the eternal election of the one community of God by the existence of which Jesus Christ is to be attested to the whole world and the whole world summoned to faith in Jesus Christ."[1] The discussion is organized around Barth's notion of double predestination, but this notion does not refer to the community as the object of election. Rather it refers to the manner in which the one community in its two forms gives concrete expression to the double predestination enclosed and revealed in Jesus Christ who is the electing God and the elect/rejected human. Barth deduces the nature and function of the community from the twofold electing will of God as this applies to the divine self in the act of becoming the God-human. The twofold form and determination of the one community thus corresponds to the twofold form and determination of Jesus Christ. Beginning with the conjoined Subject and object of election in the God-human, Barth develops a construct of the community and its election in which the community is viewed as an extension and manifestation of the twofold determination of the election of Jesus Christ, and not as an independent election.[2] He establishes a formal, material and functional correspondence between Jesus Christ and the community by appropriating the categories of election evident in the election of Jesus Christ in such a way that the community is seen to have its reality only as the reflection, reiteration and extension of his election. What we will endeavor to show in this section is the fact that in Barth's construction, the notion of the one community has its basis in the noetic function of election as a dogmatic category, and its reality is seen to consist entirely in its objective participation in and extension of the identity of election and revelation/incarnation, i.e., its participation in election as the means of the knowledge of God.

 1. The Extension of Objectivity. Barth contends that the relation between Jesus Christ and the community consists in the fact that the election of Jesus Christ includes (*eingeschlossen*) the election of the community in such a way that it corresponds to (*entspricht*), reflects (*spiegelt*), and repeats (*wiederholt*) the election of Jesus Christ, and that therefore the election of the community is neither outside nor independent of his election.[3] As the God-human, Jesus Christ is the

---

[1] *C.D. II,*2:195.
[2] See especially Barth's discussion at *C.D. II,*2:197-200.
[3] See *C.D. II,*2:195-98. The theme of the election of the community does not figure prominently in the literature on Barth's doctrine. When reference is made to it, the

concrete elect human in unity and relation with God, and his person therefore represents the archetype and the reality of the union of God and humanity.[4] In Barth's view, this inclusiveness means that the actuality of the God-human relation in Jesus Christ contains within itself the possibility of the God-others relation by virtue of the humanity which God takes upon the divine self in the execution of election: "... we have to see our own election in that of the man Jesus because His election includes ours within itself and because ours is grounded in His."[5] The humanity which God elects for Godself is the concrete humanity of Jesus of Nazareth, and the nature of this humanity is inclusive in that it implies and renders possible the electional movement from the particularity of the human Jesus to the particularity of the community.

The key to understanding Barth here is the abrogation of the polarity of the general and the particular in what can be called *the inclusive extension of the particularity of election*. The one God elects this human being, and therein is the particularity of the Subject and object of election. The community is included in this one object in that it signifies and extends the relation and function of God and the human in Jesus Christ. To his particularity and the nature and function of his election, there corresponds the particularity of the community and the nature and function of its election. It is this inclusion and correspondence that constitutes the origin, objectivity and function of the community.

The community is an "object" of election with Jesus Christ in its character as a communion whose essential life consists in its relatedness to God. The objectivity of Jesus Christ determines the objectivity of the community in the form of the reflection of Jesus Christ's election. In Barth's construction, the primary expression of this reflection is the fact that the community has two forms, corresponding to the twofold determination of the God-human Jesus Christ:

---

discussion generally overlooks the noetic function of the community's election, and focuses instead on the interposition of the community between Jesus Christ and the individual, and the correlation of the election of the "many" in Jesus Christ and the historical nature of the community. For otherwise useful discussions of Barth's view of the election of the community, see Berkouwer, *Triumph*, pp. 107-11; Buess, *Zur Präd.*, pp. 13-17, 25-27, 52-56; Camfield, *Ref.*, pp. 76-77; Hartwell, *Theology*, pp. 143-46; Hendry, *Review*, pp. 399-401; Polman, *Barth*, pp. 41-42; Woyke, *Doctrine*, pp. 260-65. For discussions which do not take up Barth's doctrine, but which reflect a similar approach to Jesus Christ and the community, cf. Cullmann, *C. & T.*, pp. 115-16, 157; *Christ.*, pp. 161, 172; Daane, *Freedom*, pp. 99-107, 121-47; Jocz, *Theo. Elec.*; Maury, *Pred. & Other*, pp. 64-66; Rowley, *Election*; and Weber, *Found.*, pp. 438-86.

[4]See especially *C.D. II*, 2:117-18.

[5]*C.D. II*, 2:120. See also p. 195. Though he does not have Barth directly in mind, still Daane's notion that God creates what God elects is apropos here in that the God-others relation is effected on the basis of the God-human relation actualized in the election of Jesus Christ. See *Freedom*, pp. 100-106.

The Extension of Election

If the election of the community is included in the election of Jesus Christ, if in and with Jesus Christ it is the object of this primal act of the free love of God, then we must inevitably expect that in its election too we will encounter this twofold (and in its twofoldness single) direction of the eternal will of God.[6]

Double predestination as the twofold determination of Jesus Christ is thus extended to the community; the unity and differentiation of the twofold form of the one community has its origin in the twofold objectivity and signification of the God-human Jesus Christ. In relation to the community, this twofold determination of Jesus Christ is expressed this way:

> Jesus Christ is the crucified Messiah of Israel. As such He is the authentic witness of the judgment that God takes upon Himself by choosing fellowship with man. As such He is the original hearer of the divine promise. As such He is the suffering inaugurator of the passing of the first human form of the community....
> Jesus Christ is also the risen Lord of the Church. As such He is the authentic witness of the mercy in which God in choosing man for fellowship with Himself turns towards him His own glory. He is as such the original pattern of the believer. He is as such the triumphant inaugurator of the gracious coming of the new form of man.[7]

This is the manner in which Barth views the particularity, objectivity and concreteness of the twofold determination of Jesus Christ, and it is this which is rendered objective and concrete in the reality of the community.

The objectivity of the negative determination is extended to the community as it exists in the form of Israel, who as such reflects Jesus Christ's election by signifying that the human who is elected for fellowship with God is the human who is disobedient in his/her unbelief, and who therefore stands under divine judgment. However, rejection and judgment are not extended to the community. Rather Israel's objective

---

[6]*C.D. II,2*:197. Barth introduces and briefly describes the concept of *Gemeinde* ("community") at *C.D. II,2*:196, and indicates some important delimitations for its meaning. Barth's preference for *Gemeinde* as over against *Kirche* to refer to the people of God is well noted by John H. Yoder (see McKim, *Changed*, p. 170). Barth's usage of the term in the doctrine of election, however, makes it clear that *Gemeinde* is the higher category which includes the notion of *Kirche*.
[7]*C.D. II,2*:198.

existence signifies the one who is rejected, and thus this form of the community is an extension of the object of election only in a limited sense.[8] Israel's objectivity consists in its representation of this human being in communal form.

The objectivity of the positive determination is extended to the community as its exists in the form of the Church, who as such reflects Jesus Christ's election by signifying that the God who elects fellowship with humanity is the God of grace, love and mercy.[9] Here there is no limit to the inclusive extension of particularity because the Church also signifies the faithful human in fellowship with God: the Church itself is the object of election, and its objectivity consists in its representation of this human being in communal form.

Barth contends that the two forms of the one community cannot be separated from one another, and that it is only in their unity and differentiation that they constitute the inclusively extended object of election, extending the particularity of the twofold determination of Jesus Christ: "The community is the human fellowship which in a particular way provisionally forms the natural and historical environment of the man Jesus Christ."[10] The community is nothing less than the objective spatio-temporal arena where the execution of God's election in Jesus Christ appears noticeably and becomes operative in humanity.

2. The Concrete Signification of the Community. In Barth's construction, the purpose and function of the community is wholly oriented to and determined by the act of election executed in Jesus Christ. It is this which requires that the community participate in the revelatory function of election and serve as an extended medium of God's self-revelation. In the being and activity of its particular existence, the community is intended to manifest the execution of election in Jesus Christ by giving evidence of the reality of that election.[11] The community has no other reason to exist than the rendering of the service of presenting the election of Jesus Christ. The peculiar *being* of the community consists in the fact that it is the ontic reality, the *humanitas* in space and time, the environment and context, where God's election is executed. The peculiar *activity* of the community consists in the fact that it noetically interposes and arbitrates the election of Jesus Christ to the many, the larger *humanitas* beyond the concrete reality of the

---

[8]See especially *C.D. II,2*:198-200.
[9]Ibid.
[10]*C.D. II,2*:196. See also pp. 199, 205, 233, 260.
[11]The verbs used by Barth to define this determination of the community's existence are *machen sichtbar, darstellen, bezeugen, zeugen, spiegeln, wiederholen* and *aufrufen* (see *C.D. II,2*:195-99, and the connotation of such terms with reference to the community clearly requires the participation of the community in both the election and revelation of Jesus Christ.

community.[12]

This being and activity of the one community is interpreted by Barth in terms of its participation in the execution of the purpose of God in the election of Jesus Christ. (1) God intends to be in a covenant relation with sinful humanity, and to save this lost humanity by taking its place so that humanity may be put in God's place. This *exchange of places* is itself the execution of the judgment and mercy of God, and this takes place only in the spatio-temporal context of the community which therefore participates in the exchange.[13] (2) God intends to reveal and offer the divine self, and to effect this revelation in the incarnation so that God can be heard and accepted by humanity. This *self-revelation of God to humanity* is itself the reality of humanity's hearing and believing, and this takes place only in the spatio-temporal context of the community which therefore participates in the revelation.[14] (3) God intends to transform the covenant partner from its sinful condition so that the partner might be exalted to new life and fellowship with God. This *transformation of humanity* is the passing of the old humanity and the coming of the new humanity, and this takes place only in the spatio-temporal context of the community which therefore participates in the transformation.[15] The depiction of these three perspectives in the exposition indicates that the community is elected primarily to be the locale where Jesus Christ's election is executed, revealed and *extended* to the whole world. It is this, therefore, that constitutes the reality of the community as the environment and medium of election.[16]

In Barth's construction, the concrete reality of the community in both its forms is necessary for the revelation of election in Jesus Christ to be executed effectively. Apart from this environment and medium, it

---

[12]Barth's notion of the election of the community as "a mediate and mediating election" and as the "inner circle" which noetically extends election to the "outer circle" of the world represents the pivotal element in his reconstruction which interposes the community between Jesus Christ and the individual. See *C.D.* II,2:195-97, 266 for discussions which constitute the foundation of Barth's view of this interposition.

[13]See *C.D.* II,2:205-6. The points we are enumerating here follow Barth's own progression in the structure of the discussion of the election of the community ("The Judgment and Mercy of God," pp. 205-33, "The Promise of God Heard and Believed," pp. 233-59, and "The Passing and the Coming Man," pp. 259-305). In our view, he would have been more consistent in his exposition if he had begun with point two below.

[14]See *C.D.* II,2:233-34.

[15]See *C.D.* II,2:260.

[16]The idea of the election of the community as an election for service to the world is the principle notion developed in Rowley, *Election*. He argues that the highest form of election, seen particularly in Israel's election, is "election to be the recipient of the divine revelation and the medium of revelation to others" (p. 45). Though he gives no evidence of familiarity with Barth's view of election, and though he focuses almost entirely on the election of Israel, the similarity between the views of Rowley and Barth on the matter of election for service as a medium of God's self-revelation should not go unnoticed.

would not be possible to perceive and understand the reality and significance of God's election. The revealing which takes place in and through the objectivity of the community consists in the specific use to which God disposes the community. The twofold determination of the community is originally and primarily the twofold determination of Jesus Christ, and the inclusive extension of particularity dictates that one form of the community must signify what God chooses for Godself, while the other form must signify what God chooses for humanity. Out of the extension of this twofold determination comes the concrete existence of Israel and the Church.[17]

Israel reveals what God chooses for Godself because Israel is the *humanitas* chosen by God for fellowship. As such, Israel manifests that God chooses to take its own particular form of existence upon the divine self in order to come to and live with this people, making God heard by them. Furthermore, Israel reveals who the humanity is whom God elects and why this election involves judgment. The *humanitas* chosen by God is an insufferable and disobedient humanity incapable and unworthy of fellowship with God, and therefore subject to the divine judgment. By electing to become this humanity, God takes their merited judgment, suffering and death away from them by taking it upon the divine self. As the unfit and unlovable humanity with whom God desires fellowship, Israel manifests the true character of the humanity taken by God upon the divine self, and Israel does this concretely when it rejects the God who comes as Messiah and delivers him up to suffering and death.[18]

God intends that Israel confirm its election by coming to faith and having its existence transformed, and from within this new reality acknowledge who it was and announce what God has done.[19] However, Israel remains disobedient and does not render its intended service, and it is this Israel that is used by God to manifest the humanity whom God chooses and what it means for God to choose fellowship with this humanity. By remaining disobedient and refusing to affirm its election, Israel discharges its actual service in a manner consistent with its obduracy. However, Israel's service is not determined by Israel, but by God. Whether Israel becomes obedient or not, the fact remains that God uses its disobedience to manifest the negative determination of the divine election of Jesus Christ.[20]

---

[17]See especially *C.D. II,*2:198, 203-4, 207, 234, 238, 261-62, 265.

[18]See especially *C.D. II,*2:206-7, 234-35, 260-61 for Barth's discussion of what Israel reveals regarding what God chooses for the divine self.

[19]See *C.D. II,*2:206-7, 233-34, 260 for Barth's description of Israel's intended service.

[20]This is vital to Barth's construction, and he emphasizes it at several places. See particularly *C.D. II,*2:207, 210-13, 235-37, 261-64. For the particularity of Israel's actual service regarding the manifesting of judgment, hearing the promise and the old and passing form of existence, see *C.D. II,*2:208-9, 236, 262.

The Extension of Election

The discussion of Israel as one form of the elect community is intended to answer the question of what it means for God to elect Godself for fellowship with humanity. But in order to show this, Barth must talk primarily about the human being who is elected. The themes of judgment, suffering and death apply to humanity, and to the extent that these are God's portion in God's self-election, they can be understood to relate to God only by looking at the humanity who is elected and whose election consists in the fact that its sinful human existence, condition and outcome are appropriated by God for the divine self. Judgment as the negative form of God's self-determination not only posits the hearing and passing determination of humanity, but the discussion of these determinations as they pertain to God and to humanity can be undertaken only in terms which fundamentally refer to humanity (i.e., unworthy, rebellious, unfaithful, disobedient, etc.). In short, to talk about what God chooses for the divine self is to talk about the human.

The Church reveals what God chooses for humanity because the Church consists of those who have confirmed their election. But in Barth's construction, the Church does not so much reveal the human who is elected as it reveals the God who chooses the human. The Church manifests that humanity is determined for believing and for a new form of existence in which it is exalted to participation in the very life, glory and mercy of God. The choice of God with respect to this humanity is that all that God is and has and does will be for it, that God will not have the divine life separate from it, and that in divine self-giving God will exalt the covenant partner into a union of fellowship.[21]

In Barth's discussion of the Church, there is no distinction between an intended and an actual service. There is no reason for such a distinction because the Church faithfully and voluntarily discharges its service of signifying the God who elects humanity. In the Church's obedience there is disclosed the life, holiness and glory of God as the positive portion extended to humanity; the Church's faithful service is used by God to manifest Godself and what this means for humanity. By remaining obedient and affirming its election, the Church discharges its service in a manner consistent with its faithfulness. Its life and activity are used by God as the means for manifesting the divine life and activity as the merciful benefactor who speaks and who lives an eternal and indestructible life. Like Israel, the Church does not determine its own service. Rather it is determined by God as the means for disclosing the positive determination of the election of Jesus Christ.[22]

---

[21] See *C.D. II*, 2:199, 210-11, 238, 265 for Barth's discussion of what the Church reveals concerning who God is and what God chooses for humanity.

[22] On the particularity of the Church's service *vis-a-vis* the disclosure of the electing God in relation to mercy, believing and the existence of the new humanity, see *C.D.*

The Hermeneutics of Election

It is clear that the revelatory function of the two forms of the elect community exhibits a symmetry determined by Barth's novel view of double predestination. Israel reveals what God chooses for Godself, and in this revealing Israel discloses that the human whom God elects is disobedient, unworthy and subject to judgment. By manifesting this negative self-determination of God, Israel also discloses that humanity is destined to hear the promise of covenant fellowship and to have its own life in an old and passing form. On the other hand, the Church reveals what God chooses for humanity, and in this revealing the Church discloses that the God who elects is faithful, merciful and ready for fellowship with humanity. By manifesting this positive self-determination of God, the Church discloses that God has given God's own life and glory to humanity, and that humanity is destined to believe the promise and to have its true life in a new and abiding form. In Barth's construction, the community's existence and function as the extended medium of the divine self-revelation consists entirely in the fact that it is the spatio-temporal arena in and through which election as revelation/incarnation is executed in Jesus Christ.

3. The Relation of the Two Forms. The fact that election is primarily a noetic category for Barth, and the fact that the reality of the one community consists in its noetic participation in the objective extension of the election of Jesus Christ is underscored by the manner in which Barth relates the two forms of the one community. His discussion at this point places the emphasis not upon two discrete, historically identifiable communities, but upon the life and activity of one community whose only purpose is to manifest the two dimensions of the single election concretely executed in Jesus Christ. The question therefore does not have to do with two communities, but with two forms of a single community,[23] and the priority at all points in the interpretation of the two forms is given to the singularity of the community.

The fact of the matter is that Barth does not really discuss two

---

II,2:2l0-11, 237-39, 264-65.
    [23]If one were to anticipate that Barth's discussion at this point would be concerned with the question of the historical continuity and co-existence of Israel and the Church *vis-a-vis* the people of God, only disappointment would follow. This question is not an issue or a problem here for Barth. Rather the point of departure is the supposed fact of one elect community. He simply ignores this question, and the resulting construct lacks historical viability and integrity. However, it should at least be stated that, while his one community remains an ideal, it is nevertheless described in some proximity to historical Israel and the Church, and it is this description which gives his otherwise amorphus picture of the one community some credibility. Cf. Buess, *Zur Präd.*, p. 55; Bromiley, *Intro.*, p. 97; Hartwell, *Theology*, pp. 142-47; Jocz, *Theo. Elec.*, pp. 134-36; Polman, *Barth*, pp. 41-42. For studies of the election of the community which bear a marked similarity to Barth's view, but which allow the concept of election to be shaped more directly by the picture of Israel as reflected in the Old Testament, and which have a greater appreciation for the historic life of Israel, see Daane, *Freedom*; Rowley, *Election*; and Weber, *Found.*

forms of one community. Rather his exposition suggests that we have to do with two distinct services or modes of revelation used by God to achieve the purpose of the divine election. The relation of the two forms of the one community is really the relation of two services undertaken by one community and expressive of the twofold self-determination of the one electing God. This relation is therefore a noetic relation in that God's purpose in the election of the community is the revelation and extension of the electing and election of Jesus Christ. What we find in the discussion of the two forms is in fact an intra-penetration and mutual dependence of two distinct services rendered by the one community:

> In this its twofold (Old Testament and New Testament) form of existence there is reflected and repeated the twofold determination of Jesus Christ Himself. The community, too, is as Israel and as the Church indissolubly one. It, too, as the one is ineffaceably these two, Israel and the Church. *It is as the Church indeed that it is Israel and as Israel indeed that it is the Church.*[24]

From a theological rather than an historical point of view, Barth's discussion is to be interpreted as the positing of an Israel-service and a Church-service by the one community relative to the signification of God's election. From the standpoint of Israel and its service, the intra-penetration and mutual dependence is to be seen in Barth's idea of the pre-existence of the Church in Israel. From the standpoint of the Church and its service, the intra-penetration and mutual dependence is to be seen in the notion of the fulfillment of Israel in the Church. Israel is the one community because it contains within itself a Church-service, and the Church is the one community because it contains within itself an Israel-service.

Barth's notion that Israel is the secret origin of the Church corresponds to the idea that the crucified Messiah of Israel is at the same time the secret Lord of the Church. The nascent presence of the Church in Israel represents the fact that the context of Israel's disobedience is the mercy and faithfulness of God, apart from which Israel's service cannot signify anything regarding either the negative self-determination of God or the unwillingness, incapacity and unworthiness of humanity. Israel cannot signify the judgment of God or the fact that humanity is determined to hear the promise and to have its life in an old and passing form unless there is signified at the same time the mercy of God and the

---

[24] *C.D. II,2*:198. Emphasis mine. See also pp. 210, 238, 266. This intermingling of Israel and the Church does not effect an identity. What unites and differentiates them is not their spatio-temporal presence and co-existence, but their mutual and complementary signification of God's election.

fact that humanity hears in order to believe and has its life in an old and passing form in order to receive its life in a new and coming form. In brief, the context of Israel's signification is the Church-service which expresses the positive self-determination of God and its concomitant determination of humanity. The point of Israel's service requires a Church-service as its counter-point. In Barth's view, the election of God in its twofold determination has always been signified even before it achieved its complete and perfect revelation in the appearing of the elect human Jesus Christ. In this respect, Israel represents an ante-signification of Jesus Christ in the period prior to his coming. The fact that Israel appears in time before the Church does not in the least alter the fact that the Church-service is present in Israel as the context of the signification of its message. Quite the contrary, this is what Barth means to suggest by the pre-existence of the Church in Israel. His discussion of this matter can only be understood as the signification of God's mercy by the presence within Israel of those who have apprehended, believed and experienced the promise, and have known the transforming and consoling power of God in God's salvation. This is precisely the signification of the positive self-determination of God; this is the Church-service in Israel.[25]

In Barth's scheme of relation, the Church recognizes itself in Israel and acknowledges in Israel's Church-service the paradigm of its own service. The elect in Israel who discharge this Church-service represent for Barth not only the origin of the Church as such, but more importantly the hermeneutic for the Church's own existence.[26]

Barth's notion that the Church is the fulfillment of Israel's election corresponds to the idea that the risen Lord of the Church is at the same time the revealed Messiah of Israel. The revealed presence of Israel in the Church represents the fact that the context of the Church's faithfulness and obedience is the judgment and obduracy of humanity, apart from which the Church's service cannot signify anything regarding either the positive self-determination of God or God's good-will, readiness and honor with respect to the covenant partner. The Church cannot signify the mercy of God or the fact that humanity is determined by God's election to believe the promise and to have its life in a new and coming form unless at the same time there is signified the judgment of God and the fact that, if left in its own sinful self-determination,

---

[25]For Barth's argument on the pre-existence of the Church in Israel, see *C.D. II,2*:198-99, 206, 211-13, 239-40, 266-67. The presence of the pre-existent Church does not alter or minimize the special determination of Israel to manifest the negative determination in God's election. On the contrary, the fact of the Church-service in Israel only confirms Israel's election, and Israel discharges its negative service only because of the presence of the pre-existent Church.

[26]See especially *C.D. II,2*:213, 240, 267. Because of the Church-service in Israel, Barth can maintain the singularity of the one elect community in spite of its two forms, the existence of which might otherwise require the positing of two communities.

humanity cannot and will not believe even though it hears, and that its own choice is to remain in its old and passing form of existence. In brief, the context of the Church's signification is the Israel-service which expresses the negative self-determination of God and its concomitant determination of humanity. The point of the Church's service requires an Israel-service as its counter-point. In Barth's view, the twofold self-determination of God in eternal election achieves its fullest and most complete expression in Jesus Christ, and in this respect the Church represents a post-signification of Jesus Christ in the period after his coming. The temporal emergence of the Church after Israel is in no way to be viewed as a displacement of Israel from the elect community, or as a nullification of its own service. Quite the contrary, the emergence of the Church constitutes a further disclosure and confirmation of Israel's election and service, and this is what Barth means to suggest by the fulfillment of Israel in the Church. However, his discussion of this matter can only be understood to suggest the faithful, obedient and voluntary signification of the negative determination of election by those within the Church itself who attest the judgment of God and who have moved on from hearing to believing, from an old and passing form of existence to a new and abiding one. This is precisely the intended service of Israel itself, the signification of the negative self-determination of God; this is the Israel-service in the Church.[27]

Barth argues that the twofold signification of election by the one community is in fact rendered by the Church in spite of (or even because of) the absence of Israel as a whole. The Church is the consummate form of the one community because it includes the Israel-service within itself; the purpose for which Israel is elected is fulfilled in the Church. Israel as such does not come to faith and enter the Church to contribute its peculiar witness to the signification of the one elect community. Rather Israel's actual life and activity are used by God in the Church to accomplish this signification, and therein Israel's determined purpose is

---

[27]For the discussions relating to the fulfillment of Israel in the Church, see *C.D.* II,2:198-99, 200-201, 206-8, 210-13, 233-36, 237-39, 260-63, 264-67. Barth argues that Israel will perform its intended service if and when it becomes obedient and enters the Church. At that point its message will constitute the "undertone" [*Unterton*] (p. 208), "background" [*Hintergrund*] (p. 260) and "foreword" [*Vor-wort*] (p. 265) to the Church's positive service. However, the fact that Israel has not come into the Church means that in Barth's construction, the one elect community lacks an internal unity, and therefore cannot present one voice with a twofold message to the world. Barth's view of the one elect community has no temporal reality, and remains only an eschatological ideal. On the other hand, Barth's view suggests that whether or not Israel as such ever voluntarily renders this service is finally immaterial. Since Israel itself will not provide this service from within the Church, this service is nevertheless provided by the Church. To the extent that such service is a constituent element in the Church's signification, it can only be called an Israel-service, not because Israel renders it but because what is rendered is peculiarly Israel's signification.

fulfilled *in the Church*, i.e., in the Israel-service discharged by the Church as the consummate form of the one community. In Barth's scheme, it is this presence of the Israel-service that constitutes the Church as "the perfect form of the one elected community."[28]

We may summarize Barth's view of the election of the community by stating that it emerges formally and materially from the notion that the singular purpose of God is the extension of the self-revelation which has taken place in the election of Jesus Christ, and that because this election is twofold in its determination, there is required within the one community a twofold service, one in the form of Israel and the other in the form of the Church. The unity of the services consists in their being rendered by one community, and their differentiation consists in the disclosure of two distinct dimensions of God's single election. The unity and differentiation which constitutes the relation refers, therefore, to the intra-penetration and mutual dependence of two modes of presentation of the divine election executed in Jesus Christ. In Barth's scheme, Israel and the Church appear to collapse into each other because he is concerned not with two historically identifiable communities, but rather with the one self-revelation of God in Jesus Christ and the signification of this by the inclusive extension of particularity. The uniqueness of Barth's view of the election of the community consists in the fact that his emphasis upon revelation constitutes the substance and signification of the singular community, the two forms of which are determined by election to correspond to the self-determination of God.

B. The Election of the Individual

Barth's view of the individual extends his polemical reconstruction into a vital nerve center of the traditional views of predestination. His revision requires that the matter of the individual be placed at the end of the discussion, not because the individual is least important, but because

---

[28]This appears to be Barth's favorite term to describe the Church as a form of the elect community. See e.g. *C.D. II,2*:210, 211, 213, 237, 239, 264, 265. We should not understand Barth to be saying that this Israel-service refers to the presence of Jewish Christians in the Church, though such presence does lend this negative signification. Whether or not the Israel-service is present in the Church is not contingent upon the presence of such Christians; the presence of Jews in the Church is not the same as the presence of Israel as a whole in the Church. It is precisely the fact that Israel as a whole is not in the Church that constitutes the basis for the Israel-service in the Church. Barth's comments about Jewish Christians in the Church are rather vague in themselves (see e.g. *C.D. II,2*:213, 234, 235, 240, 267). Nevertheless it is clear that the Israel-service in the Church does not refer to the presence of Israel as such, any more than the Church-service in Israel refers to the presence of the Church as such. It is not a matter of identity, but one of mutual signification and representation. This is what *pre-existent Church* and *fulfillment of Israel* mean for Barth.

the individual is not the most important element in the doctrine. What is ultimately important for Barth in the doctrine of election is not the status of the individual *vis-a-vis* election, but the position, determination and domination of Jesus Christ as the preeminent Subject and object of election.[29] The election of the individual in Barth's construction is a notion used to expound and interpret further his view of the election of Jesus Christ.

The election of the individual, like that of the community, is included in Jesus Christ's election, and extends that election into the new sphere of the being and activity of the individual human being. In Barth's construction, however, the *telos* of the individual's election in Jesus Christ does not consist primarily in the achievement of personal salvation. Rather the primary concern here is the reality and interpretation of the election of Jesus Christ, and the function of the individual in relation to this election. With Barth, the individual's election refers to something more than just salvation or what is traditionally understood to constitute salvation; election and salvation are not coterminous for Barth. Rather salvation is included in election as one of its components, and we find with Barth a unique view of salvation which is itself defined in terms of his particular view of election. The individual is not so much elected to salvation as he/she is saved for the purpose of election.[30] Barth's discussion of the individual is determined by the noetic function of election, and consequently the individual is seen to have his/her reality as an objective representation and interpretation of the election of Jesus Christ. The question is not so much whether and how the individual is saved as it is what the individual signifies regarding the election of Jesus Christ and the manner in which he/she participates ontically and noetically in Jesus Christ's election.

The motif which informs Barth's construction at this point is the

---

[29]Barth argued that once this position of Jesus Christ in the doctrine of election has been firmly established, the order in which the doctrine takes up its usual topics is inconsequential (see *C.D.* II,2:309). However, given his methodology both in and outside the *C.D.*, it would be difficult to imagine a "Barthian" doctrine of election which begins with the individual and ends with Jesus Christ for the reason that such a methodology would be an illustration of a theology which begins with humanity rather than God, and this was abhorrent to Barth. At the very least, even if the priority in understanding was given to Jesus Christ, such an order would threaten the doctrine and put it at a greater than necessary risk with regard to the tendencies toward anthropological determination inherent in a methodology which begins with the human. In the final analysis, Barth's particular order is the only one possible if the doctrine of election is to have Jesus Christ as its principle Subject and object, and if election is to be maintained as a noetic category.

[30]See especially *C.D.* II,2:306-11, 417-18, 423-24, 427-28, 430, 449. Barth's view of the *telos* of the elect individual, in correspondence with the *telos* of the election of Jesus Christ, constitutes the basis for his critique of the individualistic approach of the traditional views of predestination. With the elect individual as an active participant in the context of the community, Barth has set a limit on individualism and a privatistic view of salvation.

notion that the being and activity of two distinct yet mutually related individuals is required for the fulfillment and manifestation of the election of the one individual Jesus Christ, and that the existence of these two individuals is to be interpreted solely in terms of how they function in relation to his election as the God-human. Just as two forms of one community signify the election of Jesus Christ, so two individuals manifest the reality *and telos* of his election. Once again, Barth's reconstructed view of double predestination constitutes the principle by which the discussion is organized, and it unfolds here in terms of the determination of two individuals to correspond to, participate in and manifest, not the double predestination of two individuals, but the twofold determination of Jesus Christ and his election. Double predestination simply does not apply to the individual as such. The nature and function of the necessary two individuals is deduced from this twofold determination which applies exclusively to Jesus Christ as *the* object of election. In the last analysis, there is only one teleological determination of the individual, and it is for the purpose of signifying this one determination that Barth deduces two classes of individuals.

Our task in this section will be to demonstrate that in Barth's view, the predestination of the individual as an object of election has to do finally with only one individual. We will seek to show that Barth's revision of the notion of the individual as the object of election is a vital component to his overthrowing the symmetry and equilibrium of the old double predestination in the *decretum absolutum* of the traditional formulations. In this regard, we will see that election in Barth's view is to be understood as the knowledge of the being and act of God and the individual's participation in God's own life and self-revelation as its objective extension toward others who do not yet know God.[31]

1. The Individual as Object of Election. In his discussion of the election of the individual, Barth does not begin with a view of the individual as an historical being in time and then bring this view to bear on the question of the individual's election. The anthropological presupposition in this approach was a problem of the traditional doctrine which Barth wished to avoid. Rather Barth's understanding of the

---

[31]For other places where Barth's discussion sheds light on his view of the relationship between the individual, his/her participation in Jesus Christ and his/her knowledge of God, see *C.D. I,2*:362-454; *Sov.*, pp. 19-25; *Know.*, pp. 81-91; *Adam*, pp. 4-7. For germane (but otherwise short-sighted) discussions of Barth's view of the individual in election, see Bloesch, *Victor*, pp. 32-42, 60-71; Bouillard, *KB*, vol II, pp. 135-41; Buess, *Zur Präd.*, pp. 17-22, 56-60; Camfield, *Ref.*, pp. 78-82; Hartwell, *Theology*, pp. 112-41; Hausmann, *KB Doct.*, pp. 39-60; Klooster, *Signif.*, pp. 57-64; Küng, *Just.*, pp. 54-58; Park, *Man*; Polman, *Barth*, pp. 42-53; Woyke, *Doctrine*, pp. 185-214, 260-70. On the individual and election, cf. Berkouwer, *Div. Elec.*, pp. 172-217; Cullmann, *C. & T.*, pp. 217-21; Jewett, *El. & Pr.*, pp. 47-106; Jocz, *Theo. Elec.*, pp. 135-64; Maury, *Pred. & Other*, pp. 59-69; Rowley, *Election*, pp. 95-172; Vogel, *Gemina*, pp. 222-42; and Weber, *Found.*, pp. 465-80, 493-507.

individual follows from his view of Jesus Christ and his election, and this means that the individual as a human being in time and space is quite simply human being elected by God. The individual is not first a particular human being who then becomes the object of election as the result of God's choice. Rather the individual as such is an individual *precisely because he/she is first the object of election*. It is election that constitutes the origin and determination of the other in the sense that he/she is brought into existence as the object of God's election; the determination of the individual to be the object of election precedes and constitutes his/her individuality.[32] The singularity of the individual as the object of election is based on the singularity of the electing God as Subject who desires to have the divine being and activity in a fellowship with an other.[33] What this means is that the humanity of the individual is conditioned by election; he/she is created and determined through election to be an individual who is other than God, but also to be the covenant partner of God.

The question then is not whether an individual is the object of election, but whether *as the object of election* the individual has or has not yet fulfilled his/her divine pre-determination. In Barth's view, election as God's eternal predestination of the individual means that the individual is eternally intended and envisioned by God as the object of election.[34] Barth's definition of the individual has its basis in the ontic reality of Jesus Christ as the eternal and temporal individual whose being and act constitute the beginning of all God's ways and works. Whatever else may be said about the individual must acknowledge that his/her divine determination to be a particular individual who is elected supercedes all other natural, human and historical determinations.[35]

The correspondence between Jesus Christ's election and the individual's election means that the unity and differentiation that characterizes Jesus Christ's election also characterizes to some extent that

---

[32]The christological re-orientation to the discussion of the individual and his/her election is a major element in Barth's attempt to revise and correct the older doctrine (see especially *C.D. II,*2:41-45, 51, 58-76, 116-55, 168-88, 325-26). The idea of individuality for Barth does not consist primarily in the particularity of a human being *vis-a-vis* the group. Rather a human being is an individual because the human being is the object of election; the concept of individual is analytic to the concept of the object of election for Barth (see *C.D. II,*2:310-14).

[33]See especially *C.D. II,*2:140-41, 314-18, 343. The elements of concreteness, particularity and individuality in the ontological movement from God through Jesus Christ to humanity figure prominently in the strategy adopted by Barth in his study of Romans 5 (see *Adam*, pp. 4-6).

[34]There is no other meaningful way to interpret Barth's discussions at *C.D. II,*2:155-188, 321-40, 343-45, 362-401, but cf. Balthasar, *Theo. KB*, p. 115; Bloesch, *Victor*, pp. 32-42; Buess, *Zur Präd.*, pp. 39-40; Camfield, *Ref.*, pp. 78-80; and Park, *Man*, pp. 60-114, 187-89.

[35]See *C.D. II,*2:410-11.

of the individual. The issue for Barth has to do with the nature and extent of the individual's participation in, correspondence to and interpretation of the election of Jesus Christ. As the object of election, Jesus Christ is a single individual who is both rejected and elected, and for Barth's movement this means that the rejection and election that are together in a unity and differentiation in him are constitutive of the individual.[36] In order to extend and manifest the election of Jesus Christ, a duality consisting of an elect individual and a rejected individual is required. But in this duality, the two are to be held together so that they interpenetrate and mutually interpret each other in conformity with the twofold determination of the one individual Jesus Christ. The essential difference between an elect and a rejected individual is simply that the former is one whose life is distinguished by a relationship to God in fulfillment of his/her election, while the latter is one who lacks this relationship. The elect individual is one who lived as a rejected individual isolated from God, but now lives as one in whom his/her election is fulfilled in fellowship with God.[37]

In Barth's view, therefore, it is necessary to speak of two individuals, one elect and the other rejected, because it is only in these terms that the reality and significance of Jesus Christ's election can become manifest. The fact is that, for Barth, the individual who merits rejection, the individual whose self-determined life is lived in sinful opposition, resistance and isolation so that he/she deserves only wrathful judgment, is precisely the object of God's election.[38] The possibility of actually living such a godless life of the rejected to its ultimate and bitter end is forever annulled and removed in Jesus Christ.[39] The single

---

[36]See the discussions at *C.D. II*,2:117, 308-25, 350-54, 450-55, and the exegetical passages at 372-75, 420-22 and 458-65.

[37]See *C.D. II*,2:340-46, 410, 449-51. This matter of the unity and differentiation of the individual is underscored in detail in Barth's discussion of recollection and expectation where it is obvious that unity and differentiation have to do not with two individuals but with the individual *per se* as the object of election (see *C.D. II*,2:347-54). The individual lives either as one for whom rejection is no longer the characterization of his/her life, or as one for whom election is not yet the characterization because his/her eternal predetermination remains unfulfilled. Either way, he/she is, like Jesus Christ, the single individual. The fact that the individual is both rejected and elected means that "individual" is a higher category for Barth than the polar categories of "rejection" and "election," and that the unity is given precedence over the differentiation. Although Barth does say: "There are, in fact, these two classes of men, the called and the uncalled, the believing and the godless, and therefore the elect and apparently rejected,..." (p. 351), he does so only to draw attention to the differentiation which reflects the twofold determination and significance of the election of Jesus Christ. In this respect, he has moved beyond his earlier lectures on election where he was reluctant to speak in terms of categories which delimited two separate classes of humanity (see *G.G.*, pp. 26-28, 49-51).

[38]See *C.D. II*,2:306, 318, 449-50.

[39]See *C.D. II*,2:316-17. The negation of the individual's self-determined status as a godless human who is rejected by God ultimately means that his/her status as a rejected

individual who is the object of election is variously described by Barth as a rejected individual who is nevertheless elect, or as an elect individual who was rejected. In any case, the seeming opposition between the two can only be relative and not absolute.[40] The solidarity, therefore, is not between two separate individuals, one elect and the other rejected. Rather it is an ontological solidarity of one individual with Jesus Christ in whom is found the being of the rejected individual transformed and superseded by the being of the elect individual. The one who lives as a rejected individual is the object of election in that he/she has his/her existence only in relation to Jesus Christ and the fulfillment of election in him.[41]

2. *The Actualization of Election.* In Barth's construction, we learn through the revelation of election in Jesus Christ that election means the predetermination of the individual by the will of God to be and to live as an elect individual in covenant fellowship with God and in correspondence with Jesus Christ in whose election his/her own is included. As we noted previously, this will of God refers positively to what God intends and negatively to what God does not intend. That which is not willed stands in opposition to that which is willed, but this opposition is not inherent in God's will; there are not two opposing wills of God. Rather this opposition reflects the fact that one thing is willed and intended (elected) while another is not willed and excluded (rejected). In this respect, the election revealed in Jesus Christ discloses the fact that it is not the individual *per se*, but the individual's *rejection* that is decisively excluded. The individual is not determined by God to be rejected; rather precisely as a rejected individual he/she is predetermined by God to be the object of election and *represent* what it is that God does not will for the covenant partner: "He wills that the rejected should believe, and that as a believer he should become a rejected man

---

individual has no permanence or ontological validity. God's choice of precisely this godless, self-determined individual precedes and supersedes the individual's negative choice and self-determination (election precedes creation and the object of election is *homo creabilis et labilis*), and the result is that the individual's status as a rejected individual is only conditional and potential; he/she can only live *as though* he/she was rejected. What we have in Barth's position, therefore, is a single individual with a twofold determination, one who is both rejected and elected, but whose rejection is eternally annulled by the divine determination to be the object of God's election *in and with Jesus Christ.*

[40]See especially *C.D. II,2*:326-29, 350, 372-78, 419, 450-53.

[41]See *C.D. II,2*:328, 347-48, 354, 372, 451-53, 456. The unity and differentiation of the individual as the object of election makes it possible to describe Barth's view as one in which the elect individual *pre-exists* in the rejected individual, and the rejected individual finds his/her *fulfillment* in the elect individual. When Barth describes the rejected individual as the embodiment of "the pure object of election--the elect 'before' and without his election, the elect without his appropriate determination" (p. 456), the distinct implication is that the elect individual can only be described as the rejected *after and with the fulfillment* of his/her election, the rejected *with* his/her appropriate determination.

elected."[42]

Unlike the traditional doctrine, Barth's concept of the actualization of election does not have its basis in the mutually exclusive categories of two separate individuals. Rather it has to do with the single individual and how it is that he/she ceases to live as a rejected individual and begins to live in the fulfillment of his/her election. The fact that the individual's predetermination is unfulfilled does not mean that he/she is not elect. It simply means that his/her election has not yet been actualized in his/her concrete life; he/she has not yet made the transition to his/her predetermined life.[43]

In Barth's scheme, this transition presupposes a dichotomy between the being of the individual and his/her act as such, and it has to do with the extent to which an identity of being and act is actualized in the individual. The fact that the individual may live as a rejected individual does not alter his/her ontic determination to be the object of election. Rather this fact merely indicates that his/her actual life is in conflict with his/her ontic determination; there is no identity of being and act in that he/she does not give expression to his/her essential being in and through his/her act. The transition about which Barth is concerned here is nothing less than the idea that the fulfillment of election consists in the establishment of an identity of being and act in the individual. To be and to live as an elect individual is to be and to live in correspondence with God, i.e., to have a being which is wholly determined by election and which is integrally expressed and confirmed in activity.[44]

The transition takes place when the individual's true being is disclosed to him/her in revelation, and he/she learns that he/she *is* an elect individual who is now to *live* as such.[45] What differentiates an elect from a rejected individual, therefore, is not that the being of one is determined by God's election while that of the other is not. Rather it consists in the fact that the true being of one has been disclosed and confirmed while that of the other has not yet been disclosed and remains

---

[42]*C.D. II,*2:506. See also pp. 141, 315-16, 319, 346-47, 352-53, 421-22, 450, 453-55, 496. This idea of the rejection of rejection in Jesus Christ is the most important element in Barth's denial of a balanced system of election and rejection as well as his denial of the individual's foreordination to sin and evil (see especially pp. 127-45). For the discussion of the divine determination of the elect, see pp. 410-17; and for the determination of the rejected, see pp. 449-58 and the related discussions at pp. 377-87, 458-60, 470-71, 477, 504-6. The existence of the rejected individual is not determined by God's non-willing (cf. Camfield, *Ref.*, p. 82). Rather the freedom and will of the individual as such is established in Barth's view by the fact that the individual can and does *determine him/herself* as one over against God, and thus as one whom God will not have and therefore "rejects," but who precisely as such is used by God to manifest what it is that God does not will.

[43]See *C.D. II,*2:321-22, 341-43, 410-11, 413.

[44]See especially *C.D. II,*2:321, 343-44.

[45]See *C.D. II,*2:322, 340-41, 345, 348, 443-44.

unfulfilled.

For Barth, election and the identity of being and act are actualized in the individual's faith, i.e., his/her believing response to the election promised and revealed in Jesus Christ. It is in this act that the correspondence between God and the individual is achieved. Faith is the divine determination of the individual's life which enables his/her living and acting to be transformed and brought into a harmonious unity with his/her being; it is the individual's act which is itself determined, effected and evoked by God's election. This response to the divine election "rests on Jesus Christ as the promise of divine compassion towards the ungodly, and it does so as a work and gift of the Holy Spirit."[46] The individual who lives in the fulfillment of his/her election is thus one who knows God as the Elector in the act of Election and Electing, and lives with God in the fellowship of mutual relatedness; the individual who lives as though he/she was rejected is one who does not yet know God to be and act as such. There is no knowledge of God apart from the execution of this election and its actualization in the faith of the individual.

3. The Signification of the Individual. In Barth's doctrine, the existence of the individual, whether as rejected or elect, serves as a manifestation of the reality of Jesus Christ's election in its twofold determination, and this means that the individual is constituted as a medium of the revelation of the election of Jesus Christ. The life of the rejected and the elect individual represents and explains the meaning of his/her election by extending it out to the world. In correspondence with Jesus Christ, the individual is a witness who participates in God's self-revelation,[47] and an instrument in and through whom God's election is

---

[46]*C.D. II,2*:327. See also pp. 339. This is the first of Barth's merely passing references to the role of the Holy Spirit in the election of the individual (cf. pp. 345, 348-49, 350, 351, 414-15, 426, 457-58). What seems to be implied in these passages is the idea that the Holy Spirit is the revealing and active presence of God in the actualization of the individual's election; it is the divine being and act in, with and for the particular individual. However, Barth makes no attempt to develop in any significant way the role played by the Spirit in the individual's election. Nevertheless, it should be observed that Barth rejects the idea that faith is the cause of the individual's election. Faith does not precede, but rather follows election as its expression. It is the *response* which perceives, acknowledges and cooperates with the calling and transition which God effects in his/her life. Faith as such is a divine act in that God enables the individual to respond, and it is a human act in that the individual responds in a particular way to the self-revelation of God and the announcement of his/her own election. Thus Barth can say that whether the individual lives in the fulfillment of his/her election "is something which is not decided in the word of promise. It is decided in the adoption of the attitude which this subject adopts to the address made to him, and in which he shows whether he is instructed or uninstructed by the promise, that is, whether he is converted or unconverted" (p. 324). For Barth's discussions on the relation between faith and election, see pp. 126, 157-61, 177, 197, 200, 233-35, 237-40, 244, 322, 326, 333-34, 427, 453-54.

[47]For the important discussions regarding Jesus Christ and the individual as witness, see *C.D. II,2*:306, 339-40, 342, 345-50, 351-54, 364, 389, 411-19, 421-26, 428, 430-32, 444, 449,

accomplished.[48] The content of the individual's witness is Jesus Christ, and the mode of his/her instrumentality is patterned after the objectivity of the incarnation in that it consists in the particularity of the individual's human being and activity in and through which God's election is actualized. Together the elect individual and the rejected individual noetically represent and extend the twofold determination of God's election executed in Jesus Christ:

> Thus Jesus Christ is the Lord and Head and Subject of the witness both of "the elect" and also of "the rejected." For all the great difference between them, both have their true existence solely in Him.... The elect are always those whose task it is to attest the positive decree, the *telos* of the divine will, the loving-kindness of God. And the rejected must always accompany them to attest the negative decree, that which God in His omnipotence and holiness and love does not will, and therefore His judgment. But it is always the one will of the one God which both attest.[49]

In Barth's construction, nothing at all can be posited concerning the rejected individual unless it acknowledges that *the* rejected individual is Jesus Christ. The individual him/herself is not rejected. Rather God rejects what the individual chooses for him/herself and what this life therefore expresses: sin, godlessness, rebellion, isolation. God's choice disqualifies the individual's choice, and there is no rejected being in the individual which can be authentically expressed in his/her action. What the individual chooses is not a possibility given to him/her. Because the ontic determination to be the rejected individual is eternally limited to the God-human Jesus Christ, there can be no other individual whose life emerges in continuity with, and as the expression of, this ontic determination. Therefore the concrete life of the rejected individual cannot be the actual expression *of his/her own actual rejection*. In this respect, his/her life is an illusion, and any attempt to actualize such a life is ineffective and an ontological contradiction.[50]

Nevertheless, the individual does participate in rejection to the extent that his/her life manifests the basis and reality of Jesus Christ's

---

455-58.

[48]For the discussions germane to Barth's view of Jesus Christ and the individual as instrument, see *C.D. II*,2:311, 314, 342-43, 345, 413, 423-24, 428-49.

[49]*C.D. II*,2:353. See also p. 347.

[50]On these observations regarding the rejected individual and his relation to Jesus Christ, see especially the discussions at *C.D. II*,2:315-19, 346-48, 352, 416, 421-22, 450, 453-54, 494-97.

rejection. Because his/her own rejection is excluded, the individual's existence can only attest the rejection which has been borne by Jesus Christ. In Barth's view, the rejected individual participates in Jesus Christ's election only to the extent that his/her life serves as a medium in and through which God's self-revelation and election are extended. The life of the godless individual appears to attest to humanity's rejection by God, but this witness is false. It is not the individual's rejection which is attested, but the rejection of Jesus Christ, and it is precisely as a false witness to his/her own rejection that the individual's witness is used by God in the service of revelation. This individual presents what has been removed from him/her and laid on Jesus Christ. The objectivity of his/her life therefore *re-presents and re-produces* the negative side of the reality of Jesus Christ's election, and participates in his rejected life only to the extent that it serves to signify it. The instrumentality of the rejected individual's life consists, therefore, in the signification of the individual for whom election is intended and to whom it is announced: lost, sinful, godless and isolated humanity who precisely as such is the object of election.[51]

On the other side, nothing at all can be posited concerning the elect individual unless it acknowledges that *the* elect individual is originally and primarily Jesus Christ. However, unlike Jesus the rejected, Jesus is not the only elect individual. The individual is elected. In contradistinction to the rejected individual, the elect individual is the one whose life and activity are the authentic realization and expression of the one ontic determination which represents the only possibility for his/her existence, namely "the possibility of transition from his mistakenly chosen and intrinsically impossible life as a rejected man to his proper life, the life determined for him by God's prevenient choice, his life as an elect man."[52] This individual is the one whose human being as the object of election is confirmed in his/her act; it is in his/her life that the divine determination is fulfilled. This is the positive side of Jesus Christ's election that applies directly to the individual. This means that the actuality of the life of Jesus Christ as the elect human constitutes the only basis on which the objective possibility and actuality of such a life for the individual can be posited.[53] The life of this individual has a definite objectivity in which the congruity of his/her being and act is manifest: "he lives and manifests the very presupposition and distinction peculiar to his being; he fulfils his personal predestination."[54] The fulfillment and

---

[51]See especially *C.D. II*,2:317, 347, 352-53, 453-58, 496-97.
[52]*C.D. II*,2:322. See also p. 319.
[53]See *C.D. II*,2:310, 313-15, 321-22, 349, 351, 410-11, 421. For other important discussions on the grounding of the elect individual's possibility and actuality in the actuality of Jesus Christ's election, see pp. 309-10, 315-16, 319, 322, 341, 345, 347-50.
[54]*C.D. II*,2:342. "The difference between the elect and other men, and therefore their

concrete manifestation of the individual's election brings him/her into conformity with the positive side of the election executed in Jesus Christ, and only confirms the fact that rejection is not applicable to him/her.

Therefore, the individual participates in election to the extent that his/her life manifests the reality and *telos* of Jesus Christ's election, and extends it out into the world. Because it is election rather than rejection that is actualized in the individual, his/her existence can and does attest the election originally executed and revealed in Jesus Christ. In Barth's scheme, the one who lives in the fulfillment of personal election can have and live his/her life only in the service of presentation of Jesus Christ's election. Personal election is not the *telos* here. Rather it is in and through the fulfillment, confirmation and manifestation of the individual's election that the *telos* of Jesus Christ's election is accomplished. The individual participates in Jesus Christ's election only to the extent that his/her life serves as a medium in and through which God's self-revelation and election are extended to humanity: "Believers 'are' the elect in this service [of revelation] so far as they bear witness to the truth, that is, to the elect man, Jesus Christ, and manifest and reproduce and reflect the life of this one Elect."[55] In conformity to Jesus Christ's election, the elect individual attests to the positive side of God's decree (i.e., what God has willed for humanity), but this particular signification of the individual is predicated entirely on his/her actual participation in God's being and act:

> But what is meant by gratitude, and therefore blessedness, and therefore being loved by God? Clearly, participation in the life of God in a human existence and action in which there is a representation and illustration of the glory of God Himself and its work.... The elect man is chosen in order to respond to the gracious God, to be His creaturely image, His imitator.... He can possess his own life only in imitation of Him, of the gracious God. What else is the elect Jesus Christ, the incarnate gratitude of the creature, but the original of this representation and illustration of the gracious God which is free of all self-will and therefore joyful, the true imitator of His work?[56]

The participation of the elect individual in the election of Jesus Christ is constituted by the actualization of his/her knowledge of God and his/her service as a witness. It is this which manifests the congruity

---

calling, is the execution, the objectively necessary expression of their election" (p. 345). See also pp. 341, 343-45, 348-52.

[55]*C.D. II*,2:347. See also pp. 343-45, 348, 351, 353, 410-18, 424-25, 429, 444-49.

[56]*C.D. II*,2:413-14.

of the individual's being and act, and it is this which constitutes the individual's conformity to and participation in the congruent being and act of the electing and self-revealing God. In and through the instrumentality of the individual's self-witness *to Jesus Christ*, the self-witness of God *in Jesus Christ* is extended out into the world. The individual's election is actualized only to the extent that he/she hears and believes the divine self-witness in Jesus Christ, *and embodies and expresses* this witness in his/her own life: "The fact that the elect is himself a witness to his election means that he himself may witness to the election of Jesus Christ, and to his own election in and with it."[57] The individual's election cannot be fulfilled apart from this witness, for it is only in and through the objective medium of the individual and his/her witness that those who live as though they were rejected can also be confronted with the promise of their election. In Barth's view, therefore, the knowledge and activity of the elect individual is necessary; this individual must be and act as a witness to the election of Jesus Christ in order both to actualize and confirm his/her election as well as to extend the execution of election to others.[58]

It is clear that, in Barth's view, we do not have two individuals, but rather a twofold reality, a *not yet* and a *no longer*, which has its basis in, and stands as a representation of, the twofold determination of God's election as executed and revealed in the God-human Jesus Christ. It is only on this basis and in relation to his reality that anything meaningful can be said of the individual who either lives the impossible life in contradiction to his/her ontic determination, or lives the actual life in its fulfillment.

---

[57] *C.D. II,*2:339. See also pp. 341-44, 413-18, 423-49, 484-506.
[58] See especially *C.D. II,*2:416-17, 455-58.

Chapter Four

The Dogmatic Implications of Election

To this point we have observed how it is that the execution of God's gracious election in and through Jesus Christ constitutes the centrifugal force that propels the reality of God's being and act outward from the intra-divine life of the triune God toward the sphere which is external to that life. It is precisely this execution that noetically determines and effects the structure, content and means of the knowledge of God. However, the being and act of the electing God cannot be said to achieve its intended effect in this outward movement unless and until it evokes a quite specific response from the human subject to whom this activity is directed. This subsequent response, in both its uniquely divine and human determination, is itself a joint action that stands as an ontic and noetic implication of the precedence of God's action. It is itself a centripetal force that propels the knowing subject back toward the One who occupies the center of the divine act of election. As a subsequent act, this human act of determined response not only fulfills the knowledge of God but also enables the knowing subject to participate ontically and noetically in the being and act of the divine Subject. For Barth, this human act in response to God's election comprises the fundamental core of theological ethics in as much as it is the preeminent ethical act of human existence. This is to say that, as participation in the knowledge of God, this human act is constrained by the centrifugal and centripetal forces paradigmatically at work in the execution of the divine decree of election in the God-human Jesus Christ. It is necessary that we inquire at this point into the nature of this uniquely human ethical act of response in order to round out a comprehensive understanding of the entire movement of the reality and extension of election. Such an inquiry will in turn provide the noetic context and orientation for an examination of the so-called problem of universalism in Barth's construction, a problem which is widely perceived to be itself an "implication" of his doctrine. We will then find ourselves in a position to articulate a preliminary description of the distinctive christology which both originates from Barth's doctrine of election and determines the later christological construction in *C.D. IV*.

The Dogmatic Implications of Election

A. Election as the Command of God

The actualization of the knowledge of God achieved in the fulfillment of the individual's election opens the way for Barth's discussion of the characteristic human action of response to the electing action of God. The covenant relation effected in election brings the divine action and human action into harmony, and the relation between election and command is to be seen in the fact that God wills something *from* humanity at the same time that God wills something *for* humanity as the covenant partner. Precisely in his/her determination by God as the object of election, the individual is placed under a divine claim which can only be satisfied by a particular human response to God's self-giving. Barth completes his construction of the doctrine of God by bringing humanity more fully into its content; the indicative of who God is and what God does for humanity is followed by the imperative of what God demands from the one for whom God is and acts. The human individual is not just the answer to the question of God's gracious election. He/she is the acting subject whose peculiar response is determined and required for the actualization of the covenant, and for Barth this fact constitutes the essence of theological ethics. Our task in this section will be to show that the noetic significance of election in Barth's thought requires that the fundamental orientation to ethics as both a human problem and dogmatic category consists in the fact that it addresses the *implications* of election for the human subject in terms of his/her response to and active participation in the knowledge of God. We will observe that for Barth, election is not fulfilled unless and until the correct answer is given by the individual to the question put to him/her in his/her knowledge of God which is grounded in God's electing action.

Barth's remarks at the opening of the chapter on the command of God make it apparent that a preoccupation with, and critical discussion of, the doctrine of election itself which excludes his discussion of the command of God is thereby immediately rendered suspect.[1] If election is to be understood as the divine determination of humanity as God's covenant partner, then this raises the question of human self-determination and the extent to which it is made to correspond to God's

---

[1] A review of the literature on Barth's doctrine of election at this point indicates that discussions of the ethics of election are surprisingly conspicuous by their absence. There is a significant body of literature that deals with Barth's ethics as a whole, as well as its relation to dogmatics. But critical discussions of his doctrine of election and the significance it plays in the orientation of his ethics are absent for the most part from the literature that concentrates on his view of election. For discussions that do perceive this linkage of ethics and election, see Bromiley, *Intro.*, pp. 99-106; Camfield, *Ref.*, pp. 86-99; Come, *Preach.*, pp. 222-32; Hartwell, *Theology*, pp. 154-64; Jüngel, *Legacy*, pp. 105-26; and Weber, *Found.*, pp. 104-16.

determination. The fact of God's election and the knowledge of God's election have implications for the individual as the object of this election, and therefore the articulation of election cannot be completed without an understanding of the divine command directed to humanity in election. As Barth argues:

> The truth of the evangelical indicative means that the full stop with which it concludes becomes an exclamation mark. It becomes itself an imperative. The concept of the covenant between God and man concluded in Jesus Christ is not exhausted in the doctrine of the divine election of grace. The election itself and as such demands that it be understood as God's command directed to man; as the sanctification or claiming which comes to elected man from the electing God in the fact that when God turns to him and gives Himself to him He becomes his Commander....
>
> ... For who can possibly see what is meant by the knowledge of God, His divine being, His divine perfections, the election of His grace, without an awareness at every point of the demand which is put to man by the fact that this God is his God, the God of man? How can God be understood as the Lord if that does not involve the problem of human obedience?[2]

For Barth, the knowledge of the divine command, and of God as the divine Commander, is an implication of the execution and fulfillment of election, and this means not only that ethics is grounded in election, but that there is no knowledge of God or of God's election apart from humanity's particular and determined response to the self-revelation executed in election. Ethics begins with the knowledge of the electing God and the elect human, and finds its origin and expression in the command and claim placed upon humanity by the electing action of God. It is this orientation that constitutes the uniqueness of Barth's view of ethics and its departure from other views.[3] The reality and knowledge of the divine command is nothing less than a distinct form of the reality and knowledge of Jesus Christ as the God-human, and for this reason the construction of the doctrine of the command of God emerges from the decisive noetic categories established in the election of Jesus Christ. He alone is the original and paradigmatic reality of the elect human who

---

[2] *C.D. II*,2:512. See also pp. 515-18.
[3] See especially his critical discussion and reconstruction of the foundation of ethics at *C.D. II*,2:515-48, the exposition of the basis of ethics at pp. 552-65, and related discussion at pp. 575-76.

rightly responds to the electing God. Thus the knowledge of God, and the knowledge of God's election and command is determined throughout by the knowledge of Jesus Christ.[4] In Barth's view, it is the command of God in the election of Jesus Christ that manifests God's electing decision and determination on the one hand, and the personal nature and character of the individual's election and response on the other. It is this command that expresses the unambiguous demand that the individual act in a way that corresponds to his/her determination in the divine decision.[5]

In Barth's construction of the doctrine of God's command, the implications of the knowledge of God and God's gracious election are developed around four central ideas, each of which presupposes the noetic significance of election and the fact that God has already acted to effect the knowledge of the divine self in the human subject, but that there remains the requisite response on the part of the human subject to complete the knowledge of God.

1. The Basis of Knowledge and the Response to God's Command. Barth understands the command of God to be an event in which the self-revelation of God executed in election calls for a response from humanity; from what God has done for humanity in the self-revelation executed in election, we know what God wants with us and from us as God calls and claims us:

> God's command, God Himself, gives Himself to be known. And as He does so, He is heard. Man is made responsible. He is brought into that confrontation and fellowship with Jesus Christ. And his action acquires that determination. The command of God is the decision about the goodness of human action.... It is as God gives man His command, as He gives Himself to man to be his Commander, that God claims him for Himself, that He makes His decision concerning him and executes His judgment upon him.[6]

---

[4]The fact that Barth grounds the discussion here in the knowledge of Jesus Christ, that the knowledge of Jesus Christ as the electing God and elect human decisively determines the understanding of the command of God, and that no meaningful exposition of ethics can take place apart from this knowledge is readily apparent in the discussions at *C.D. II,2*:517, 536-40, 549-50, 557-62, 567-68, 582-83, 605-6, 609, 632-35, 660, 662, 709, 736-41, 748-51, 757-63, and 777-81 where his concern is to show that the knowledge of the divine command is possible and actual only because of the concreteness of the identity of Jesus Christ and the command.

[5]See especially *C.D. II,2*:594-97, 631-36, 653-57, 708-13, 733-41.

[6]*C.D. II,2*:548. On the knowability and concreteness of the divine command given in God's self-revelation, see also pp. 509, 535-38, 543, 551, 559-61, 566-69, 669-70, 675-76, 777-78. For Barth's discussion of the manner in which the Bible as one form of the Word of

In particular, what God wants is the response of belief in Jesus Christ and the gracious act of election executed in him. In the noetic encounter with the human subject, God demands that who God is and what God has done be apprehended, accepted and affirmed as the only possibility determined for him/her. God commands that as the human hears and is confronted with God's claim and the divine decision concerning him/her, he/she acknowledges that he/she is a helpless transgressor under judgment, but that God is for him/her, and he/she is now to live for and with God as a forgiven sinner.[7] In Barth's view, the reality of this believing response is grounded in, and therefore only possible in, the knowledge of faith effected by the Word of God in which the human subject knows God and him/herself as the forgiven covenant partner of God. The faith which is demanded is itself the acknowledgement and acceptance of who God is and what God has done. Faith is the *only* answer that is acceptable in the face of the particular decision of God in the divine election because faith is itself the divinely determined response which corresponds noetically to this decision.[8] Faith therefore is not only a noetic response to election, but a response in election, i.e., a response made possible solely from within the divine execution of election. Thus the basis, possibility and actuality of the response demanded by the command and claim of God is the knowledge of God given in the execution of election.

2. *Human Freedom in the gospel Under the Law.* In Barth's construction, the command to believe the election of God in faith is the law contained in the gospel which announces who the electing God is and what the electing God has done, and it is the sum and substance of God's gracious election proclaimed in and through the gospel that gives humanity the necessary freedom and capacity to know and believe, and therefore fulfill the law placed upon it by God's claim. This is to say that the command of God is revealed and known only on the basis of, and in the execution of, God's gracious election. Barth contends:

> The Law is completely enclosed in the Gospel. It is not a second thing alongside and beyond the Gospel. It is not a foreign element which precedes or only follows it. It is the claim which is addressed to us by the Gospel itself and as such, the Gospel in so far as it has the form of a claim

---

God concretely attests and mediates God's self-revelation as his command, see pp. 671-708.

[7] See especially *C.D. II,* 2:583, 735-39, 746-58, 768-74.

[8] For the discussions germane to the demand for faith as the knowing response to God's election and the claim that accompanies it, see especially *C.D. II,* 2:603, 766-68, 772-81.

addressed to us, the Gospel which we cannot really hear except as we obey it. For Jesus Christ is the basis on which we may believe in God, the Word in which dwell the light and force to move us to this event. He Himself is the Gospel. He Himself is the resolve and the execution of the essential will in which God willed to give Himself to us. The grace of God, of the God in whom we may believe, is this. In Jesus Christ the eternal Word became flesh.[9]

In him/herself, the individual has no capacity to hear or know or obey the command or the gospel which contains it. Rather it is the command itself, given in the execution of election, that summons and liberates the individual to act responsibly in the divinely bestowed freedom which is proper to him/her. Because this command takes its form in the gospel, it too is determined by grace, and as such it signifies the order and content of the human response. The command of God is the imperative in election which orders that the individual be free, and which gives him/her the permission to exercise this freedom decisively in such a way that his/her action corresponds to his/her determination as the object of election. The law which demands the individual's submission is the command of God which gives him/her the freedom, capacity and willingness to respond accordingly, and which removes from him/her the possibility of being and acting in any other way.[10] Therefore, we can say that because the command of God which frees the individual is given only in the revelation executed in election, the only way to comprehend Barth's view of the free and responsible action of the elect individual in faith is to view it as the implication, determination and fulfillment of the knowledge of God.

   3. *Human Existence in the Act of Obedience Under Divine Judgment.* Barth contends that the free and responsible act which characterizes the existence of the elect individual is the act of obedience to the divine command. It is this act of obedience, enabled by the electing grace and command of God, that effects the identity of the intended being and action of the elect individual and constitutes the fulfillment of his/her divine determination. In the face of God's self-giving, the individual must choose and decide what he/she is to be and do, and to act rightly is nothing less than to become obedient to the revelation of God and to live as one to whom grace has come in Jesus Christ. Barth states:

---

[9] *C.D. II,2:*557. See also pp. 510-15.
[10] See especially *C.D. II,2:*552-57, 583-88, 593-97, 602-5, 609-12, 717.

> The goodness of human action consists in the goodness with which God acts toward man. But God deals with man through His Word. His Word is the sum and plenitude of all good, because God Himself is good. Therefore man does good in so far as he hears the Word of God and acts as a hearer of this Word. In this action as a hearer he is obedient. Why is obedience good? Because it derives from hearing, because it is the action of a hearer, namely, of the hearer of the Word of God. It is good because the divine address is good, because God Himself is good.[11]

The obedience which God demands is the individual's decision for Jesus Christ. This decision alone stands as the repetition and confirmation of God's electing decision. Because of God's election, neutrality and disobedience are excluded as possible choices for the human subject. Only an obedient act can give witness to the electing will and action of God, for it is only obedience to the divine command that actualizes the covenant relation:

> The thing we are to hear as we hear the command is that we may belong to Him. To obey God's command is to accept this invitation to live as those who belong to Him, and therefore to rejoice as we stand in fellowship with this One who has been judged.[12]

In Barth's construction, it is only within the actuality of the election of God, and therefore within the reality of the knowledge of God, that the elect individual's self-determining decisions of obedience affirm and conform to his/her predetermination in God's eternal decision regarding him/her, and therefore the act of obedience is an implication of the knowledge of God effected in divine election. All other human actions are excluded:

> If we know and discern that He and no other calls us, we definitely have no choice between obedience and disobedience. The decision has been made even as we are confronted by it. There is absolutely no place for disobedience, unbelief and impenitence. Evil becomes for us the absolutely excluded possibility that it is for God Himself. It is the shame that we can only leave under us

---

[11]*C.D. II,*2:546. See also pp. 511, 516-17, 535-40, 559, 562, 568-69, 575-76, 580-83.
[12]*C.D. II,*2:738. See also pp. 609-13, 632-36, 649, 659, 678-79, 704, 744-45, 768.

and behind us. When we obey we do the only thing that we are free to do; the thing that we can do only in real freedom.[13]

Because obedience is the response determined and demanded in the electing command of God, the being and action of the elect individual is a continuous answer to the self-revelation of God, and as such it stands continually under God's judgment. Whether human action is obedience or not is something that God judges in the light of the divine electing decision. As the individual is called upon to realize the true purpose of his/her election to be the covenant partner of God, he/she is judged by the divine command in terms of the extent to which his/her determination is fulfilled in his/her actions. The one who is so judged is the rejected individual who is chosen, acquitted and justified in grace and love by God to be and to live as God's covenant partner. As Barth states:

> The presupposition of the divine judgment is that God wills to have man for Himself. The execution of this judgment is that He creates right for the man who is in the wrong before Him, setting him in the right against himself. Its goal and purpose is that man should be the one who passes from this judgment, the one who is judged by His command. It is as such that God wills to have him for Himself. It is as such that man can and should live in covenant with Him.[14]

The fact is, however, that in Barth's construction, this continual judgment under which the one who lives as an elect individual stands has its basis in the idea that disobedience, disbelief and the life of the rejected individual have themselves been eternally excluded in the election of Jesus Christ, and as such this judgment presupposes the reality of the knowledge of God on the basis of which it is possible for the individual to act obediently in freedom. Obedience under the judgment of God is an implication of the knowledge of God.

4. Human Existence in Conformity to the Divine Life. It is obedience to the command of God in the divine self-revelation that constitutes for Barth the actualization of the knowledge of God and the conformity of the divine and human being and action: "As the one Word of God which is the revelation and work of His grace reaches us, its aim

---

[13]*C.D. II,2:*779.
[14]*C.D. II,2:*764. For important discussions regarding the nature and extent of the divine judgment exercised on the individual who seeks to live in obedience, see also pp. 633-36, 641-45, 655, 733-41, 748-63.

is that our being and action should be conformed to His."[15] In this manner, the life and activity of the elect individual participates in, attests and interprets the reality of the electing God. All that this individual is and does as one who lives in the fulfillment of his/her election is predetermined to confirm and conform to the divine decision; his/her being and action as one who knows God and who lives in free obedience will be a concrete manifestation of God's own life. In this regard, Barth states:

> It is the grace of God which is attested to us by the claim of God. The grace of God wills and creates the covenant between God and man. It therefore determines man to existence in this covenant. It determines him to be the partner of God. It therefore determines his action to correspondence, conformity, uniformity with God's action.... What is involved is that man and man's action should become the image of God: the reflection which represents, although in itself it is completely different from, God and His action; the reflection in which God recognises Himself and His action.... Eternal life is God's own life, and the life of the creature when it is uniform with God's own life. What God wills of man when He establishes the covenant between Himself and man, when He is gracious to him, is that his creaturely life and being and action, his thoughts and words and works, should acquire this uniformity.... The determination of man is always to reflect this. The covenant of grace alone constitutes the real relationship between God and man. Man is determined only to be the partner of the gracious God. What other claim can be considered in relation to this partner, indeed what other claim can be known by man at all, except that he must be one to whom God is gracious, and think and speak and act as such?[16]

The claim and command of the electing God demands human action that attests the divine action. It is in this command as an implication of the knowledge of God that we find an important element to Barth's view of the possibility and actuality of the service of the elect individual. The service of witness in which the individual participates in

---

[15]*C.D. II*,2:512.

[16]*C.D. II*,2:575-76. For discussions germane to the individual's conformity to and participation in the being and action of God under the rubric of the individual's obedience to the command of God, see pp. 537, 540, 543, 553, 567, 576-83, 631-33, 644-45, 669-71, 750, 756, 766.

The Dogmatic Implications of Election

the being and activity of God is commanded in the execution of his/her election, and as an implication of his/her knowledge of the electing God, this service is freely and voluntarily rendered in obedience in such a way that the individual's election is fulfilled and confirmed in his/her own life. Apart from the knowledge of God executed in election, and apart from obedience to the command of God which requires as an implication that the individual participate in and attest the divine life in faithful and obedient service, there is no election or elect individual. There is only one who lives as though he/she was rejected and whose election has not yet been fulfilled.

B. The Problem of Universalism

There is no question but that Barth's view of election raises the specter of a universalist view of salvation, and it is generally recognized that his tendency in this direction is an implication of the christologically oriented construction of the doctrine.[17] Our task in this section is neither to confirm nor deny that Barth is a universalist. Rather it will be our task to show that Barth's refusal to confine himself to the usual alternatives to the problems of election and his reconceptualization of election as a primarily noetic category represent a positive and creative (though not entirely unambiguous) contribution to the problem of a theological reflection on the reality of God's election.

There are numerous passages in Barth's doctrine that can be read to suggest that universal salvation or *apokatastasis* can and perhaps even must result from the argument presently advanced in the construction.[18] Those who contend for a universalism in Barth's view point to two progressions of ideas in the construction, each of which tends to call into

---

[17]A considerable number of Barth's interpreters have either accused him outright of holding universalist views or argued that universalism is the necessary outcome of his doctrine of election. See e.g. Balthasar, *Theo. KB*, pp. 48-52, 151-64, 179-80; Berkouwer, *Triumph*, 111-22, 223-43, 262-96, 361-68; *Div. Elec.*, pp. 228-34; Bloesch, *Victor*, pp. 32-42, 60-71, 137-39; Bouillard, *KB*, vol II, pp. 155-64; Brunner, *Chr. Doc.*, 334-39, 346-53; Buess, *Zur Präd.*, pp. 17-20, 27-29; Duthie, *Ult. Tri.*, pp. 158-60, 165-68; Gloege, *Prädest.*, pp. 198-200, 243-52; Hartwell, *Theology*, pp. 67-87, 101-2, 178-88; Hausmann, *KB Doct.*, pp. 11, 39-44, 54-60, 67-72, 83-89; Hendry, *Form*, pp. 310-12; *Review*, 399-404; Klooster, *Signif.*, pp. 41-44, 59-74; Küng, *Just.*, pp. 82-88, 278-80; Mueller, *K. Barth*, pp. 107-10; Polman, *Barth*, pp. 31-55; Van Til, *Modernism*, pp. 75, 100-4, 157-59; Weber, *Found.*, pp. 453, 474-78; Woyke, *Doctrine*, pp. 265-75, 293-95, 335-37; Yu, *KB Elec.*, pp. 255-60. For two studies that contend that Barth is not a universalist and that his view does not require universalism as an outcome, see Bettis, *Univ.*, pp. 423-37; and Park, *Man*, pp. 115-221.

[18]See e.g. *C.D. II,2*:116-18, 148-49, 166-75, 195-96, 309-10, 316-27, 333, 345-54, 415-17, 453-58, 496, most of which appear in the discussion of the election of the individual. Overall, these tend to be the passages most often cited in the criticism of Barth's doctrine on the question of its implicit or explicit universalism.

question an element in the traditional view of election which is believed to be so vital that its elimination can only mean the denial of the gospel attested in Scripture. These progressions and their apparent outcome can be summarized as follows:

First, Barth teaches that the basis for creation and the existence of the individual is his/her election to be the covenant partner of God, and that he/she is predestined to bear the image of God's glory. This predestination is determined wholly by God's grace and consists in the acceptance of humanity in the one will of God. There are not two opposing wills or an equilibrium with respect to the object of predestination. Rather there is only the one predestined individual who lives either now or not yet in the fulfillment of his/her election. The object of this predestination is precisely the sinful, disobedient and unworthy one who as such should only be rejected, but who is nevertheless the one chosen to live in covenant fellowship with God. Because the knowledge of this election comes only from the knowledge of God's will revealed in the life, death and resurrection of Jesus Christ, there can be no knowledge of an actual election *and* rejection of humanity. Because of the nature of God's election, faith is not the appropriation of salvation, but the acknowledgement of one's election which supercedes one's merited rejection. In the minds of Barth's critics, this progression appears to limit and discount God's freedom, sovereignty and holiness in the eternal judgment of the unbeliever who refuses to come to faith; God is not wholly free and truly just in that God cannot reject the individual who disobeys and repudiates God.

Second, Barth teaches that double predestination means that God has taken rejection upon the divine self in Jesus Christ. As the elect human, Jesus Christ is the *only* rejected individual. All individuals are elect in Jesus Christ because the election of others is included in his election, and these others attest his rejection though they do not actually experience it. They do, however, participate in and experience his election. Living as one who is rejected is the result of one's own godless choice which nevertheless cannot supplant or nullify God's prior choice of election. When the individual endeavors to live the life of one rejected, he/she actually usurps what God has reserved for Godself, and the choice of disobedience, unbelief and evil is an impossible choice and as such excluded. The individual is not free to choose and actualize rejection as the expression of the identity of his/her being and act. In the minds of Barth's critics, this progression means that Barth does not take human decision and responsibility seriously. He appears to vilify the freedom and responsibility of the individual in that his emphasis upon the fact of election already accomplished renders human faith and decision meaningless.

The usual solutions to the problem of election have tended to fall into one of three categories, and there are certainly elements in Barth's view that appear to conform to elements in each of these options. When the problem is posed in terms of how it is that some are saved while others are not, those who hold to a traditional view of double predestination and a double decree argue that the answer lies in God's decision to elect or to reject. In this construct, the individual is not free to choose to be elect; he/she can only choose disobedience, evil and rejection. Furthermore, he/she cannot oppose and successfully resist God's decision to elect or reject; no act of the individual can constrain or limit God's judgment or grace. Election and rejection are wholly the work of God, and the individual is elect or rejected solely on the basis of God's decision. The obedience and faith of the individual follow his/her election, while his/her disobedience and unbelief result in his/her rejection. The salvation of all is neither possible nor necessary. Though Barth has rejected this view of double predestination, there are elements in it that are part and parcel of his view. Still, this traditional view represents a rather restrictive view of humanity's freedom and autonomy, and a speculative and exaggerated view of God's freedom, power and sovereignty.

Others have attempted to solve the problem by arguing for an Arminian or Pelagian view, saying that the answer lies in the individual's decision in which he/she chooses or does not choose to believe. In this construct, the individual is and remains free to choose to respond with belief or unbelief. He/she may successfully oppose and obstruct God's decision to elect and thereby constrain God's grace by his/her own act. The actualization of the individual's election is a synergistic work, for the individual is elected or rejected based on whether or not he/she believes. Salvation follows belief, and rejection follows unbelief. In this view the salvation of all is possible, but not necessary. Without question, Barth has rejected this view as well, though again there are elements here that can be found in Barth. Nevertheless, this construct represents an exaggerated view of the individual's freedom and power, and a rather narrow and restrictive view of God's freedom, power and sovereignty.

The alternative usually offered to both of these answers to the problem is a universalism which in general is more concerned with who is saved, rather than how or why. This view is a blend of elements in the previous two. The individual is free to choose, but his/her salvation is not necessarily contingent upon the choice of obedience and belief. In fact, he/she plays no significant role one way or the other in effecting salvation. He/she can oppose or thwart God's will to save now, but in the end this opposition is really irrelevant. Salvation is wholly a work of the love and grace of God which is defined entirely in terms of what God does for humanity. This view requires that the goodness of divine love consists entirely in the salvation of humanity, and the salvation of all is necessary as the logical outcome of God's love and grace. God necessarily has to save to be consistent in the divine loving. However, this alternative is to be rejected because it does not take human sin, disobedience and unbelief seriously, and ultimately represents a denial of justification. As one which metaphysically, logically and necessarily excludes the possibility and actuality of rejection, this view emphasizes God's love at the expense of God's justice, and ultimately separates the two, putting them over against one another.

Barth is accused of being a universalist, or inclining toward universalism, because he has categorically rejected the first two options to the problem. In the minds of his critics, this rejection necessarily means that he holds the third option. But Barth has decisively rejected the idea of *apokatastasis* or universalism as well.[19] He perceived in this idea a faulty point of departure which in the end called into question the Christian understanding of both God and humanity. In his opinion, *apokatastasis* worked from an abstract, exaggerated and optimistic view of humanity in which the number of elect individuals was the unqualified totality of all individuals. It was this abstract humanity as such that was predestined, and not individuals *per se*. *Apokatastasis* contends that God necessarily has to save all humankind in order to be God and be true to Godself, and for Barth this view disallows the sovereign freedom of divine love and grace by making them necessary in the scheme of things. He saw in this view a thorough repudiation of the significance of the human decision because there was no real threat of rejection hanging over humanity. Furthermore, he failed to see how there could be any real and truly significant forgiveness and regeneration if all individuals were elect. Such a view could not take seriously the fundamental transformation in human existence that occurs when the circle of the elect is opened up and enlarged. Over against the view of *apokatastasis*, Barth argued that individuals are elect precisely in order that the circle of the elect should be expanded. When the election of the individual is executed, the number is indeed expanded, and for Barth this implies that the circle is *not* fixed, either narrowly restricted to some or opened to the totality of all. Nowhere in Scripture could Barth find an unambiguous example of a hopelessly rejected individual or the conclusion that all will be saved. He refused to limit and eviscerate the love and grace of God; to *say* that the number of the elect is limited either to some or to all does not *make* it so. To say "God must save all" or "God cannot save all" is to speak in abstractions in both cases, and both are "formal conclusions without any actual substance."[20]

---

[19]For Barth's discussions and rejection of *apokatastasis*, see *C.D. II,2*:186-87, 295, 299-301, 305, 313-14, 321-24, 417-19, 421-23, 476-77, *C.D. IV,3,1*:475-78, and outside the *C.D.*, see *G.G.*, pp. 26-32, 48-54; *Hum.*, pp. 59-61; *Message*, pp. 33-34, and *Credo*, pp. 171-72. The description of Barth's understanding of *apokatastasis* which is to follow draws upon his comments in these passages.
[20]*C.D. II,2*:418.

The Dogmatic Implications of Election

In the final analysis, Barth's rejection of *apokatastasis* results from the fact that it is an argument based on necessity and a presumptive and pretentious knowledge of God. But it is also the presence of these two components in the other options that bring Barth to reject them as well. Barth rejects the necessity, implicit or explicit, in these alternatives which contend that God either must save all or cannot save all. But he does not reject the possibility. He argues that we simply do not *know* that there *cannot* be a final opening up of the circle of the elect to include all humanity, but that there is no basis to contend that this is necessary. All we can know is that there have been, are and will be elect individuals because of God's gracious decision and work alone.

Barth's rejection of the three usual alternatives stands on the fact that election is primarily a noetic category. His solution to the problem of election is set within the context of the actual knowledge of God as an acting Subject, and not that of how it is that some are saved while others are not. This is to say that the problem for him is how the individual comes to know who God is and what God has done, not why has God done this and not that. The context of the problem is epistemological, and not primarily soteriological. Indeed, it is only because election is a noetic category that it is also a soteriological category. The strength and integrity of Barth's solution lies in the fact that he avoids the problem of necessity adherent in the other views, and maintains the tension between the freedom and sovereignty of God on the one hand and the responsibility and decision of the individual on the other. We can fairly represent Barth's solution to the problem and the fact that he does not address it within the same conceptual construct by articulating the following elements which characterize his alternative:

1. The purpose of election is not the salvation of some to attest God's glory and the rejection of others to attest God's judgment. Rather the purpose for which individuals are elected is to live in covenant fellowship with God here and in eternity, and to participate in God's revealing and reconciling work. The purpose is therefore to attest the being and act of God to the world as an objective medium which extends God's self-revelation and to live in conformity to God by expressing the identity of one's being and act.

2. The decree of election is a decree made in eternity before creation, but this decree does not imply that history or the lives of individuals are the necessary unfolding of this decree. The divine decree is made in eternity and executed in the form of new decisions each moment in time which provide the occasion for the fulfillment of the eternal decree.

3. There is no right, basis or authority to deny God the ability to elect *and* reject. The doctrine of predestination cannot be based on necessity or rational consistency. There is universal election, but this does not necessarily imply universal salvation. Nowhere in Barth's view is there

any indication that all who are objectively elected will realize this subjectively either here or in eternity. Whether or not an individual lives in the fulfillment of his/her election, he/she is and remains the one for whom God has acted; he/she stands as the one to whom the gospel is proclaimed; he/she lives always as the one for whom election is intended and therefore always in either the possibility or actuality of his/her election. Those who do not live in the fulfillment of their election still remain as the object of God's election and still attest (in this case) the negative side of Jesus Christ's election. In him/herself, every individual is and remains a rejected individual, even in God's grace and in the fulfillment of the divine election. There is no necessity in Barth's view which requires that all who are elect will live in its fulfillment.

4. The emphasis upon the freedom and sovereignty of God is not made at the expense of human freedom and decision, and Barth refuses to separate God's justice from God's love. The love in God's justice denies vitality, effectiveness and endurance to the individual's disobedience and unbelief, but this does not mean that Barth denies the seriousness of human rebellion and unbelief. God allows disobedience to be real, but God hinders its intention to defy God successfully. If disobedience were effective in its intention, it would mean that God is limited to the extent that God is unable to resist it and deal effectively with it. On the other hand, a necessary restoration of all things would remove the substance and thrust of Barth's view of the command of God where election is articulated as God's sovereign act which must be proclaimed to humanity and responded to in faith. It is only on the basis of the freedom of God to disallow the effectiveness of disobedience that Barth can maintain the seriousness of human responsibility and the call to faith. In Barth's view, the actuality of election executed in one individual makes it impossible to affirm that one can believe in rejection, disobedience and the effectiveness of evil in the same way that one believes in the power, freedom and sovereignty of God. If evil is overcome in one place, in the life of one individual, there can be no basis to affirm that evil has the staying power to resist God. But this does not necessarily imply that evil is not real, or that it is overcome in all individuals.

In the end, what Barth is arguing for is the idea that the understanding of predestination cannot come from a speculative analysis of the human condition, human destiny, human nature or history. It must come from the knowledge of faith conditioned and determined by the existence of Jesus Christ and the revelation in him. Barth's view of election is an explicit acknowledgement that the answer to the problem of election cannot be based on necessity. The only answer that can be given is one that emerges from within the actuality of the knowledge of faith. There is simply no basis to contend that the fulfillment of the election of any or all is not possible; it is not given to faith to know the answer to the question whether all will be saved. Neither the absolute and eternal rejection of an individual other than Jesus Christ nor the universal restoration of all things are data given to the knowledge of faith, and therefore there is no basis for a doctrine which contends that any or all necessarily will or will not live in the fulfillment of election. What is known is that individuals are elect who do not deserve it and cannot effect it. Thus from a human point of view, there is no reason not to proclaim the election of all in God's grace and the urgency of the human decision in response.

The vitality and creativity of Barth's doctrine lies therefore precisely in his refusal to construct a doctrine out of an unknown possibility for God. In our judgment, the problems, issues and contours of a universalist solution to the problem of election are imposed upon Barth's doctrine by those who hold to one or the other of the usual solutions. The only way Barth can be indicted for holding a universalist view or a doctrine which results in universalism is if one retains necessity either with respect to God or to humanity as a component to the doctrine of election, and imputes a necessity to Barth's doctrine, a necessity which Barth decisively rejects.

C. The Electional Christology

We now bring this chapter to a close with a description of the basic christological construct that emerges from Barth's doctrine of election. Barth's doctrine is actually a complex mosaic of christological themes and perspectives finely woven to produce a picture of the unity of God's being and action in Jesus Christ. Apart from God's election, there could be no Jesus Christ for us, no temporal reality of the God-human, and therefore no knowledge of God. What we have in Barth's doctrine is an electional christology, i.e., a christology constructed in terms of election. Our immediate concern is with grasping the manner in which the categories of election condition and qualify the christological issues of the deity, humanity and unity of the God-human Jesus Christ. It can be seen that it is the identity of God's being and act, concretely established and expressed in election and its identity with incarnation and revelation, that substantiates Barth's christology. In other words, Barth's christology is shaped by the doctrine of election to the extent that election as the primal being and act of God is understood to be the origin and basis of incarnation and revelation. Consequently, it is Barth's view of election that gives the primary meaning, substance and breadth to the affirmation that Jesus Christ is "very God and very human." So much is this the case that one can contend that the christology in the doctrine of election is preeminently the christology of Barth's theology.[21]

In Barth's construction of the doctrine, there is a quite explicit connection between election and a "two natures" christology. The preliminary articulation of christology in *C.D. I,2* is brought over into *C.D. II,2* as the noetic point of departure for the exposition of the election of Jesus Christ which constitutes the substance of the doctrine. Christology is found in *C.D. I,2* because there the concern is the question of the actuality and possibility of revelation as the basis for the knowledge of God and dogmatics, and the answer for Barth is to be found in the identity of incarnation and revelation. But the question of the *basis, origin, determination and execution* of this identity is given its substantive answer in *C.D. II,2* with the reality of God's eternal and temporal election of Jesus Christ. In the discussions of christology in *C.D. I,2*, revelation is oriented by and grounded in the incarnation. But in the discussions in *C.D. II,2*, revelation and incarnation as christological categories are themselves oriented by and grounded in election. It is precisely this contention which we want to make evident in this concluding section by describing the basic christological contours of Barth's doctrine of election.

In *C.D. I,2*, Barth undertakes a discussion of the incarnation in terms of the "two natures," and this discussion takes the form of an exposition of John 1:14. He contends that the acting *Subject* here is God the Son or Word, God in the second mode of existence as the triune God. The Father does not become flesh, nor does the Holy Spirit become flesh. Rather the *Word* becomes flesh. As Godself, the Word remains as such even in the act of becoming flesh, and at no time does the Word cease to be the Word. The fact that the Word becomes *incarnate* signifies that the Word is not without the flesh, but in and through the flesh. The Word is the acting Subject, and not the flesh. The Word derives divine being not from the flesh, but from God. Though the Word becomes flesh, the Word never ceases to be the Word. Nor does the Word as such undergo a change in essence or nature as God. Precisely in this becoming, the Word is and remains fully God, participating in the divine reality and existence of the triune God. In the incarnation, the Word is

---

[21]While we will attempt to describe the basic substance of Barth's christology as it appears in the doctrine of election, a fuller discussion of the influence of election on Barth's christology must await the discussion in Chapter Seven of the present study. A discussion of the distinctly christological substance of Barth's doctrine of election is lacking in the literature which is concerned with his view of election. For discussions which do manifest some interest in this regard, see Amberg, *Christol.*, pp. 133-38; Balthasar, *Theo. KB*, pp. 155-70, 100-108; Berkouwer, *Triumph*, pp. 17-19; 93-103; Bouillard, *KB* I, pp. 119-48, 221-43; II, pp. 114-23; Camfield, *Ref.*, pp. 71-85; Gloege, *Prädest.*, pp. 201-17, 233-43; Hausmann, *KB Doct.*, pp. 1-14, 29-44, 67-72; Jenson, *Alpha*, pp. 21-140; Jüngel, *Trinity*, pp. 42-83; Mueller, *K. Barth*, pp. 61-76, 94-139; Park, *Man*, pp. 8-33, 115-71; Sparn, *Revision*, pp. 49-69; Sykes, *Studies*, pp. 17-54; Thompson, *Perspec.*, pp. 1-135; Woyke, *Doctrine*, pp. 147-215, 255-71, 287-99, 313-20.

and remains the preeminent *Subject*.[22]

The *object* of this incarnation is the *flesh* which the Word becomes. For Barth, the fact that the Word became flesh means that the Word became a true and real human, and therefore the incarnate Word is to be seen as a particular expression of human essence and existence, a unique human being in the space and time between birth and death. The human being whom the Word became had no prior, separate or independent existence apart from the Word. The concrete reality of this one human is itself the work of the Word of God, the work of becoming, and thus the concrete human being of this one has no other existence than that which the Word gives to it by taking its existence upon itself. This one is and has concrete existence only in so far as the Son or Word of God is this human, only in so far as God the Son or Word assumes or adopts or appropriates the human essence and existence of this one human being for the divine self, only in so far as the Word of God actualizes the possibility of the existence of this particular individual. By becoming this human being, the Word does not cease to be the Word, nor is this human being something other than human because it is what the Word becomes. Rather the Word becomes what the Word was not before, namely a human being, while this particular human being as such comes into concrete existence. But in this "God and human," it is God as the Word who is the *acting Subject* of this one particular concrete existence.[23]

For Barth, the relation and unity of this Subject and object in the incarnation is the reality of the action of *becoming* which unites the Subject and object in oneness. This becoming is an act of the Word which is undertaken without any compulsion or necessity other than the Word's own free and sovereign willing and doing. In no way is it an act of the human nature or being. Human being as such has no power to become the Word, and in this act the human being is not the Subject. Rather this becoming signifies the incorporation of human nature and being into the divine nature and being so that the human being as such is the Word's being. Here again, the Word does not cease to be the Word in this becoming. Rather it makes human being its own being together with its divine being. God's presence in this particular individual means not only that this human being is identical with God; more particularly it means that God is the living and acting Subject in this concrete human existence which has no existence apart from the fact that the divine mode of being of the Son or Word acquires this particular human existence. At the same time, however, it must be said that this human nature as such does in fact have existence. But it has this

---

[22]See the discussion of the *Word* at *C.D.* I,2:132-39.
[23]See the discussion of *flesh* at *C.D.* I,2:147-59.

existence only in its union with the Word. This union of the divine and human natures in the concrete existence of this one means that God the Word or Son does not exist for us apart from the human being and existence of this one. It must be emphasized, however, that in Barth's view, the origin of this human being's existence is the Word, and in this respect the becoming of the incarnation means that the Son or Word of God claimed for the divine self the one specific possibility or potentiality of the human being who would be born of Mary, and actualized that possibility in the birth, life and death of Jesus of Nazareth. In this one particular individual is to be recognized a subject who is God in all the fullness of divine being, and a human in all the fullness of human being, and therefore one subject who is God and human being together in unity. In Jesus of Nazareth, the Word or Son of God is the Subject of a real human being and acting.[24]

We have taken note of the fact that incarnation as revelation is identical with election. Barth's contention that Jesus Christ is the electing God depends on the identity of election and incarnation/revelation. The establishment of the direct identity of the human Jesus Christ and God the Son or Word is the point of the exegesis of John 1:1-2 which opens the first subsection of §33 in *C.D. II,2,* "Jesus Christ, Electing and Elected." Barth's principle concern in this exegesis is to ground the idea of Jesus Christ as the electing God and the elect human on the same biblical passage which deals with the incarnation of the Word in the human being Jesus of Nazareth. Barth intends to establish the fact that Jesus Christ is the electing God because he is the Son or Word of God who is the electing Subject, and who precisely as such becomes the acting Subject incarnate in the elected object, the human being Jesus Christ. The electing God is predicated of Jesus Christ because the human Jesus is who the Son becomes and therefore is. But for Barth, predicating God the Son or Word to Jesus Christ does not mean that the human Jesus became the Son. There never was a time when the human Jesus was not the Son; Jesus Christ's divinity, his *being* the Son of God, is not something that began either in eternity or in time. Barth understands John 1:1-14 to mean that the Son or Word of God never was apart from Jesus Christ, but that the Word was concretely manifest in this identity only in time. All that is predicated of God the Son is to be predicated of Jesus Christ, because Jesus Christ is identical with God the Son. Furthermore, because neither the possibility nor the actuality of the one human being Jesus Christ ever existed apart from his being God the Son, the *electing God* must be predicated of Jesus Christ. Apart from the eternal being of the Son of God, the human Jesus Christ does not exist in time or in eternity. But as God the Son, the human Jesus does exist,

---

[24]See the discussion of *egeneto* at *C.D. I,2*:159-72.

first in eternity and then in time. This identity of God the Son and the human Jesus Christ goes back to the beginning, to God's being with Godself in eternity, before and outside all created reality and temporal being and time. Because of this eternal identity and oneness, it is the elect human Jesus Christ who is with God, and who is himself God.

There are two fundamental propositions which are essential to the christology in the doctrine of election. In the light of our discussion in Chapter Two, and under the rubric of these two propositions, we can make several observations about Barth's christology as it is reflected in his doctrine, and thereby arrive at an understanding of the basic christological orientation which informs the *C.D.*

1. Jesus Christ is the electing God. God the Son is the Subject of an authentic becoming in which God does not cease to be God, but is and remains the acting Subject in this real human being. In the incarnation, becoming is a movement from God to humanity. It is not at all a case wherein a previously existing human becomes God. This movement of becoming means that God is both Subject and object: as Subject, God is a real human being in existence, and as object, this human is a real divine being in existence. For Barth, Jesus Christ is to be understood first and foremost as the eternal Son or Word of God, the second person of the trinity. His deity is therefore an intrinsic attribute of his being. His pre-existence means that he shares in the essential divinity of the triune God prior to and apart from his existence as a human being. But it also means that the human Jesus possesses an essential unity with the Father and Spirit before he takes on concrete human nature in the actual incarnation. Divinity is not predicated of Jesus because he is a human in a unique relation to the Son of God. Rather it is predicated because it is in fact his essential nature. For Barth, there are not two persons or personal subjects in Jesus Christ, God the Word and the human person Jesus. Rather there is only one truly personal subject involved in the concrete existence of this human being, and that is God the Son who adds human nature to the divine nature. To say that Jesus Christ is the electing God is to say that in Jesus Christ, we have to do with the self-determining God who elects to have fellowship with humanity and to effect this by becoming a human being who lives as such in the sphere of human nature and existence, and who takes the merited judgment and rejection of sinful humanity upon the divine self.

2. Jesus Christ is the elect human. In Jesus Christ, God becomes a particular human being in concrete existence. In this reality, God becomes what God is not in the divine self: a human being. In Barth's view, this human has no existence prior to, apart from or independent of God. He is not a separate human person who is selected by God to be united with God after his coming into existence. Rather his existence is identical from first to last with God's existence as a human being. The only possibility of this human's existence is as the concrete human being whom God would become. This human does have his own existence, but only as the human being and existence of God. In Barth's view, therefore, Jesus Christ is the divine person who is also human. The unity of this one person is a unity between the person of God the Son in God's divine nature and the complete human nature which in itself is not a person. This human nature cannot be or act on its own, apart from the divine person who takes it upon the divine self. Rather the human being and actions of this person are the being and actions of the Son or Word of God who remains the dominant factor in the union. The human Jesus is therefore fully identical with God in as much as he is the concrete human nature taken by God in the incarnation. For Barth, therefore, the elect human Jesus Christ is seen as the particular instance of human nature and existence as created by God for exaltation, union, harmony and fellowship with God. He is the one authentic paradigmatic reality of human existence which has its true origin, basis and goal in the election of God. To say that Jesus Christ is the elect human and that all others are elect in him is to say that the basic determination of human nature is to exist in fellowship with the electing God, and that it is only in the concrete humanity of this one that the reality of election is fulfilled for human existence.[25]

---

[25]This basic description of the christological contours found in the doctrine of election clearly marks Barth's orientation to christology as Alexandrian, rather than Antiochian. Waldrop has very persuasively demonstrated this in his recent study of Barth's christology (see Waldrop, *KB Christ.*). However, his investigation is flawed by the fact that he bases his constructive argument entirely on the identity of reconciliation and revelation as articulated in the doctrine of the incarnation in *C.D. I,2* and the major treatment of christology in the doctrine of reconciliation in *C.D. IV,1-2*, and entirely overlooks the christological formulation in the doctrine of election, to say nothing of the identity of election with incarnation/revelation. In spite of this oversight, Waldrop's study remains an important one for exhibiting the Alexandrian orientation of Barth's christology.

Part III

The Biblical Hermeneutics
of Election

Chapter Five

The Core of
Election Hermeneutic

The creativity and novelty of Barth's reconstruction of the doctrine of election makes it necessary that we inquire into the exegetical basis of the doctrine. This necessity is only intensified by the fact that Barth claims to construct his dogmatics as a whole on the exegesis of the Bible as the witness to God's self-revelation. In the light of this claim, there are two fundamental questions which we must engage and attempt to answer before proceeding further in our investigation of the role Barth's view of election plays in the *Church Dogmatics*, namely: (1) is Barth consistent in the application of his hermeneutic when he turns to exegete the biblical passages which constitute the foundation of his doctrine of election, and (2) does his exegesis in fact call for and support the dogmatic construction given to the doctrine? Before we turn to Barth's exegesis and endeavor to answer these questions, we need to have a basic grasp of the fundamental orientation and shape of the biblical hermeneutic employed in the *Church Dogmatics*. In order to accomplish this, we will focus our attention in the first section of this chapter on the hermeneutic program articulated by Barth in *C.D. I, 1-2*.[1] With this as the immediate background

---

[1]It is outside the scope of this investigation to undertake a comprehensive and critical review of the origin, development and application of Barth's biblical hermeneutic. For discussions on the development and application of Barth's hermeneutic *vis-a-vis* the historical and dogmatic environment out of which it emerged, consult G.C. Berkouwer, *A Half Century of Theology*, trans. and ed. Lewis B. Smedes (Grand Rapids: William B. Eerdmans Publishing Co., 1977); Hans W. Frei, "The Doctrine of Revelation in the Thought of Karl Barth, 1909 to 1922: The Nature of Barth's Break with Liberalism" (Ph.D. dissertation, Yale University, 1956); Van Harvey, *The Historian and the Believer* (New York: Macmillan Co., 1966); David Kelsey, *The Uses of Scripture in Recent Theology* (Philadelphia: Fortress Press, 1975); James M. Robinson, ed., *The Beginnings of Dialectic Theology*, vol. I (Richmond: John Knox Press, 1968); James M. Robinson and John B. Cobb, Jr., eds., *The New Hermeneutic*, New Frontiers in Theology, Vol. II (New York: Harper & Row, 1964); Klaas Runia, *Karl Barth's Doctrine of Holy Scripture* (Grand Rapids: William B. Eerdmans Publishing Co., 1962); James D. Smart, *The Divided Mind of Modern Theology: Karl Barth and Rudolf Bultmann 1908-33* (Philadelphia: Westminster Press, 1964); and James D. Smart, ed., *Revolutionary Theology in the Making: Barth-Thurneysen Correspondence, 1914-1925* (Richmond: John Knox Press, 1964).

For general discussions of Barth's biblical hermeneutic in the context of his dogmatic construction, see Camfield, *Ref.*, pp. 142-56; Casalis, *Portrait*, pp. 83-116; Come,

117

and context for our discussion, we will then take the remaining section of this chapter and the whole of Chapter Six to examine the exegesis in the doctrine itself. In this way, we will not only attempt to pose the answers to the above questions, but also identify the uniqueness of the contribution of Barth's hermeneutic of election.

A. Scripture: Revelation and Interpretation

Barth's understanding of biblical hermeneutics is intimately tied to his doctrine of Scripture. More particularly, it stands in relation to his view of the unique subject matter of Scripture in its capacity as the witness to God's self-revelation. For Barth, this means that "the object of the biblical texts is quite simply the name Jesus Christ, and these texts can be understood only when understood as determined by this object."[2] It is Jesus Christ and he alone who is identical with God's revelation; what Jesus Christ is originally and directly, the Bible is derivatively and indirectly, namely the Word of God. Scripture is therefore to be distinguished from the revelation itself, and viewed as a witness to and account of the event of that revelation. Barth makes this distinction by contending that the words of the text are not themselves revelation. Rather they are human words about the one Word of God which constitutes the one definitive revelation.[3]

Nevertheless, the human words of the text witness to the revelation of the Word, and to that extent they participate in the revelation. The uniqueness and significance of these human words lies in the extraordinary nature of the subject matter or object to which they refer. Whether the words of the text become revelation depends not upon the text itself or the reader/hearer, but on the sovereign decision of the

---

Preach., pp. 168-98; Jüngel, *Legacy*, pp. 53-104; Mackintosh, *Types*, pp. 272-319; Parker, *Karl Barth*, pp. 30-115; Sykes, *Studies*, pp. 55-87; Torrance, *Early*, pp. 33-198; Weber, *Report*, pp. 57-73; and Wingren, *Conflict*, pp. 23-44, 108-28.

The literature on Barth's doctrine of election does not reflect an intense interest in--let alone a preoccupation with-- his exegetical work in the construction of the doctrine. Among those few critics who may be considered as exceptions to this rule, there is a wide divergence of opinion as to whether the exegesis does in fact support the doctrine. (See especially Berkouwer, *Div. Elec.*, pp. 156-62; Buess, *Zur Präd.*, pp. 29-36, 42-63; Gloege, *Prädest.*, pp. 209-17, 243-53; Hausmann, *KB Doct.*, pp. 67-76; Klooster, *Signif.*, pp. 44-47, 66-71; Polman, *Barth*, pp. 31-55; Sparn, *Revision*, pp. 50-53.) Our contention on this issue is that the question of exegetical support for the doctrine is tied inextricably to the question of consistent application of the hermeneutic which is claimed to be the basis for dogmatic construction. One can not deal adequately with Barth's exegesis in the doctrine of election without dealing at the same time with the hermeneutic agenda articulated by Barth at the outset of the *Church Dogmatics*.

[2]*C.D. I,2*:727.
[3]See *C.D. I,1*:111-20 and *C.D. I,2*:457-72.

who witness to it, inspiration can also be said to be operative in the second case, i.e., when a later reader/hearer is the recipient of revelation in and through the written witness. By means of the text, later readers/hearers encounter the witness of the authors. But it is not until God again reveals the divine self that this written witness mediates the same Word of God originally encountered by the authors in the event of revelation. When this does occur, there again is inspiration, an obedient perceiving and hearing of the self-revelation of God mediated by the text. This revelation to later readers/hearers is no less inspired because it is mediated by human thoughts and responses set to writing. Quite the contrary, it is precisely through the encounter with these very human words that the self-revelation of the Word to others occurs again:

> In what they have written they exist visibly and audibly before us in all their humanity, chosen and called as witnesses of revelation, claimed by God and obedient to God, true men, speaking in the name of the true God, because they have heard His voice as we cannot hear it, as we can hear it only through their voices. And that is their *theopneustia*. That is the mystery of the centre before which we always stand when we hear and read them: remembering that it was once the case (the recollection of the Church and our own recollection attest it) that their voice reproduced the voice of God, and therefore expecting that it will be so again. The biblical concept of *theopneustia* points us therefore to the present, to the event which occurs for us: Scripture has this priority, it is the Word of God.[13]

The problem of the historicity and verifiability of the events of revelation as reflected in the text is qualified by Barth's view of inspiration which connects both writer and reader/hearer with the self-revelation of God. So far as the text as a medium is concerned, the important element is its character and usability as a divinely enabled human witness to the presence and act of God, and not its historical accuracy and verifiability. Barth's view of inspiration is built upon a distinction between two types of history. First of all, there is what Barth calls general historicity, by which he means the concrete events in space and time that are accessible to historical investigation, analysis and judgment. All events, including those described in the Bible as taking place between God and humanity, are subject to the canons of historical inquiry, but only with regard to their human, temporal side. The

---

[13]*C.D.* I,2:505-6. In this regard, see also Barth's discussion of I Corinthians 2:6-16 and II Corinthians 3:4-18 at pp. 512-26.

historical judgment which presupposes this general historicity can neither confirm nor deny the divine activity, even when such judgment is brought to bear precisely upon the human, temporal side of that activity. There is thus for Barth a second kind of history, a special historicity in addition to general historicity. In this second kind of history, historical judgment gives way to the judgment of faith which alone can perceive the activity of God in the spatio-temporal events of human history. In particular, it is the judgment of faith which recognizes the activity of God with humanity in the history narrated in the Bible. While it is true that a particular event in the Bible may be judged in its historicity according to the canons of the general sense of history, such a judgment does not touch at all the question of the special historicity of the activity of God with humanity. An event judged by general historical criteria to be non-historical may still be recognized as a special historical event: "The question which decides hearing or non-hearing of the biblical history cannot be the question of its general historicity; it can only be that of its special historicity."[14]

With this view of two types of history which are related and yet distinct, Barth overcame the problem of the extent to which the biblical history could be a component in general history and yet remain free from human control and critical judgment in terms of general historicity. The biblical history is the narration of revelatory events that took place in a specific place and time involving particular persons. But accessibility to this special history within the sweep of general history is denied to the judgments of human historiography and opened only to faith as itself given in the execution of the revelation. As Barth says:

> Part of the concept of the biblically attested revelation is that it is a historical event. Historical does not mean historically demonstrable or historically demonstrated. Hence it does not mean what is usually called "historical." We should be discarding again all that we have said earlier about the mystery in revelation if we were now to describe any of the events of revelation attested in the Bible as "historical"; i.e., apprehensible by a neutral observer or apprehended by such an observer. What a neutral observer could apprehend or may have apprehended of these events was the form of revelation which he did not and could not understand as such. It was an event that took place in the human sphere with all the possibilities of interpretation corresponding to this sphere.

---

[14]*C.D.* I,1:327. Barth's discussion of the two types of history occurs in the context of his treatment of revelation as the root of the doctrine of the trinity. In this regard, see especially pp. 324-33.

The Core of the Election Hermeneutic

In no case was it revelation as such.[15]

Because the events of the Bible have to do with the judgments of faith, and not with the canons of critical judgment exercised under the rubric of general historicity, there is no threat posed by the use of the historical-critical method. Rather there are limits placed upon the usefulness of the method to the extent that it is oriented to the human, temporal side, and as such it cannot on its own terms access the divine revelation which takes place in a special way within particular events of human history.

In Barth's view, it is the first moment of inspiration that is operative in the human side in the original event of revelation that takes place as an historical event. That is, it is inspiration that effects the faithful perception of the activity of God with humanity in its original form. But it is the second moment of inspiration that is at work in the human side when a later reader/hearer faithfully perceives the activity of God in the original historical event, and this perceiving is itself the repetition and confirmation of the original revelation in and through the medium of the author's witness. That is, it is inspiration that accesses the special history of God's action with humanity there and then, and makes it recognizable and intelligible here and now. We can therefore represent Barth's view of the interrelation between history, revelation, biblical text and inspiration in this way: when the biblical text is used by God as a medium for self-revelation to the present reader/hearer, and the voice and activity of God are heard and perceived there and then (and thus here and now), then the two moments of inspiration have been connected as a single piece and there has taken place a continuation of an event of special historicity, and no amount of historical judgment based on general historicity can confirm or deny this occurrence, either then or now.

The starting point for Barth's hermeneutic program is the fact that "God's Word comes to man as a human word."[16] For Barth, this means that the human word is itself a continuing witness to the event of the Word becoming flesh, and that the interpretation of this human word is itself an act of the Word of God.[17] The proclamation and hearing of the Word of God demands interpretation and explanation for the simple reason that this Word takes on the form of human words. Barth contends that the Word of God in itself is clear, but that the human words in which it comes to the reader/hearer are not. This ambiguity and

---

[15] *C.D.* I,1:325. The German word translated here as "historical" is *historisch*.

[16] *C.D.* I,2:699.

[17] *C.D.* I,2:710. The context of this remark is the discussion of human freedom under the Word and the responsibility for the exposition of the biblical witness to the divine self-revelation (see pp. 695-722). This freedom and responsibility are understood as "the genuine effective interpretation and application based upon and connected indissolubly with the Word of God" (p. 710).

obscurity of human language in the service of the Word of God requires that the concepts, images and understandings brought to biblical interpretation must be subordinated to the biblical text as the primary human witness to revelation.[18] The interpretation of the Word of God is possible only in the interpretation of the human words of witness, and genuine hearing and perceiving require the subordination of all previous thoughts and ideas:

> To interpret God's Word must and can now mean to interpret Holy Scripture. And because the interpretation of the Word of God can take place only through man's subordination, this subordination now comes concretely to mean that we have to subordinate ourselves to the word of the prophets and apostles; not as one subordinates oneself to God, but rather as one subordinates oneself for the sake of God and in His love and fear to the witnesses and messengers which He Himself has constituted and empowered.[19]

Barth articulates the actual process of biblical interpretation by identifying three discreet, yet interrelated phases. The first phase consists in the explanation (*explicatio*) of the *sensus* of the words in their original, historical context and situation; it is concerned with the words of the text and the authors who used them in a particular literary-historical environment. This phase is thus one held in common with general hermeneutics. The task here is to hear and understand the meaning of the authors' words, and attempt to reproduce the image, theme or reality reflected in and controlled by those words. Subordination to the text in this phase means that the possibilities of the textual referents cannot be pre-determined or limited to the ideas and categories of understanding brought to the text. Rather there must be a genuine hearing and attempt to understand the object referred to in the text, and a re-presentation of that object which is determined by its own form and not one imposed upon it by the reader/hearer. The success of this phase depends on whether the literary and historical investigation of the text aids in this re-presentation so that an accurate picture of the object can be formed. In short, the issue is whether or not this phase of interpretation enables the

---

[18]See *C.D.* I,2:715-20.

[19]*C.D.* I,2:717. It is to be noted that if (as Barth contends) the human words are not themselves identical with the Word, with the reality of God's self-revelation, but rather the human witness to that Word, then the human words of the text are themselves an *interpretation* of that reality. What this means for Barth's construction, therefore, is that the interpretation of the biblical text is nothing more nor less than an interpretation of an interpretation.

re-presentation of Jesus Christ who alone is the object of the biblical text.[20]

The second phase of interpretation consists in the act of reflection (*meditatio*) on what is said in the text *vis-a-vis* its object, and as such it represents a transition from what is said to the thought of the reader/hearer. In this phase, the interpreter is legitimately entitled to invoke a scheme of thought to assist in the exposition and to provide a frame of reference for hearing and understanding the text subjectively. But though the utilization of some scheme of thought is appropriate and indeed required, Barth identifies five components which serve to limit the usefulness of any particular logic, philosophy or epistemology as a tool for biblical interpretation. He argues that: (1) The interpreter must be aware that such a scheme is being imported to the task, that it is different from that found in Scripture and that no scheme in itself is fitted for the apprehension and explanation of the text. (2) A scheme of thought can therefore function only as an hypothesis in an experimental and provisional manner, and whether it can and actually does aid in the explanation of the text and its referent is something determined ultimately only by the Word of God and not the interpreter. (3) Because the scheme of thought is imported to the text, different from the text and ultimately in itself unfit for definitive interpretation, it can never become an end in itself or claim an independent status over the text. (4) Given this basic and inherent unfitness and relativity of schemes of thought, there is no fundamental reason for precluding one scheme or preferring another in the task of interpretation. (5) Therefore any scheme of thought is legitimate to the extent that it is determined and governed not by itself, but by the text and its referent, and allows itself to be subject to criticism under the text.[21]

---

[20]See the discussion at *C.D.* I,2:722-27.

[21]See the discussion at *C.D.* I,2:727-36. Barth's discussion of this second phase of interpretation seems to contradict his earlier discussion of the subordination and submission of all human thoughts, ideas, images and convictions to those of the text (pp. 715-22). How can an interpreter subordinate a scheme of thought to the text when a scheme of thought is required for the understanding of the text? If a scheme of thought is a necessary "key" to interpreting the text, what else can this mean except that in some sense the interpreter controls the means whereby the text is to be understood? It is meaningless to talk about subordinating a scheme of thought to that of the text unless one already knows what the text is saying, unless one already knows the text's "scheme of thought" to which another scheme can be subordinated. But this textual scheme of thought or idea is something which cannot be known in advance of interpretation. Indeed, it cannot be known at all unless the interpreter brings a scheme of thought to bear on the text, and this exercise is anything but the subordination of all human thoughts, ideas etc. Furthermore, Barth's discussion here begs the question as to whether the interpreter and his/her scheme do not in fact determine the nature and understanding of the objective referent of the text. In the light of Barth's five limitations to a human scheme, it is appropriate to ask Barth: How do you know that another interpreter offers a correct or incorrect interpretation of the object of the text unless you yourself stand in a position

The third phase of interpretation consists in the appropriation and application (*applicatio*) of the meaning and understanding of the text. It is at this point that examination and reflection achieve their *telos* in that the interpreter is enabled to think the text for him/herself, to assimilate its meaning into him/herself, and to assume in his/her own existence the witness to the reality of the text's objective referent. In this regard, Barth contends:

> When the Word of God is appropriated, it means that each individual who hears or reads it relates what is said to himself as something which is not spoken generally or to others, but to himself in particular, and therefore as something which is to be used by him.[22]

The interpretive task, therefore, is one which decisively issues in concrete response-ability to Jesus Christ as the object reflected and encountered in the text, i.e., an internal, subjective acknowledgement and appropriation of what is spoken to the reader/hearer by the Word in and through the text, and the faithful act of human obedience and witness which can then be used by God to further the divine self-revelation. Barth completes the discussion of the interpretive task by contending for the idea that biblical interpretation is finally a faithful human act of response:

> By faith we ourselves think what Scripture says to us, and in such a way that we must think it because it has become the determining force of our whole existence. By faith we come to the contemporaneity, homogeneity and indirect identification of the reader or hearer of Scripture with the

---

above both text and interpreter, holding the correct "key" to interpretation, and therefore in a position to judge the text, its object and its interpretation? Is this not a judgment exercised from the perspective of a human scheme of thought, one exercised according to the criteria implicit in a particular scheme of thought? If it is not, then ultimately there is only an infinite separation of all schemes of thought (including the human scheme of thought in the Scriptures) from that reality or content which interpretation claims can be perceived and understood, but only by a (or any) scheme of thought.

Even more, we must ask Barth: On what basis can one interpret and understand the biblical scheme of thought, and then be in a position to subordinate one's own scheme to that of the Bible, except by the use of another human scheme? Does not subordination presuppose knowledge of the biblical scheme? Is not subordination then merely an exchange of one human scheme for another (albeit biblical) one? If it is not, then there is in fact a divinely chosen and determined human scheme which we have only to discover by means of an interpretation which is oriented by a non-chosen scheme.

In the light of these questions, and with reference to Barth's discussion of the matter of subordination and the matter of the use of a human scheme of thought, we can only observe that at its best, Barth's argument is circular; at its worst, it is ludicrous.

[22]*C.D. I,*2:737.

witnesses of revelation. By faith their testimony becomes a matter of our own responsibility. Faith itself, obedient faith, but faith, and in the last resort obedient faith alone, is the activity which is demanded of us as members of the Church, the exercise of the freedom which is granted to us under the Word.[23]

With this basic understanding of Barth's hermeneutic and his description of the interpretive task, we can now focus our attention on the major exegetical passages which are used to support the construction of the doctrine of election.

B. The Subject and Object of Election

The credibility of Barth's construction of the doctrine of election as a whole depends on the exegetical establishment of the notion that Jesus Christ is himself the electing God and the elect human. The biblical interpretation which lies at the foundation of the construction of this notion moves in a direction which represents a reversal of the direction taken by previous constructions of the doctrine, and it is this reversal which represents the basis for the christological orientation of the construction. Jesus Christ is at the center of the doctrine, not because he is the electing God and the elect human. This is a constructive conclusion which is itself based on the exegesis which supports the elements that come together and call for such a conclusion. Rather Jesus Christ is at the center because he is the concrete self-revelation of God, and as such he constitutes the only basis on which it is possible to know and say anything at all about the being and activity of God. The exegesis at the basis of this notion is intended to establish the identity of revelation/incarnation and election (or the fact that election constitutes the center of revelation/incarnation), so that it becomes necessary to speak of one of these elements only in terms of, and in direct relation to, the other. The exegesis at this point is meant to demonstrate that revelation/incarnation can be meaningfully grasped only under the rubric of election, and that election cannot be discussed apart from revelation/incarnation. Every component in Barth's doctrine depends ultimately on the exegetical demonstration of the identity of election and Jesus Christ in the biblical witness to God's self-revelation. Our task in this section will be to analyze the exegetical passages in §33, "The Election of Jesus Christ," in order to grasp the interpretive juxtaposition which calls for the dogmatic construction as it presently stands, and

---

[23]*C.D.* I,2:740. For Barth's discussion of this third phase of interpretation, see pp. 736-40.

thereby expose both the reversal represented in Barth's work as well as the uniqueness of his exegetical contribution to the doctrine of election.

1. The Identity of Subject and Object. The exegesis of John 1:1-2 which opens the discussion of §33 is intended to support the notion that Jesus Christ is the *election* of God, and on that basis he is the *Word* of God, the *decree* of God and the *beginning* of God.[24] Barth begins with these two verses because they establish the eternal deity, consubstantiality and personhood of the Word (or Son) as co-equal with God the Father: The Word is itself God, participating fully and eternally in the perfection of the one divine being and its activity. Then, in the light of the declaration in vs. 14 that "the Word became flesh and dwelt among us", Barth correctly links the being and activity of the Word with the human Jesus of Nazareth: this human is himself the person of God in the mode of being as the Word (or Son) of God. When vs. 14 is connected to vs. 18 ("No one has ever seen God; the only Son, who is in the bosom of the Father, he has made him known."), it is possible to contend not only that Jesus Christ is himself God, but that he alone is the one who can and has made God knowable and known to humanity: Jesus Christ is identical with the divine self-revelation, and he is so in the form of the incarnation. Barth thus begins the exegetical work at the base of his doctrine by establishing the fact that Jesus Christ is the "Word" of God who is as such in the "beginning" with God, and who now is the concrete medium of God's revelation. In other words, Barth begins by establishing the identity of revelation and incarnation as the basis on which it is possible to know God.[25]

While it is true that the first chapter of John's gospel supports the declaration of the identity of Jesus Christ with revelation/incarnation, it does not in itself call for the identity of Jesus Christ with *election* and *decree*. It is precisely at the point of this identification that we find the reversal and uniqueness of Barth's exegesis. The Johannine prologue which calls for the identity of Jesus Christ and revelation/incarnation is itself interpreted in terms of the biblical concept of election or predestination. This is to say that the revelation/incarnation motif

---

[24]See *C.D. II,2*:94-102. The exegesis is found at pp. 95-99.

[25]Implicit in Barth's discussion at this point is the question of the pre-existence of the *human* Jesus. Based on the discussion in the doctrine of election, it is fairly obvious that Barth's position calls for a strict understanding of the eternal pre-existence of the human Jesus. It is not possible to engage this issue in the present discussion. However, it should be pointed out that the christological discussions which precede the doctrine of election are ambiguous. There are passages which seem either to assume or require an eternal pre-existence of the human (see e.g. *C.D. I,1*:392-400, 412-16, 424-27, 433-41, *C.D. I,2*:12-25, 44, 136). At the same time, there are passages which can clearly be read to suggest the contrary (see e.g. *C.D. I,1*:402-11, *C.D. I,2*:35-40, 134-35, 147-71). In any event, it is not finally decisive how one resolves the question with regard to Barth, for it does not alter his position on the identity of the human Jesus and revelation/incarnation.

focused concretely in the human Jesus Christ and articulated in the prologue has imposed upon it a hermeneutic which is conditioned by the biblical categories of election. The ideas of election and decree are brought to the task of interpreting the prologue. In this respect, what Barth's exegesis reflects is this: if the triune God is the electing God, then it can be said that the Son who is also God and therefore with God in the beginning is also the electing God. To the extent that the Son is the acting Subject in the human Jesus, it can legitimately be said that the human Jesus is the electing God. To the extent that the human Jesus is the one whom God chose to become, it can be said that the Son in the human Jesus is the *elect human*. However, these contentions can be recognized in John 1 only when the passage is interpreted in the light of such passages as Romans 8:29, 9:6-18, Ephesians 1:4-13, 3:3-5 and other New Testament passages which deal explicitly with Jesus Christ and election, and this is clearly what Barth is doing. The reversal is therefore the fact that the revelation and incarnation motifs of John 1 are set within the context of, and interpreted with reference to, the concept of divine election, as opposed to the tendency to interpret the election passages either in isolation from, or with only indirect reference to, a concept of revelation which may or may not be christologically oriented. The uniqueness of Barth's construction at this point is the fact that he exegetically connects the reality of election to the concrete and definitive self-revelation of God in the human Jesus Christ, and contends that nothing at all can be known or posited regarding election apart from its connection with the divine revelation. In short, the prologue of John's gospel figures prominently in the doctrine of election, indeed constitutes its foundation, because it links the reality and knowledge of election to the focal point of God's self-disclosure. Though this linkage in itself does not yet establish the identity of revelation/incarnation with the election of Jesus Christ as Barth has constructed it, it nevertheless constitutes the noetic basis for exegetically pursuing this identity in the categories of election, and this is what Barth intends to accomplish with the remaining exegetical sections in §33.

   2. The Covenant Relation. The categories of election are not only taken from New Testament passages, but from Old Testament passages as well. In one exegetical passage, Barth contends that the concept of predestination is to be traced back to the Old Testament concept of the covenant in which God commits the divine self to entering into a relation with the as yet to be created humanity.[26] Barth argues that this idea of covenant is meant to express the fact that from eternity God has committed Godself to a relationship with a reality outside the divine self, and that this commitment constitutes the beginning and the

---

[26]See the discussion of covenant at *C.D. II,2*:102-3.

determination of God's relationship with that external reality. The biblical passages cited in support of the eternal and steadfast nature of this covenant commitment are interpreted to suggest that the whole of creation is to be understood as the arena in which the covenant relation with humanity is worked out.[27] Again, however, it is the linkage of this concept of covenant with the idea of revelation/incarnation that for Barth evokes the election hermeneutic as a way of grasping more comprehensively the significance of the role played by Jesus Christ. Building on the confluent interpretations of John 1 and the election passages in the New Testament, Barth contends that the covenant motif as descriptive of the eternal resolve of the triune God must itself be understood in terms of election, and that this alone explains the origin of revelation/incarnation on the basis of which we can know God:

> In the beginning it was the choice of the Father Himself to establish this covenant with man by giving up His Son for him, that He Himself might become man in the fulfilment of His grace. In the beginning it was the choice of the Son to be obedient to grace, and therefore to offer up Himself and to become man in order that this covenant might be made a reality.[28]

The biblical idea of the covenant is thus intended to support the notion that the origin of revelation/incarnation is to be found in God's decision or *election* or *decree* before creation to unite Godself with humanity. This idea underscores, qualifies and substantiates the notion that Jesus Christ was with God and was himself God at the beginning, and as such he is the one "whose person is that of the executor within the universe and time of the primal decision of divine grace, the person itself being obviously the content of this decision."[29] By interpreting the biblical motif of covenant in terms of an eternal decision manifest in the incarnation and revelation executed in Jesus Christ, Barth has not only linked the knowledge of God's primal election and decree to Jesus Christ, but he has also posited an identity between revelation/incarnation and election, concretely manifest in Jesus Christ.

    3. The Human Jesus is the Electing God. Barth then moves to establish the notion that the *human* Jesus is to be understood first and foremost as the electing God, participating in the divine election as an

---

[27]In particular, the Old Testament passages are Genesis 9:14, 17:7f, Isaiah 55:3, Jeremjah 32:40, 50:5, Ezekiel 16:60, 37:26.

[28]*C.D. II,*2:101. The New Testament passages cited in support of this contention are Acts 2:23, 4:27f, Ephesians 1:3-5, 9-11, 3:4, II Timothy 1:19, I Peter 1:20, Hebrews 9:26, and Revelation 13:8.

[29]*C.D. II,*2:103.

electing Subject together with the Father and Spirit, and that only on that basis can he be understood as the elect human. The exegesis at this point focuses largely again on John's gospel, and the passages selected for citation have to do with Jesus' acting as a divine Subject as well as with the intimacy of his relationship as the Son with the Father.[30] The emphasis here is upon the mutual relationship and the mutual working of the Father and the Son Jesus. Against the background of this mutuality and co-equality, Barth singles out Jesus' selection of the disciples as illustrative of his divine electing activity as a human:

> In the light of these passages the electing of the disciples ascribed to Jesus must be understood not merely as a function undertaken by Him in an instrumental and representative capacity, but rather as an act of divine sovereignty, in which there is seen in a particular way the primal and basic decision of God which is also that of Jesus Christ.[31]

The apparently simple act in which Jesus chooses his disciples is thus interpreted by Barth in the context of a mutuality between Father and Son that is maintained even in the incarnation so that the act of the human Jesus is understood as the act of the divine electing Subject. John 1 is thus evoked to support the notion that the action of the human Jesus is first of all the action of the electing God. In short, God's eternal electing is the basis for understanding the discrete actions of the human Jesus as the actions of the electing God in the sphere of the divine self-disclosure. The exegetical linkage between revelation, incarnation and the electing action of the divine Subject in Jesus Christ is thus established:

> But if He and the Father are one in this unity of the divine name and glory ... then it is clear that the Son, too, is an active Subject of the *aeterna Dei praedestinatio* as the Son of Man, that He is Himself the electing God,... For trust in the divine decision depends upon whether that decision can be and actually is manifested to us as God's decision. And this is impossible unless it can be and actually is manifested to us as the decision of Jesus

---

[30]See *C.D. II,2*:106-15 for the excursus on this point. Most of this passage is given over to a critical discussion of the traditional views of the role played by the human Jesus in election and the noetic problem inherent in the affirmation of the *decretum absolutum*. The Johannine passages cited are 3:35; 4:34; 5:19, 26, 30; 6:37, 44-45, 65; 13:18; 14:1, 6, 10, 28; 15:1-2, 5, 16, 19; 17:1-6, 9-10, 24. Barth also appeals to other New Testament passages to support his interpretation of the Johannine material: Matthew 11:27; 16:17; Galatians 1:4; 2:20; Ephesians 5:2; Philippians 2:7-8; I Timothy 2:6; and Hebrews 5:8; 7:27; 9:14.
[31]*C.D. II,2*:106.

Christ.[32]

This establishment of the linkage between both the self-revelation of God and the electing action of God in the human Jesus constitutes a crucial element in Barth's rejection of the *decretum absolutum*. The clear implication of his exegesis at this point is that unless Jesus Christ is held first of all to be the electing God precisely as the human Jesus, there is no other place to locate the basis for election than in an indeterminate and abstract good-pleasure of God.

4. *Jesus is the Elect Human.* Barth opposes the idea that Jesus Christ is one of the elect, or that his authority and instrumentality comes from the fact that he is the object of election. He argues rather that it is because of his deity and his activity as an electing Subject that he is understood to be the head of the elect and the instrument in and through whom election is executed.[33] The "in him" of Ephesians 1:4 is thus interpreted in the light of the exegetical confluence of election and incarnation in John 1. Jesus Christ is the elect human because it is in him that the basic decision of God is fulfilled, and he is to be singled out in a category of his own because he is the electing God precisely as the elected human. Thus it is the identity of the Subject and object of election that constitutes the substantive reality of the original elect human.

Barth contends that "the basic passage in Jn. 1:1-2 speaks of the man Jesus. In so doing, it contains self-evidently this second assertion, that Jesus Christ is elected man."[34] Thus for Barth, the fact that the human Jesus is the elect human materializes exegetically from the confluence of election, covenant and revelation/incarnation (i.e., from the identity of Subject and object), and not from an exegetical analysis of the biblical witness to his humanity. As the object of election, Jesus Christ is not only the reality of the exaltation of humanity to participation in the divine life, but he is also the revelation of this exaltation, the one in whom both a representative and all-inclusive election is accomplished. Thus God's way and purpose with this human as the object of election is the manifestation of God's way and purpose with human nature. But it can be understood as such, and exegetically established as such, only on

---

[32]*C.D. II,*2:107.

[33]See the discussion at *C.D. II,*2:117-20.

[34]*C.D. II,*2:117. This second proposition can be "self-evident" (*selbstverständlich*) only when the passage is read in the light of the priority of the first proposition and the confluence of revelation/incarnation and election which is itself developed by linking John 1:1-2, 14, 18 with the election passages in the New Testament, i.e., when the election hermeneutic is imported to the text. If the proposition is so self-evident, it would be unnecessary to interpret it in the light of other passages which speak explicitly of the human Jesus as being chosen by God (John 17:24; 19:4-5; Luke 9:35; 23:35; Acts 2:23; 4:27f; I Peter 1:20; Hebrews 2:11f; Revelation 13:8).

the basis of the identity of election and revelation/incarnation.

5. Jesus Christ, the Only Rejected Individual. Having exegetically established the notion that Jesus Christ is both the electing God and the elect human, Barth now has a hermeneutic basis on which to build his contention that Jesus is the only rejected individual. This election hermeneutic is brought to bear on those passages which speak of the necessity of Jesus' suffering and dying as the God-human.[35] As the object of election (who is also the divine Subject of election), the human Jesus is predestined to confront Satan and Satan's power, to suffer and die, and in the resurrection finally to triumph over the power of evil and sin which humanity cannot otherwise resist. In particular, Philippians 2:6-11 and Matthew 4:1-11 are singled out as illustrative of Jesus' peculiar predestination. However, neither passage in itself speaks of rejection. Rather rejection as the signification of God's wrath and judgment upon sin and evil is imported into these texts in order that the suffering and death of the God-human Jesus might be qualified and substantiated in the categories of election. This is to say that rejection as the negative side of election is utilized as the motif for expositing the reality of Jesus' suffering and death. Barth interprets the two biblical passages to this effect:

> In this one man Jesus, God puts at the head and in the place of all other men the One who has the same power as Himself to reject Satan and to maintain and not surrender the goodness of man's divine creation and destiny; the One who according to Mt. 4 actually does this, and does it for all who are elected in Him, for man in himself and as such who does not and cannot do it of himself. The rejection which all men incurred, the wrath of God under which all men lie, the death which all men must die, God in His love for men transfers from all eternity to Him in whom He loves and elects them, and whom He elects at their head and in their place. God from all eternity ordains this obedient One in order that He might bear the suffering which the disobedient have deserved and which for the sake of God's righteousness must necessarily be borne. Indeed, the very obedience which was exacted of Him and attained by Him was His willingness to take upon Himself the divine rejection of all others and to suffer that which they ought to have suffered.[36]

---

[35]See the discussion at *C.D.* II,2:122-27.

[36]*C.D.* II,2:123. The appropriation of the electional category of *rejection* in the interpretation of these passages is what allows Barth to press on to contend that

Thus the suffering and death of the God-human Jesus Christ, so clearly attested in Scripture, is interpreted in terms of the negative category of rejection, a category which is necessary for both the comprehensive understanding of election and the materializing of the focal point of the revelation and execution of that election as it pertains to others.

6. *The Election Hermeneutic.* The contention that the will of God is the election of Jesus Christ is intended by Barth to be the basis for his opposition to the notion that ultimately the electing God and the elect human are unknown. But the identification of Jesus Christ with both the electing God and the elect human can be posited only when revelation in the form of incarnation is understood to be identical with election, and this means only when the biblical passages which deal with God's self-revelation in the God-human Jesus Christ are themselves interpreted in the light of the categories of election, i.e., when an election hermeneutic is juxtaposed on the text. Once the categories of election are appropriated to interpret and understand Jesus Christ as the self-revelation of God, then it is only a relatively small step to interpreting the whole of Scripture (as the biblical witness to this revelation) in those same categories. Because the knowledge of God is tied to the Word of God incarnate in Jesus Christ, and because the Word of God is interpreted in terms of election, everything that is to be said about God and God's relation to God's creation is to be expressed with reference to the divine electing. Even though the biblical passages which deal with

---

predestination is not only "double" predestination, but that the negative side applies only to God in the human Jesus Christ: "That the elected man Jesus had to suffer and die means no more and no less than that in becoming man God makes Himself responsible for man who became His enemy, and that He takes upon Himself all the consequences of man's action--his rejection and his death" (p. 124). This contention comes as a constructive conclusion to the exegesis of Philippians 2:6-11, and it is the closest Barth gets to establishing an exegetical foundation for his view of double predestination. It is worth noting that when he addresses directly the notion of double predestination, there is no exegesis whatsoever (see pp. 161-75). He does acknowledge, however, that "this interpretation of double predestination stands or falls, of course, with the view that the divine predestination is to be understood only within the election of Jesus Christ. It stands or falls with the view that in regard to the electing God and elected man we must look and continue to look neither to the right hand nor to the left but directly at Jesus Christ" (p. 174). Thus Barth's view of double predestination can be correlated only indirectly with an exegetical foundation, and seen only as a reasonable dogmatic inference drawn from the notion that Jesus Christ is the elect human.

We should also pause here to note that the discussion of the Supra- and Infralapsarian controversy follows on the heels of the discussion of Jesus' predestination to suffering and death as the rejected individual, and brings the subsection on Jesus Christ's electing and election to a close. This progression would suggest that the discussion of the controversy is to be understood against the background of Jesus as the Subject and object of election (i.e., the identity of revelation/incarnation and election), rather than the problem of the individual as the object of election and the polarity of election and rejection as applicable categories for understanding the individual.

election *per se* are few in number, they nevertheless constitute the starting point and thus the explicitly biblical basis for a hermeneutic by which the whole of the Bible may be accessed in interpretation. "The decisive point is the reading of the Bible itself."[37] The linkage between revelation/incarnation on the one hand and election on the other is thus grounded exegetically in the fact that Scripture as the witness to this revelation does speak of election as the act of God, and no act of God can be known apart from revelation. To the extent that election is revealed and known, it is so only in and through the form determined by God for the divine self-revelation, and this means only in and through Jesus Christ as the Word of God, and thus penultimately in and through Scripture as itself the Word of God. The coalescence of the Subject and object of election in the human Jesus Christ is thus grounded noetically and exegetically in the juxtaposition of those passages which deal with election and those which deal with the incarnation. But for Barth, it is ultimately the election passages which determine the hermeneutic:

> Is it not the case that all God's dealings attested in the Bible can be understood only against this background, as the dealings of the elected God with elected man? In exegetical considerations of this kind we may well be in full agreement with all the classical exponents of the doctrine. As regards the content of this concept it could hardly be otherwise: it is one of those comprehensive concepts which underlies all that the Bible says about God and man, and of which account must always and everywhere be taken even where it does not appear directly.[38]

In summation, if election is understood primarily as the execution of revelation/incarnation, then everything that can be known and acknowledged about God and Jesus Christ can be appropriately articulated in the categories of election. But for Barth, this orientation depends on whether the identity of revelation/incarnation in John 1 can be made to include election, i.e., whether there is exegetical support for locating revelation/incarnation in the context of election. It is clear that

---

[37]*C.D. II*,2:148.

[38]*C.D. II*,2:148-49. The context of this remark is Barth's critical discussion of the older hermeneutic which guided the exegesis of the election passages, and which he believes to have been flawed by the fact that it did not hold itself at this point to God's self-revelation in Jesus Christ (see pp. 146-54). Over against their hermeneutic, Barth argues that the election passages "must be read in the context of the whole Bible, and that means with an understanding that the Word of God is the content of the Bible" (p. 152), and that "at no point, then, and on no pretext, can we afford either to dispense with, or to be turned aside from, the knowledge of Jesus Christ" (p. 153).

for Barth, election is the higher category in his hermeneutic scheme, and because it is identical with revelation/incarnation it qualifies everything that is to be said *vis-a-vis* the person and work of Jesus Christ. It is also clear that the point of Barth's exegesis in §33 is the interpretation of the revelation of God in Jesus Christ *as this is attested in the scriptural witness to that revelation*. The point is not the interpretation of the election passages, except as their contextual and thematic proximity to Jesus Christ provides the basis for their use as a hermeneutic key to the interpretation of Jesus Christ as the self-revelation of God attested in Scripture. The question at this point is whether Barth has imported an external human scheme of thought into his exegesis of both the election and the revelation/incarnation passages, or whether he has subordinated his own thoughts, concepts etc. to those of the text, and has made a biblically defensible hermeneutic decision to interpret revelation/incarnation in terms of the biblical concept of election. Clearly Barth's own position on this question is the latter option.[39] His belief that the text is the Word of God and can be understood as such only with reference to Jesus Christ, his desire to be open and submissive to this subject matter who alone controls the meaning and understanding of the text, and his conviction that no understanding is possible apart from the execution of revelation in and through the text all coalesce in the proposition that knowledge of God's election and electing is constrained by the objective reality of God's self-revelation in Jesus Christ, and that therefore the act of divine election cannot be separated from revelation.

What Barth has done in his exegesis here is tie the knowledge of election to revelation/incarnation. In our judgment, the priority of election as the biblical category by which the revelation of God in Jesus Christ is to be interpreted is both legitimate and defensible in Barth's construction. He has succeeded in establishing a sound exegetical basis for his view of Jesus Christ as the electing God and the elect human, and has done so on the basis of the confluence of biblical passages which heretofore have not been brought together. But it must be noted that Barth is able to do this by interpreting the biblical witness to revelation in terms of the biblical witness to election, i.e., by accessing the textual witness to the Word of God by means of the structures and symbols of election as these are reflected in the text. In short, Barth's notion that election constitutes the means of the knowledge of God has exegetical integrity. His views on the election of Jesus Christ as the concrete decree, the beginning of God's ways and works, the self-determination of God and double predestination can be defended exegetically.[40]

---

[39] This position is articulated unambiguously in *C.D. II,2*:146-54.

[40] As we pointed out in n. 36, the one possible weak link in this chain of electional components is Barth's notion of double predestination which is not grounded directly on exegesis. However, Barth's dogmatic construction at this point does build upon the

confluence of election and the concreteness of God's self-revelation in the life and death of the God-human Jesus Christ. While Barth's view of double predestination does depart radically from the traditional formulation, it must be noted that it does so to a great extent because of his refusal to impose the older exponent's scheme of symmetry between election and rejection with reference to individuals as objects of election. Barth views this scheme as external to the text, and therefore invalid. In its place, he interposes the revelation/incarnation categories of the Subject of election, and what it means for this Subject to enter into fellowship with humanity concretely by becoming a human in Jesus Christ. Again, it is a construct which depends on the identification of election with revelation/incarnation which is itself exegetically grounded.

Chapter Six

The Perimeter of
The Election Hermeneutic

Just as we observed in the construction of the doctrine that Barth's dogmatic movement consists in the extension of the reality of election from the christological center outward, through the community as the environment in which God's election is executed, to the individual as the penultimate object of election, so too the exegetical movement can be seen to consist in the extension of the hermeneutic of election into the biblical substructures which suggest the contours for comprehending the community and the individual. As we turn now to the investigation of this extension in Barth's exegetical engagement with the biblical materials, we can discern in his work an evocative and ingenious utilization of the hermeneutic which calls for both a fresh evaluation of the biblical texts which summon a notion of election as well as a reappraisal of the foundations on which the doctrine of election as a whole is constructed.

A. The Medium of the Community

It would appear that Barth is on secure ground in his exegesis of the biblical materials in support of the election of the community. As the *locus classicus* for the doctrine of predestination, Romans 9-11 deals explicitly with the election of Israel and its relation to the Church as the people of Jesus Christ. However, Barth does not come to this passage without the election hermeneutic articulated in §33. His exegesis of these three chapters presupposes the identity of revelation/incarnation and election, and can be seen to consist in the interpretation of an objective reality (Israel and the Church) which he finds imaged in the text. The truly significant element in this exegesis is the fact that it is not so much the interpretation of biblical revelation as it is an interpretation of a medium which is itself an interpretation of revelation. This is to say that the exegesis of Romans 9-11 is an interpretation of an interpretation. Jesus Christ is *the* revelation, and Barth views the existence of the community as an interpretation of that revelation. Thus Barth interprets the community in its two forms in terms of the primary reality of Jesus Christ's election. It is only in the light of the election executed in Jesus

Christ that it is possible to interpret and understand the community as an object of election.

Barth's exegesis here is overwhelmingly typological; the one community is interpreted as a type of Jesus Christ whose twofold election it signifies and interprets in the attestation which constitutes its twofold life. With the aid of this particular typology, Barth links the event of Jesus Christ with the emergence of Israel as a nation and the rise of the Church, all within the historical framework of revelation. His principle interest is to demonstrate the analogies and correspondences which manifest the continuing theme of God's electing activity in and through history. However, Barth's typology embraces more than the establishment of correspondence between events and persons in the history of Israel in the Old Testament and the Church in the New. Rather it attempts to articulate the manner in which Israel and the Church in correspondence to Jesus Christ prefigure, foreshadow and materialize the reality of election comprehensible only in him. Both Israel as the Old Testament type and the Church as the New Testament type are regarded as important not in and for themselves, but for what their existence has to say about the election of Jesus Christ, and what this means is that Barth's typological interpretation of Israel and the Church is ultimately inimical to their historical reality in itself, to say nothing of the historical sense of the text. Barth's exegesis at this point is, after all, theological rather than historical, and he is as little concerned with the actual histories of these two realities as he is with the historical-critical method in general. The typological interpretation employed here assumes the unity of the two testaments and the unity of divine revelation, and seeks to articulate the reality of the community in terms of types which are either inherent in or deduced from the text, and which ultimately find their formal and material substance in Jesus Christ as the electing and elect God-human.

In our discussion of Barth's dogmatic exposition of the election of the community, we noted that the fundamental contention is that there is a single elect community existing in two forms, one revealing what God elects for Godself and the other revealing what God elects for humanity, and that both together constitute the environment and the extended medium for the execution of revelation in the election of Jesus Christ. The question before us in the examination of Barth's exegesis has to do with whether and to what extent Romans 9-11 is capable of calling for and supporting this contention. Our task in this section will be to describe and analyze Barth's election hermeneutic in so far as it is grounded in the identity of revelation/incarnation and election on the one hand, and oriented by a particular typology on the other.[1]

---

[1] In spite of (or perhaps because of) its typological orientation, Barth's interpretation of Romans 9-11 represents a singularly impressive piece of work *vis-a-vis* the biblical basis for a doctrine of election. Though his exegesis of this passage in *C.D. II,2* reflects a

The Hermeneutics of Election

1. Mercy and Judgment [Romans 9:6-29].[2] Barth begins his
exegesis with the problem posed by the fact of Israel's disobedience and
rebellion in the face of their election and the appearance of their
Messiah. The Old Testament evidence for Israel as the elect people of
God is overwhelming and beyond dispute, and in the light of this fact,
Barth sees Paul confronted with the problem of why it is that Israel as
such has not lived in faithfulness and obedience to its election, and
whether Israel's unbelief has in fact rendered its election void. This
problem is only compounded by the fact that the salvation brought by
Israel's Messiah has now been given to the Gentiles who have thus
become heirs and recipients of all that constituted Israel's election. In the
light of the faithfulness and obedience of the Church, the question which
forces itself on Paul is: How can Israel be the elect people of God when
they are so disobedient? Is not their rebellion an indication that God has
rejected them and turned toward a new people, putting them in the place
once occupied by Israel? The answer which Barth correctly sees in Paul's
response is a resounding No, and the general course of Barth's exegesis
consists in the declaration that Israel's disobedience is not only a sign of
their election, but is in fact required for the revelation of the election
which can only be understood in relation to Jesus Christ. For Barth, the
question thus becomes: In the light of the execution of election in the
revelation of Jesus Christ, how are we to understand the disobedience of
Israel in the face of their election, and the fact that the Church is now
the heir and recipient of the promises given in God's covenant with
Israel? In the light of the election of Jesus Christ, what constitutes the
election of Israel, and what is the relationship between Israel and the
Church?

The master typological motif which informs Barth's exegesis takes
its fundamental shape from the one individual Jesus Christ in whom is
seen the rejected human under God's righteous judgment and the elect
human living by God's gracious mercy. In brief, the motif is: one who is,
and who therefore signifies, two; or, two together who ultimately signify
one. With regard to the origins of the community, Barth interprets
Romans 9:6a-13 in terms of this motif, and then proceeds to unfold it in
the exegesis of verses 14-29. From the figure of Abraham, Barth moves
out in two directions of signification: (1) Abraham, Ishmael and Esau
who correspond to "Israel as such," and (2) Abraham, Isaac and Jacob

---

different agenda and a more mature application of his hermeneutic, it can nevertheless
be seen as a continuation of the themes expressed in the exegesis of Romans 9-11 in his
Romans where an albeit different typology is to be found. At several crucial junctions in
the exegesis in *C.D. II,2*, we find further development of ideas which have their initial
articulation in the earlier work. As we proceed in our discussion, we will take note of the
earlier formulations in an effort both to illustrate further the argument in *C.D. II,2* as well
as to show the continuity between the earlier and later work.
[2]See *C.D. II,2*:213-33.

who correspond to "the pre-existent Church in Israel." He thus moves from the interpretation of a single figure to that of the two categories of multitudes. The single figure of Abraham represents the origin of the one elect community, and all of his descendants are members of this one elect community:

> They were certainly appointed members of the one elected community of God. This is something that none of this race can be deprived of; this is something that not one of this race can decline, not even if his name is Caiaphas or indeed Judas Iscariot; this is what Jews, one and all, are by birth.[3]

They are so on the basis of God's election of Abraham and the fact of their biological descent from him. This act of God constitutes the election and origin of "Israel as such." But in addition to this first election, there is, according to Barth's interpretation, a second one, one which does not apply to all Abraham's descendants, but which distinguishes and differentiates:

> For it is (vv. 6b-7a) not at all the case that according to the Word and will of God all who belong to the race of Abraham, all bearers of the name Israel, were appointed to become members of the Church.... But they were not all appointed members of the Church hidden in Israel and revealed in Jesus Christ.[4]

This is the election which constitutes "true Israel," or the "pre-existent Church in Israel," or "the Church hidden in Israel." This is the second election which applies to only some of Abraham's offspring, only some of "Israel as such," and which comes about "by God's special choice."[5] In

---

[3] *C.D.* II,2:214.
[4] Ibid.
[5] Ibid. In his earlier commentary on Romans, Barth described the one community as "the Church" which is divided by the Word of God into "the Church of Esau" and "the Church of Jacob." He states: "The two Churches do not, of course, stand over against one another as two things. The Church of Esau alone is observable, knowable and possible. It may be seen at Jerusalem, or Rome, or Wittenberg, or Geneva. The past and the future can be comprehended without exception under its name. The Church of Esau is the realm where failure and corruption may be found, the place where schisms and reformations occur. But the Church of Jacob is capable of no less precise definition. It is the unobservable, unknowable, and impossible Church, capable neither of expansion nor of contraction; it has neither place nor name nor history; men neither communicate with it nor are excommunicated from it. It is simply the free Grace of God, His Calling and Election; it is Beginning and End. Our speech is of the Church of Esau, for we can speak of none other. But we cannot speak of it without recollecting that its theme is the Church

short, what Barth sees in Romans 9:6b-13 is not the origin of Israel as such, but the origin of the Church in Israel, and this is constituted by a differentiation within a differentiation. According to Barth, from the very beginning there is within the one elect community a distinction based solely on God's call, promise and mercy, and it is this second separate election that effects the origin of the now pre-existent and hidden "Church." As the objects of the second separate election, Abraham, Isaac and Jacob have their reality for Barth as types of the Church which will later become manifest in the community which surrounds the risen Lord Jesus Christ. As the objects of the first election who are denied the second election, Ishmael and Esau have their reality as types of "Israel as such" which will later become manifest in the nation of Israel constituted at the Exodus. In short, all Abraham's children are "children of the flesh" who are recipients of the first election. But within this group, there are also "children of the promise" who alone are recipients of the second election. Abraham is the father of "Israel" who is made by Barth to include Ishmael and Esau. But because Abraham is also the father of Isaac, the child of the promise, he is also the father of "the elected Church gathered from Jews and Gentiles."[6] Barth's exegetical interest in the pairs of Isaac and Ishmael and Jacob and Esau as they come from the one human Abraham is not concerned with these individuals as historical figures at the beginning of the life of the chosen people. Rather it is in the typology of the contrasting pairs within a single reality. For Barth, the priority of Isaac over Ishmael and Jacob over Esau signifies not election and rejection, but the separation of the Church within Israel: "The issue is the separation of the Church in Israel."[7] The two emerging from one are interpreted as nothing more than types of what will become the two forms of the one community.[8]

---

of Jacob. The very life of Esau, questionable as it is, depends upon Jacob; and he is Esau only because he is not Jacob" (*Romans*, p. 341-42).

[6]*C.D. II,2*:216.

[7]Ibid. "The totality of those who are of the *seed of Israel*, the type--they are not more than this--of all who lift up hands to God in prayer, stand, then, under the KRISIS of the twofold nature of the Church: or, putting it another way, they are under a 'Double Predestination'. All are confronted by the eternal two-sided possibility, which moves and rests in God alone. As the *seed of Israel*, they are elected or rejected; as *children of the flesh*, they inhabit the House of God or are strangers to it; with the Word of God ringing in their ears or on their lips, they belong to the Church of Jacob or to the Church of Esau" (*Romans*, p. 343).

[8]"Only because He elects and rejects, loves and hates, makes alive and puts to death, can He be apprehended and worshipped by men of this world. The paradox that eternity becomes time, and yet not time, is the tribulation of the Church and the revelation of God. He makes Himself known in the parable and riddle of the beloved Jacob and the hated Esau, that is to say, in the secret of eternal, twofold predestination. Now, this secret concerns not this or that man, but all men. By it men are not divided, but united. In its presence they all stand on one line--for Jacob is always Esau also, and in the eternal 'Moment' of revelation Esau is also Jacob" (*Romans*, pp. 347).

What Barth overlooks in this exegesis, however, is the fact that the line which begins with Abraham and runs through Isaac and Jacob is viewed by the Bible as precisely the origin of "Israel as such," the people of God who are so disobedient and rebellious that their status as the chosen people is called into question in the face of the reality of the Church, so much so that Paul must defend their election. If we take Barth's construction seriously, what Paul is defending in Romans 9-11 is the separate election of the Church (typified in Isaac and Jacob), and not the separate election of Israel as such (typified in Ishmael and Esau). Furthermore, with his contention that Ishmael and Esau typify a portion of the one elect community, Barth appears to ignore the fact that nowhere does the Bible speak of these two figures in a manner which suggests that they can and should be viewed as a type of "all Israel as such," or that they represent the remainder of Israel who does not receive the second election. Quite the contrary, the Old Testament speaks of these two as excluded from the chosen people precisely by God's election. Paul certainly does not regard them as a type of all Israel or as part of the elect community. This fact is not mitigated by the notion that God is also the God of Ishmael and Esau, or that God has a purpose for them too. Only by importing the hermeneutic informed by the election motif can Barth typologically interpret the text the way he does at this point.

In the interpretation of Romans 9:14-29, Barth is concerned with the typological development of the signification of "Israel as such" and "the pre-existent Church," and it continues to unfold again in terms of the motif of one signifying two, and two signifying one. In this passage, the motif takes two forms. First, the figure of Pharaoh (representing Israel as such and the execution of judgment) is placed alongside Moses (representing the pre-existent Church and the execution of mercy), both of whom are elect in that they serve the manifestation of God's purpose in election. The key to Barth's interpretation of Romans 9:6b-29 is found in verses 17-18 where Pharaoh's "election" is for the purpose of God's self-disclosure in the form of the judgment necessary as the context for Moses whose "election" is for the purpose of the disclosure of God's mercy. Pharaoh is interpreted by Barth as a type of that form of the elect community which does not receive the second election, but which is nevertheless elected to manifest the withholding of mercy. In this regard, Pharaoh is viewed "as a representative of reprobate and rebellious Israel,"[9] the "Israel as such" or the remainder who are not appointed to be in "the Church," but whose election is nevertheless certain and determined for the purpose of displaying judgment. The figure of Pharaoh thus extends the line which began with Ishmael and Esau, while Moses extends the Isaac and Jacob line. Both Moses and Pharaoh are

---

[9] *C.D. II,2*:220.

understood here as types of a single election which contains within itself a differentiation of purpose. Together, these two figures signify the one election of God:

> And [God's willing] is determined in this sense that it has this twofold direction. On both sides, although in different forms, God wills one and the same thing.... It is just this purpose which, according to vv. 15-17, both Moses and also Pharaoh must carry out. They do so in different ways and to this extent the single will of God has a differentiated form. He chooses Moses as a witness of His mercy and Pharaoh as a witness of the judgment that in and with this mercy becomes necessary and is executed. Thus He determines Moses as the voluntary, Pharaoh as the involuntary servant of His power and His name. He renews His mercy with regard to Moses. He refuses this renewal to Pharaoh.[10]

The parable of the potter offers the second form of the motif, i.e., the one lump from which two vessels are made, each of which represents a quite distinctive expression of God's election. Barth interprets this parable by identifying the vessels of dishonor with "Israel as such" and the vessels of honor with "the pre-existent Church in Israel." The one elect community is represented by the lump from which is made the vessel of Israel as such who signifies God's judgment, and the pre-existent Church within Israel who signifies God's mercy. Together, these two vessels signify the one purpose and action of God in election:

> He uses them both as witnesses to Jesus Christ, each in its own way.... Without prejudice to the seriousness of the divine purpose on both sides, the relationship between the two sides of the one divine action is one of supreme

---

[10]*C.D. II,2*:221. "Moses, it is true, was *raised up* in his invisible office to be the man of God; but so also was Pharaoh, when he acted as the visible opponent of Moses. In predestinating Pharaoh to hardening, God pays no attention to his human qualifications. Moses has no human pre-eminence over Pharaoh. Both stand humanly under the harshness of God; and from this point of view Moses and Pharaoh are interchangeable.... The purpose of the rejection of Pharaoh could be, and in fact is, identical with that of the election of Moses. Both are servants, not masters: servants of the will of God. The one manifests the 'Yes' of God, the other His 'No'; the one His mercy, the other His hardening; both, the good and the bad, are made use of to maintain and expose the invisible glory of God.... If the Church desires to be altogether Moses--and what Church or conventicle does not so desire?--then it must recognize and ponder the fact that it is Pharaoh, the Church of Esau. By this recognition and by this pondering room is made for the absolute miracle; and when the Church bows before this miracle, it can be Moses, the Church of Jacob" (*Romans*, pp. 352-53).

incongruity, supreme asymmetry, supreme disequilibrium.... If the 'vessels of dishonour' are appointed to demonstrate the impotence and unworthiness of man, of the 'lump' out of which they and the 'vessels of honour' are taken, 'the vessels of honour,' shaped by the same hand, stand in relation to them as a demonstration of what God's will and purpose are with this man.[11]

The identity of "Israel as such" (typified in Ishmael, Esau and Pharaoh) with the vessels of wrath, and the identity of "the pre-existent Church in Israel" (typified in Isaac, Jacob and Moses) with the vessels of mercy together enable Barth to extend the line of twofold prefiguration from the appearance of Abraham right up to the appearance of Jesus Christ in whose election the judgment and mercy of God are unequivocally executed and manifest. Barth's exegesis is clearly guided by the notion of the rejection and election of Jesus Christ. Because of his election, the vessels of wrath cannot be regarded as rejected: "Because He bore in His own Son the rejection which falls on mankind, the fact of Ismael's rejection, of Esau's, of Pharaoh's, of all Israel's also, is in the end superseded and limited; it is characterised as a rejection borne by God."[12] Rather "God endured these vessels in order to reveal the riches of His mercy through the others."[13] The signification of the line that runs through Ishmael, Esau, Pharaoh and "Israel as such" who are the vessels of wrath is interpreted in terms of the *rejected* human Jesus Christ; this line is to be understood as the necessary context for the emergence of the second line. On the other hand, the signification of this second line that runs through Isaac, Jacob, Moses and "the pre-existent Church in Israel" who are the vessels of mercy is interpreted in terms of the *elected* human

---

[11]*C.D. II,*2:223-24. "Why is God the God of Esau and of Jacob? Why is He the God of anger and of mercy? We know the question to be childish and formulated in mythological terms. For in God is no 'and', nor any duality. In Him the first is dissolved by the second. He is One. In eternity He is the God of Jacob manifesting Himself to men. But our thought cannot escape from dualism. We know that we are unable to comprehend otherwise than by means of a dialectical dualism, in which one must become two in order that it may be veritably one" (*Romans*, p. 358).

[12]*C.D. II,*2:226.

[13]*C.D. II,*2:225. "But what if the process of the revelation of this one God moves always from time to eternity, from rejection to election, from Esau to Jacob, and from Pharaoh to Moses? What if the existence of--vessels of wrath--which we all are in time!--should declare the divine endurance and forbearance (3:26), should be the veil of the long-suffering of God (2:4), behind which the vessels of mercy--which we all are in Eternity!--are not lost, but merely hidden? What if the man Esau, who is--fitted to destruction--to whom also the man Jacob belongs--endures the wrath of God only in a representative capacity, in order that the road may be prepared for the man Jacob, who is fitted for glory--to whom also the man Esau belongs--to enter the righteousness of God, which is hidden in His wrath and which emerges from it?" (*Romans*, pp. 359.)

Jesus Christ; this line is to be understood as the *telos* of the first line, namely the proclamation of God's purpose for humanity. As Barth states:

> Israel in itself and as such is the 'vessel of dishonour.' It is the witness to the divine judgment. It embodies human impotence and unworthiness. For by Israel its own Messiah is delivered up to be crucified. In its midst, however, there stands in relation to it from the very first the Church with its comprehensive and final commission to proclaim to this man the work of God--the Church which in virtue of its Head, the risen Lord, is the 'vessel of honour,' the witness to the divine mercy, the embodiment of the divine goodness which has taken the part of this man.... Ishmael is called by Isaac, Esau by Jacob, Pharaoh by Moses--the Synagogue of the present by Paul.[14]

Again, in following Barth's exegesis we are confronted with the fact that the Bible nowhere explicitly speaks of a differentiation within the one elect community, at least not in terms of the two lines articulated by Barth. In itself, the passage in Romans 9:19-29 does call for the equation of Israel with the vessels of wrath and the Church with the vessels of mercy. But it does not call for the differentiation of Israel into an "Israel as such" and a "pre-existent Church in Israel." A careful reading of Paul in 9:24-29 would suggest that he understood the vessels of mercy to be not a differentiation within Israel as a whole, but rather the apostolic Church made up of the Gentiles (vs. 25-26) and Jews (vs. 27-29), both of whom are called by God in and through the divine self-revelation in Jesus Christ. The only way this passage can be made to support Barth's construction is if one assumes at the outset that (1) there is only one elect community which in its Old Testament form must include the line of Ishmael, Esau, Pharaoh and the vessels of wrath as well as the line of Isaac, Jacob, Moses and the vessels of mercy; and that (2) the distinction between the two lines is based on a first election which applies to all, and a second election which is added to the first for only some. Both assumptions are operative in Barth's exegesis. Like Paul, Barth is unwilling to surrender the election of Israel in the face of the Church which now consists of Jews and Gentiles. But unlike Paul, he establishes Israel's election in this passage by typologically including those who in the biblical view are outside God's election of Israel, and he does so in order that they might signify the judgment on sinful and rebellious humanity executed in the crucifixion of Jesus Christ. Indeed, on the

---

[14]*C.D. II*,2:224-25.

strength of the first election, they are included precisely as those to whom the second election is denied at first, but to whom the announcement of its promise and reality is to be proclaimed. The vessels of wrath are thus intended to become vessels of mercy. In fact, however, the question of whether the actual figures of Ishmael, Esau and Pharaoh will come into the "Church" (i.e., receive the second election) is ultimately irrelevant for Barth. They are simply interpreted as types of Jesus Christ with no other significance than their representation of "Israel as such." Their election, along with that of the vessels of wrath, is for the purpose of serving as a medium for the manifestation of God's righteous judgment. In order to articulate this exegetically, Barth must discount these figures in themselves and interpret them typologically. In short, it is precisely as types that Ishmael, Esau, Pharaoh, "Israel as such" and the vessels of wrath together with Isaac, Jacob, Moses, "the pre-existent Church in Israel" and the vessels of mercy serve as media for the revelation of election executed in Jesus Christ.

2. Hearing and Believing [Romans 9:30-10:21].[15] The contention that the one elect community is the spatio-temporal environment in which God's revelation is executed and the place where humanity is positioned to hear and respond to that revelation depends to a great extent on Barth's interpretation of this passage. It is the community which contextualizes revelation, and this passage provides an important element for Barth's understanding of corporate media which manifest the relation between revelation and election. The central concern here has to do with the manner in which the community stands in relation to Jesus Christ as the self-revelation of God. The exegetical development receives its focus under the rubric of Jesus Christ as the rejected and elected human on the one hand, and the response of the community to the revelation executed in him on the other. The typology of "Israel as such" and "the pre-existent Church in Israel" is put aside, and replaced with "Israel as a whole" and "the Church" as two distinct significations on either side of the human Jesus Christ. There is a continuing development of the motif, but not in terms of a duality of "election" and "rejection." Rather it now takes the form of the noetic significance of election as a whole which can nevertheless be distinguished as the first election (manifest in "Israel as a whole" and its disbelief) and the second or separate election (manifest in "the Church" and its belief). In this regard, the exegesis assumes the revelation executed in the rejection and election of Jesus Christ, and for this reason it regards election as a prior status which precedes, and therefore qualifies, the actual distinction of belief and unbelief, obedience and disobedience.

Israel as a whole is now understood to be the recipients of the

---

[15]See *C.D. II*,2:240-59.

first election; they are the elect people whose efforts to secure their own salvation have resulted in their rejection of and refusal to believe in the promised Messiah. This rejection and refusal, however, presuppose both their election and God's self-disclosure; their pursuit of righteousness on their own terms is disobedience and unbelief precisely in relation to the demand placed upon them by their first election and to the self-giving of God in their Messiah. Barth's exegesis requires this first election in order that the significance of Israel's rebellion may be made clear. Barth interprets Israel to this effect:

> By endeavouring to establish its own righteousness instead of believing it had to reject Jesus Christ. And by its rejection of Jesus Christ it was made clear that in its endeavours to establish its own righteousness it was refusing faith. But by doing this it did not keep but broke the Law as the order of life under the promise that had become its own, as the determination under which it had to live after its election. By doing this it revealed man as the rebel against the God who elects him, and indirectly, therefore, the mercy of God as the sole sufficient power over against man elected by him.[16]

Israel's disobedience and unbelief is measurable only in relation to Jesus Christ, its Messiah, the revelation of God's election. For Barth, it is this fact that qualifies the entire history of Israel and summarizes the state of its existence:

> It is with [Jesus Christ] and Him alone that the Law is concerned as the order of life under the promise. It is He who interprets this order and fulfils it. It is He who guarantees its validity. To live in obedience under this order means to believe in Him. By refusing to do this, Israel transgresses and breaks its own Law. It fails to recognise the *kelal* of it, and with all its zeal for keeping it in its individual parts, according to 9:31 it comes short of the whole, the Law as such. It becomes guilty with regard to the one manifestation of the will of its own God.[17]

The heart of Barth's exegesis of this whole passage, however, is found in Romans 10:8-17. What Israel as a whole refuses to do once it

---

[16]*C.D. II*,2:244.
[17]*C.D. II*,2:245.

has heard God's self-revelation in Jesus Christ is not just press on to belief and faith. Rather because it refuses to do this, it cannot do the one thing that ultimately establishes and fulfills its election, namely the proclamation of its witness to Jesus Christ as the elect human and self-revelation of God. The demand placed upon Israel in the light of the first election is their acknowledgement and announcement of the reality of God's gracious and merciful act of revelation in Jesus Christ:

> The real demand addressed to the elect, but also the prohibition under which they are placed, can be derived only from the fact that the Word of God is near to them, that it is put on their lips so that there remains as their own doing only the subsequent act of uttering it as their confession, that it is put into their hearts so that what is expected of them is again only the subsequent act of putting faith in it. This is what the Law in its recapitulation, in Jesus Christ, speaking to them in a living way, requires of them.... This is the meaning and substance of the Law. It demands of man this appropriate action, this response, this subsequent motion of his lips and heart.[18]

Thus the witness to what God wills for and wants from humanity is not given by Israel. In paraphrase of Paul, Barth focuses the rebuke against Israel, and contends that election and salvation can only be fulfilled in faithful proclamation:

> Let elected man make his election sure in this twofold performance--by the faith of his heart his dignity as elected man, by the confession of his mouth the salvation that falls to him on the ground of this dignity. Scripture is unambiguous with respect to this twofold performance, its necessity, and its full sufficiency.[19]

---

[18]C.D. II,2:246. A somewhat different sentiment was offered earlier: "So it is that--with heart man believeth unto righteousness, and with the mouth confession is made unto salvation. The sequence *heart-mouth* is of no particular importance, nor is the selection of these two organs of any peculiar significance; it might just as well have been feet or hands or eyes or ears. What is important is that the mention of human organs in this context secures the correct emphasis. It emphasizes the ambiguity and contingency of the course of human existence, in order to make it clear that this contingency is answered by the corresponding existentiality of the turning-point and decision. Since this occurs in Jesus, it occurs in the domain of human possibility, thought at its outer limit. The man who DOES this--that is to say, who confesses and believes--shall live by righteousness" (*Romans*, p. 382).
[19]C.D. II,2:248.

What is it, then, that confirms Israel's first election and keeps it in line with the second? Barth's interpretation of 10:14-21 suggests that the answer is to be found in the fact that there are Gentiles who did not seek God, but who now believe in their hearts and proclaim with their lips the reality of God's gracious and merciful election in Jesus Christ *to the Jews and to others*. The answer lies in the fact that there is another form of the elect community which did not receive the first election, but in whose existence is nevertheless found the positive witness to God's act in Jesus Christ. It is the reality of the existence of this form of the community that establishes the fact that the second election is acquired not by sinful humanity's willing and running, but by the free mercy of God alone:

> God caused Himself to be found by those who did not seek after Him and was revealed to those who did not ask for Him. This is what takes place in the calling and conversion of the Gentiles to the Church.... They were found by the Gospel in the same situation as the Jews; but through the Gospel they were found by God Himself and made participants in His self-revelation. Through the Gospel they were snatched from that incapacity and mischance.[20]

Because of the reality of God's self-witness in and through the Church made up of Jews and Gentiles who believe in and proclaim Jesus Christ, Israel as a whole remains in confrontation with the demand that it too press on to faith and belief. The Church's proclamation of God's merciful election comes back upon Israel in another form, i.e., the testimony of those in whom the second election is fulfilled. This reality both indicts Israel and confirms its election. Given the fact of the Church's positive witness to Jesus Christ, the movement of Barth's exegesis at this point is clear: "The proclamation based on mission has, in fact, come to the Synagogue Jews. They can therefore hear. They can therefore believe. They can therefore call upon the name of the Lord. They can therefore confess with the Church."[21] But it is precisely this unfulfilled possibility that accentuates the indictment of Israel:

---

[20]*C.D.* II,2:257-58.

[21]*C.D.* II,2:252. "And Faith is miracle. Otherwise it is not faith. The word, which enters human ears and is uttered by human lips, is the Word of God--only when the miracle takes place. Otherwise it is just a human word like any other. The Church is the Church of Jacob--only when the miracle occurs. Otherwise it is nothing more than the Church of Esau. But the miracle cannot be striven after, or attained, or boasted about. It is the unexpected, new, divine occurence among men" (*Romans*, pp. 366).

Thus the refusal to confess that Jesus is Lord--the demand which, according to vv. 9-13 sums up all the demands of the Law, and in which its fulfilment as such is prescribed to a reader--can only be understood and characterized as disobedience.[22]

Israel's disobedience and disbelief are the necessary prerequisite for the Church's obedience and faith; their reality signifies that no amount of human willing and running can effect the fulfillment and confirmation of election. In short, Israel witnesses negatively to the Church. At the same time, however, this disobedience and disbelief constitutes the point to which the Church's faithful proclamation of Jesus Christ is addressed. In short, Israel's intransigent existence confirms its election. Barth declares:

As God confirms His election of Israel by the apostolic proclamation of the good tidings sustained by the Word of Christ Himself, so Israel confirms its election, its identity with the people of former times of and to whom Isaiah spoke, by the disobedient act of its unbelief.... This very people, disobedient to the Gospel and therefore unfaithful to its own election, was and is, as the natural root of the Church called and awakened to faith by His mercy, God's chosen people.[23]

Barth's typological exegesis of this passage ultimately comes down to this: there are two stages in the election of the one community, and these stages correspond to the double predestination of Jesus Christ. The first stage is the election to hearing; the second stage is the election to hearing *and* believing *and* confessing. "Israel as a whole" is elected to hear, but disobeys and does not believe the self-revelation executed in the election of Jesus Christ. "The Church" is elected to hear, believe and proclaim that revelation. For Israel, the second election does not follow upon the first; they hear, but the gift of faith and proclamation is not given because they seek to establish and confirm themselves by their own willing and running. Israel thus represents the rebellion and unworthiness of humanity. For the Jews and Gentiles who constitute the Church, the first and second election are simultaneous; they hear, and are given the gift of faith and proclamation precisely because they did not seek it. The Church thus represents the faithfulness and mercy of God.

The whole interpretation is a recapitulation of the self-revelation

---

[22]*C.D. II*,2:253.
[23]*C.D. II*,2:255.

of God executed in the twofold election of Jesus Christ. God speaks, and God's chosen humanity hears and chooses to respond in belief or disbelief. Both the unity and the differentiation of the community is articulated in terms of the unity and differentiation expressed in the twofold reality of Jesus Christ's election. The two forms of this one elect community are what they are, however, only in the light of this correspondence to Jesus Christ and the fact that, because of their participation in God's revelation, they say something to each other. Barth's interpretation suggests that Israel's election is to hear and be disobedient so that through their disobedience others may hear the promise, see the futility of human running and willing and throw themselves on God's mercy by doing the one thing necessary, i.e., believe, and in faith proclaim the promise and its fulfillment in Jesus Christ to Israel and the whole world. This reciprocity which Barth finds in the text, however, is based on the fact that Israel's failure presupposes that it is the object of the first election, and can be comprehended only as the rejection of its election and its unwillingness to believe. Nevertheless, this failure is itself precisely the medium for the election of the Gentiles, and as such it is necessary for the complete revelation of God's election in the crucified Messiah. Thus the Church's belief and proclamation presuppose Israel's election, and as such it is necessary as the medium for the manifestation of the fulfillment of Israel's promise in the risen Lord.

Barth's interpretation of this passage indicates that the fulfillment of election is to be understood to consist in the hearing, believing and proclaiming of God's self-revelation in Jesus Christ. It is evident that the coalescence of the rejected human under God's righteous judgment and the elect human living by God's gracious mercy in the God-human Jesus Christ is the typological motif employed in the exegesis here. This one is two, and Israel and the Church signify this one. Israel as a whole receives its light from Jesus Christ the crucified and rejected Messiah, and as a consequence it serves by way of the first election as a medium of God's negative election and revelation to the Gentiles, and is the presupposition of their election. The Church made up of Jews and Gentiles receives its light from Jesus Christ the risen and elect Lord, and as a consequence it serves by way of the second election as a medium of God's positive election and revelation to Israel and the world, and is the presupposition of Israel's advance to the fulfillment of its election. In short, Barth's interpretation says that, just as Jesus' humiliation as the *God*-human (rejection) is the electional basis and presupposition for his exaltation as the God-*human* (election), so Israel's disobedience and unbelief ("rejection") is the electional basis and presupposition for the Church's faith and proclamation ("election"). Like Jesus Christ the crucified *God*-human, Israel is interpreted as the recipient of the first election in the form of rejection. Like Jesus Christ the risen God-*human*, the Church is interpreted as the recipient of the second election in the form of acceptance.

3. Passing and Coming [Romans 11:1-36]. Barth's interpretation of the types that foreshadow and materialize the revelation of Jesus Christ's election reaches its resounding crescendo in the exegesis of this passage. Here Barth sees the answer to the question of who is constituted as the one elect community and how it is in fact constituted. The outcome of his interpretation of this chapter can be seen to be the contention that ultimately there is only one elect community of God which universally embraces all humanity. It is here in Romans 11 that Barth uncovers the typology which supports a universal election and which informs the proposition that:

> The elected community of God ... *must* correspond to this twofold determination of its Head by existing itself also in a twofold form, in a passing and a coming form, in a form of death and a form of life. It fulfills its determination grounded in its election by representing *in bodily form* and attesting to the world both the death taken away by God from man and also the life bestowed on man by God.[24]

The line which began with Isaac, Jacob and Moses is now continued in the appearance of the remnant of Israel, the seven thousand who remain faithful and obedient. As such, they typify the fact that the Church has always existed in Israel, though only in a hidden way until the appearance of Jesus Christ.[25] But Barth also now interprets this remnant in terms of the type "Israel as such," so that what was previously a predominantly negative image has now become a positive one. He states: "These seven thousand ... strangely enough, represent the whole, Israel as such.... It is these seven thousand men, and not the unfaithful majority, who represent Israel as such."[26] Presumably like Ishmael, Esau and Pharaoh, the rest of Israel is hardened by God so that they are unable to respond in obedience and faith to the promise. Nevertheless, it is precisely this majority whose second election is anticipated in the typology of the remnant.[27]

---

[24]*C.D. II*,2:260. Emphasis mine.

[25]See *C.D. II*,2:272-73.

[26]*C.D. II*,2:270. "The 7,000 are not so many individuals. As one whole, they represent the vast, mighty, invisible host, encompassing the lonely Elijah: as only 7,000, as a diminished number, they represent invisibly the whole people of God in their quality as objects of election in the midst of rejection; they represent the invisible Church of Jacob in the midst of the Church of Esau. The 7,000, then, are the people of God whom He has not cast off. They stand upright--but only in the presence of God" (*Romans*, p. 395).

[27]See *C.D. II*,2:273-78.

The Hermeneutics of Election

It is Barth's interpretation of the purpose of the hardening of many and the preservation of some that opens up both the universality of election and the materializing of the two forms of the one elect community. In this respect, Romans 11:7-24 is central, and is interpreted in terms of the motif which now takes the form of mutual corporal instrumentality. On the one hand, there is Israel as a whole hardened, blinded and rejected by God because of their sin. This is how Barth understands Israel's being cut off from the holy root in the parable in vs. 17-24. But Israel (as typified in Ishmael, Esau, Pharaoh, the vessels of wrath, the majority, etc.) is hardened and cut off by God precisely in order that election and salvation might come to the Gentiles. Israel as such, the recipients of the first election, is the necessary instrument for the inclusion of the Gentiles; Israel is rejected in order that the Gentiles might be elect:

> God needed the Jews for the sake of the Gentiles. He needed their transgression. In order to bring about this trangression, He hardened them. Thus their hardening has become an integral part of salvation-history in a way that is decisive even for the Gentiles.[28]

On the other hand, there are the non-elect, lost and isolated Gentiles illumined and accepted by God. This is how Barth understands their being grafted into the holy root. These Gentiles (as typified in Isaac, Jacob, Moses, the vessels of mercy, the remnant, etc.) are grafted in precisely in order that Israel's second election and salvation might be fulfilled. The Gentiles as the recipients of the second election are the necessary instrument for the salvation of Israel; the Gentiles are elect in order that Israel might be called again to the confirmation and fulfillment of its election:

> By the transgression of these blinded rest, salvation was meant to come to the Gentiles, and this occurrence was in turn meant to provoke to jealousy the hardened rest themselves. Their transgression has brought salvation to the Gentiles. As the Jews delivered up their rejected Messiah to the Gentiles for crucifixion, the latter became with them the instruments of the divine work of

---

[28]*C.D.* II,2:279. See also pp. 278, 282-84, 288, 299-300, 304. "'But by their fall salvation is come unto the Gentiles.' The tribulation and guilt of the Church is a 'Moment' in the invisible, divine scheme of advance from rejection to election, from 'No' to 'Yes', from Esau to Jacob, from Pharaoh to Moses. By this scheme the sovereign freedom of God is set in motion. By it He makes Himself known, and reconciles the world to Himself (9:22-23)" (*Romans*, p. 401).

atonement completed by the death of Jesus Christ.... The existence of Gentiles as recipients of salvation has the meaning and purpose of a summons to these hardened Jews and therefore of a confirmation of their eternal election.[29]

The fact that Israel is hardened, cut off and rejected for the Gentiles does not mean, however, that Israel is forever lost. Their rejection is for the sake of their election, and is intended to be the instrument for the election of others as well as the signification that the death in rejection is necessary for life in election. The parable of the olive tree means:

> However it may be with that hardening of the rest of Israel, however it may be with Israel's transgression ... Israel is still the possession and work of God, and as such the presupposition without which there would be no Church, and no Gentile Christians.[30]

The fact is that not all the natural branches have been cut off. Implicit in the typology is the notion that the remnant remains, that portion of Israel who has remained faithful and obedient and therefore a continuing part of the tree.[31] These branches represent the line which began with Isaac, Jacob and Moses and now finds its fulfillment in the form of believing Jews in the Church. But most importantly for Barth, the presence of these branches together with the believing Gentiles who have been grafted in constitutes the basis for the teleological typology which finally issues in this: the fact that God has elected some means that God has not finally rejected any. Just as the seven thousand represent the whole of Israel, so they constitute "a clear proof that God has not rejected His people."[32] On the contrary, "in the existence of the seven thousand God's election is established as an election of Israel."[33] This is how it is with Israel in both its lines, i.e., from Ishmael to the "majority" and from Isaac

---

[29] C.D. II,2:278-79. See also pp. 281, 288-90, 296-97, 304.

[30] C.D. II,2:285. "Rejection is no more than the shadow of election. The 'No' of God is no more than the inevitable turning to the man of this world of the reverse side of His 'Yes'. Esau is Esau only in so far as he is not Jacob.... Election is the real and possible, though utterly incomprehensible, salvation of men from the inevitable destiny of rejection. The 'Yes' of God consists only in the transformation of His 'No'. Jacob is Jacob because he is not Esau" (*Romans*, p. 401-2). "The rejection of the elect does not destroy His *gifts* and His *calling*. They are as much established by it as they are by the election of the reprobate. Both operations are in God invisibly one and the same" (*Romans*, p. 419).

[31] See C.D. II,2:287.

[32] C.D. II,2:273.

[33] C.D. II,2:274.

to the "remnant."

At the same time, however, Barth's interpretation of the parable of the olive tree implies that much the same is to be said of the Gentiles. The fact of the presence of grafted in Gentiles means that those who were rejected, who never had any part of the holy olive tree nor shared in its root, are now elected to life. But they are so not without a rejection, cutting off and death of their own. For Barth, the fact that some Gentiles are cut off from their own natural root only to be grafted into the holy root means that God has not finally rejected all; cutting off also carries a positive signification. Barth states of these Gentiles:

> They belonged by nature to a situation where no promise and no salvation is to be expected because there is no election. Yet now against all nature they have been removed from their place. They have been cut out of the wild olive to which they belonged and in which they lived. They have been taken out of the hopeless state of their paganism, out of the absolute emptiness and destitution of their non-Israelite existence.[34]

For Barth, this election of the Gentiles, signified by the presence of believing Gentiles in the Church, means that they "have suddenly ceased to be Gentiles, that they have been taken out of the natural and necessary context of their paganism,..."[35] and thus: "These Gentiles, having been removed for their part from what is their nature, actually come to Israel, namely, to Israel's Messiah, and therefore become Israel,..."[36] If the faithful remnant means that all Israel is elect, then believing Gentiles mean that all the Gentiles are elect as well.

The culmination of Barth's interpretation of these three chapters is reached in Romans 11:25-32. Here all the various types, lines and images find their completion in a single eschatological reality which embraces the whole of Israel and the whole of the Gentile world. The "all Israel" of vs. 26 is more than the combined "Israel as such" (the line beginning with Ishmael) and "the pre-existent church in Israel" (the line beginning with Isaac). It is quite simply the fulfillment of the election of all humanity. Barth declares:

> "All Israel" is the community of those elected by God in and with Jesus Christ both from Jews and also from Gentiles, the whole Church which together with the holy

---

[34]*C.D. II*,2:296.
[35]*C.D. II*,2:297.
[36]*C.D. II*,2:297.

root of Israel will consist in the totality of all the branches finally united with and drawing sustenance from it, in the totality constituted by the remnant continuing in and with the original stem Jesus Christ, by the wild shoots added later from the Gentiles, and by the branches which were cut off and are finally grafted in again.[37]

This is how the one elect community appears from the perspective of both believing and non-believing Israel, in the light of the revelation executed in Jesus Christ. But this same reality can also be expressed from the perspective of the believing and non-believing Gentiles in the same light. This "all Israel" of vs. 26 is itself identical with "the Church." Barth declares:

> Regarded christologically and eschatologically the Church is always both *all* Israel--not only the seven thousand but also the hardened rest--and *all* the Gentile world, those who have already become believers and those who are yet to become so.[38]

In short, the one elect community as a whole is greater than the sum of its parts; "Israel" and "the Church" coalesce into the same reality when viewed typologically under the rubric of Jesus Christ's election.

It is clear that with his exegesis, Barth has moved beyond the simple typology of Israel and the Church, Ishmael and Isaac, Esau and Jacob, Pharaoh and Moses, vessels of wrath and vessels of mercy, majority and remnant. He has also completely abrogated the polarity of rejection and election as exclusive categories by which we can understand the two categories of typologies. Barth has clearly brought the categories of the election of Jesus Christ to bear on the interpretation of these chapters. In Jesus Christ, Barth sees that election means to be rejected, to come under God's judgment and to die. But also in him, Barth sees that this rejection means to be elected, to come under God's mercy and to live. The two coalesce originally and primarily in one, Jesus Christ. As media for the extended revelation of his election, they coalesce secondarily in one, the elect community.

We can summarize the scope and significance of Barth's interpretation in this way:

(1) The fact that Israel is hardened, cut off and rejected signifies God's judgment on sin, disobedience and unbelief. The grafting in of the Gentiles signifies God's mercy which is undeserved and which effects

---

[37] *C.D.* II,2:300. See also pp. 295, 298.
[38] *C.D.* II,2:280.

obedience and belief. Just as Jesus must be crucified in order to rise again, so Israel must be cut off from the olive tree in judgment in order that it may be grafted in again in mercy. Likewise, the Gentiles must be cut off from the wild olive tree in order to be grafted into the holy one. Israel's experience *vis-a-vis* rejection is to be a testimony of this judgment to the Gentiles, while the Gentiles' experience *vis-a-vis* election is to be a testimony of this mercy to Israel. The elect Israel is rejected so that the rejected Gentiles might be elect. Then, the rejected Gentiles are elect so that the rejected Israel might fulfill its election.

(2) Just as the Gentiles were used by God to execute judgment on rebellious Israel, so they are now used by God to bring mercy and the fulfillment of the promise to Israel. The fact that Israel is the necessary instrument for the Gentiles' salvation, and the fact that the Gentiles are the necessary instrument for Israel's salvation mean that rejection does not stand over against election, judgment over against mercy, death over against life. Rather it means that rejection is for the purpose of election, No is for the purpose of Yes. It means that rejection finally gives way to election, that death is overcome by life, that the rejected one becomes the elected one. The "one elect community" contains within itself the two forms which correspond to the No on its way to becoming Yes, and the Yes which triumphs over the No.

(3) Rejection and election must be viewed together, and understood as the transformation which takes place when the old sinful and rebellious life is destroyed and put to death (cut off) in order that the new faithful and obedient life might emerge in participation in God's life (grafted in). This is originally signified in the crucifixion and resurrection of Jesus Christ.

(4) In the final analysis, what Barth sees in Romans 9-11, in the light of the revelation executed in the election of Jesus Christ, is a single elect community embracing the whole of humanity and consisting of forms which are in one phase or another of the transformation determined by God's election. In the language of the parable of the olive tree, we can describe these forms the following way. The center of the community (or root) is Jesus Christ, and at the outer circumference there is in relation to him (1a) Israel, those who are part of the root but cut off; and (2a) Gentiles, those who are not part of the root at all. At the inner circumference, there is in relation to him (1b) Christian Jews, those who are part of the root and remain; and (2b) Christian Gentiles, those who have been grafted in. "The Church" as the preeminent form of the one elect community consists of Christian Jews and Gentiles. But it is precisely because of this that the remainder of the Jews *and* Gentiles must also be regarded as part of this community.

Barth's interpretation of these three chapters can indeed call for and support the dogmatic exposition of the election of the community, but only (a) if a first and a second election is modeled after and

160

substantiated by the double predestination of Jesus Christ, and (2) if the typology of contrasting pairs giving way to each other in their signification of a single reality is brought to bear on the text.

B. The Medium of the Individual

Barth's biblical interpretation which gives rise to the dogma concerning the election of the individual extends across a broad range of Old and New Testament passages, much more so than the exegesis of the biblical passages concerning the community. In every case, however, the interpretation is guided by the master typological motif in which one reality is actually twofold in nature, and therefore is ultimately to be signified by two realities. Furthermore, the exegesis presupposes both the biblical picture and dogmatic construct of Jesus Christ as the Subject and object of election in and through whom God's self-revelation is executed; at every point, the identity of revelation/incarnation and election is assumed. The fact of Jesus Christ as the primal reality of both the elect and the rejected individual casts an unequivocal light on all the texts selected by Barth; without qualification, he alone is the preeminent subject whose reality is disclosed in these passages, and apart from him the true meaning of the texts and the figures represented there cannot be comprehended.

As we observed in our discussion of the exposition of the election of the individual, the fundamental idea which constitutes the reality of the individual as an object of election has to do with the manner in which the individual participates in the reality and revelation of Jesus Christ's election and rejection, and the fact that ultimately we have to do with a single individual who either lives or does not yet live in the fulfillment of his/her election. We noted in that discussion that what is finally significant for Barth is not whether this individual is elect or that individual is rejected, but rather the extent to which the individual as such represents in his/her own existence the signification of either the election or rejection of Jesus Christ. Toward this end, the traditional symmetry and equilibrium of election over against rejection is abandoned by Barth because he sees these two are finally one, giving way to each other, in the individual Jesus Christ. Because the elect individual and the rejected individual are to be defined in terms of their signification of Jesus Christ, and as such have no independent status or reality, they must ultimately be seen together, and like Jesus Christ, signify each other and merge into each other in a single reality of signification. The traditional symmetry and equilibrium of mutually exclusive categories vis-a-vis the individual thus become for Barth the symmetry and equilibrium of contrasting shades within the single reality of the individual.

Perhaps the most innovative aspect of Barth's exegesis in this section is the fact that, for the most part, the texts selected for interpretation do not generally suggest themselves as biblical bases for the understanding of the elect individual and the rejected individual. Furthermore, the themes and ideas suggested by the selected passages have not generally been considered as constitutive of the biblical and theological agenda regarding election and rejection. But above all, the creativity and imagination of Barth's exegesis are manifest in the fact that ultimately he is concerned not with establishing the basis for the election of some individuals and the rejection of others, but rather with the extent to which biblical personalities and matters function and can be interpreted as concrete media for the signification of the reality and purpose of election and rejection as revealed in Jesus Christ. In the final analysis, Barth's view of the individual *vis-a-vis* both election and rejection is one in which the individual as such participates in God's on-going revealing and reconciling activity. Again, the question before us at this point is whether and to what extent Barth's exegesis calls for and supports his view of the election and rejection of the individual. The fact that Barth's biblical interpretation at this point takes up passages and themes not usually associated with election lends a particular sense of importance to this question.

1. The Symmetry and Typology of Election and Rejection. Barth begins the biblical exegesis on the "elect" and the "rejected" individual by examining selected Old Testament passages in which he believes can be seen not only biblical illustrations of divine rejection and election, but also the fact that at every point along the way of this biblical witness the two are seen together in a mutually determining relationship. The exegesis of these Old Testament passages is unabashedly typological in that the figures and themes are interpreted as prophetic types which can only be understood in terms of Jesus Christ who alone constitutes their fulfillment. The texts selected for interpretation are presupposed to be prophesies of Jesus Christ's election and rejection, and this means that the significance of the figures interpreted lies primarily not in themselves as such, but rather in their foreshadowing or prefiguring the reality of Jesus Christ which fulfills their signification. Two fundamental axioms emerge at the outset, and serve to guide the exegesis at every point. First, Barth understands the *elect* individual primarily as one who is a witness of God, existing in a relationship with God and sharing in the divine revealing and reconciling activity. For Barth, this is a patent and self-evident conclusion based on the observation of all those biblical figures who heretofore have been regarded as the friends of God (Abraham, Isaac, Jacob, Moses, David, the prophets etc.). In brief, the elect individual is to be understood in this way:

> Not of himself, but as an elect man, the elect is an
> authentic witness of God. It is not by chance that it is just

162

he who is active in the ministry of reconciliation between God and man, as an instrument of God's revelation. Nor is it a contradiction if he, a member and citizen of the lost world, "flesh" like all other men, is actually enabled for this ministry and function, so that this ministry is actually executed, this function discharged by him. He is enabled for it in virtue of his election, and as an elect person. His election as such is an equipment for this end because it is the conformity which he has been given with God Himself, the reflection of the divine countenance.[39]

Second, Barth understands the *rejected* individual primarily as one who is distinguishable not in him/herself, but only in relation to the elect, and that this distinction is based solely on God's sovereign choice in which the former remains in an albeit different relation to God. This axiom is referred to by Barth in these words:

> The tradition could not be clearer as to the continually operative principle of the distinguishing choice; the freedom with which this choice cuts across and contradicts all distinctions that are humanly regulated or planned on the basis of human predilections, and the relativity of the distinctions actually made; the fact that those who are cut off, who are not distinguished by actual choice, are not on that account utterly rejected, but do in their own way remain in a positive relation to the covenant of God.... It is clear throughout that those who are first condemned are also blessed in their own way, and that in their situation on the left they, too, fulfil a divinely ordained destiny.[40]

In effect, these two axioms together mean that election and rejection are the symmetrical categories which are constitutive, not primarily of the individual as such, but rather of God's self-disclosure in, through and to the individual. Furthermore, they mean that in the light of Jesus Christ, all that can be said about the biblical view of this elect figure and that rejected figure is to be understood in terms of typological or prophetic mediacy on the one hand, and mutual dependence and relativity on the other. This is clear in the first three exegetical sections in which Barth attempts to establish the biblical foundation for what may be called the signification of the elect and the rejected.

In Barth's interpretation, the significance of God's distinguishing

---

[39]*C.D. II,*2:345.
[40]*C.D. II,*2:356.

choice is disclosed in the sacrificial rites of purification described in Leviticus 14 and 16.[41] Together these two passages establish the fact that the purification which constitutes the prerequisite to God's reconciliation with humanity requires rejection. In both rites, two animals, one elected and the other rejected, together represent the one on whose behalf the sacrifice of purification is offered, and the sacrifice itself represents the action of God apart from which no purification is possible. In both cases, the death of the first animal brings a particular determination and signification for the second; the fate of one determines the fate of the other. However, this mutuality does not emerge for Barth in the mere fact of two animals. Rather it emerges from the fact that a single reality is depicted in its twofold significance. These passages present a single image in which the symmetrical relationship of God's electing action and rejecting action are reflected. Thus two animals are required to portray the significance of these actions and their implication for the one on whose behalf they are undertaken. Barth contends:

> But here, of course, we have an identity which the picture itself cannot reproduce, and which is also not to be seen in its historical counterpart, that is, in the history of the distinguishing choices as such. On the contrary, both in the picture and the fact indicated by the picture a duality is demanded. There have to be two creatures and two men, to whom the one thing intended and to be represented by both distributes itself as a duality.[42]

In the interpretation of Leviticus 16, the first goat (the one elected or used) is chosen to suffer death under the wrath of God's judgment in order that the second goat (the one rejected or not used) may be banished into the wilderness, bearing away the sin of the people. This rite signifies that God's righteous and merited judgment on sin results in a life lived in banishment from the divine presence. The fact that the first goat is elected to suffer this judgment and die means that this fate does not fall upon the people, but rather on the one who is elected by God to stand in their place. Furthermore, the death of this first goat means that the second goat is allowed to live, but only as the one laden with the people's sin and banished from the divine presence. In short, the death of the elect means a life of banishment for the rejected. Barth describes the symmetry of these two in this way: "The death of the one, which is, in fact, full of grace and salvation, is accompanied by the life of the other, which is, in fact, the essence of

---

[41]See Barth's exegesis of these two chapters at *C.D. II,2*:357-66.
[42]*C.D. II,2*:359. See also p. 361.

desolation, indeed of death itself."[43]

In the interpretation of Leviticus 14, the first bird (the one elected or used) is chosen to suffer death in order that the second bird (the one rejected or not used) may be released to freedom. This rite signifies that God's judgment on sin results in the restoration of the rejected to life in God's presence. The fact that the first bird is elected to suffer death means that this fate does not fall upon the rejected who deserves it. Again, the death of the first bird means that the second bird is allowed to live, but in this case it is a life of freedom in the divine presence. In short, the death of the elect means the restoration or resurrection to life for the rejected. Barth describes the symmetry in this way: "That which was done to the first turns to the advantage of the second.... The former is clearly used for the benefit of the unusable. The recipient of the fruit of election is obviously the non-elect."[44]

This represents Barth's formal interpretation of the two passages, and in brief we can summarize the interpretation with this statement: the vicarious death of the elect on behalf of the rejected brings about the banishment of the rejected's sin and the restoration of the rejected to life. This is evident in Barth's own summary of these two passages:

> Both are concerned with the will and way of God with men, and both affirm that death and life are decreed by God for man; first death, then life. Death is the saving judgment of God, which is necessary in the operation of His grace towards man and therefore exhibits His love for him, and through which he is cleansed and led into life.[45]

However, this formal interpretation presupposes a material interpretation which operates on two assumptions: (1) the subject to which these figures refer can not be identified with the figures in the texts, and is not identifiable from the texts as they stand; and (2) it is only by the revelation of God in Jesus Christ that this subject can be known, and therefore it is faith and not exegesis which finally decides who is the subject of these passages.[46] What these two assumptions mean is that, because revelation and incarnation are identical with election, the categories of election as reflected and determined in the revelation executed in Jesus Christ constitute the basis for the material interpretation and understanding of these texts. As Barth says:

---

[43]*C.D. II,*2:359.
[44]*C.D. II,*2:361.
[45]*C.D. II,*2:361-62.
[46]See the discussion at *C.D. II,*2:360-66.

> The elect individual in the Old Testament, so impressively and yet in so many different ways distinguished, set apart and differentiated in the Old Testament stories and pictures, is always a witness to Jesus Christ, and is indeed a type of Christ himself. It is He, Jesus Christ, who is originally and properly the elect individual. All others can be this only as types of Him, only as His prototypes or copies, only as those who belong to Him, only as considerable or inconsiderable, strong or weak members of His body, only as chastised or blessed, humiliated or exalted citizens of His community, only as in different ways His witnesses. In this sense, Jesus Christ is each of the four creatures in Lev. 14 und 16.[47]

Materially, these passages speak of Jesus Christ and the significance of his sacrificial death. He is the one elect individual, and as such he is necessarily the one rejected individual. The formal and material interpretation of these two chapters leads Barth to the conclusion that the elect is always for the sake of the rejected, and they must be seen together because they are one in Jesus Christ; the elect is rejected in order that the rejected might be elect through the banishment of sin and the restoration to life. With his interpretation of Leviticus 14 and 16, Barth brings the election motif to bear on the understanding of the priestly office of Jesus Christ.

A similar course is taken in the interpretation of the figures of Saul and David in the books of Samuel where the concern is with the Israelite monarchy as a reflection of the divine election.[48] Here Barth shows himself to be interested with the historical nature of these two figures only in so far as the events and context of their lives and their individual actions can be appropriated as types which reflect the election motif. It must be granted, however, that the interpretation of these two figures and their relation to one another brings a certain concreteness to the attempt to substantiate the picture of election and rejection *vis-a-vis* the individual.

There can be no serious question about the fact that, according to the text, the first two kings of Israel are elected by God to this function, and that the kingship now becomes the focal point of the relationship between God and the people of Israel. It is therefore most appropriate for Barth to see the direction of Israel's life as the elect people in relation to God reflected in and to some extent determined by the figure of the king who serves in a monarchy established by God's

---

[47]*C.D. II,*2:364.
[48]See *C.D. II,*2:366-93.

election. The thrust of the exegesis, however, consists in substantiating not the origins, succession, failures, and victories of the monarchy, but rather the relationship between and significance of election and rejection as embodied in the personalities and actions of the first two kings.

In Barth's interpretation, both Saul and David are divinely elected kings, first Saul and then David. Both are elected to stand before God as a representative of the people, and before the people as a representative of God. But within this general orientation, each is elected for a different purpose which is manifest finally in their inter-relationship and the particular course taken by their respective lives. Saul's election to the kingship is interpreted as the instrument of God's revelation of judgment upon the disobedience of the people in their rejection of God and their demand for a king who is different from that which God intends for them. Saul is chosen in order to embody in his own actions the autonomy and disobedience of the people on the one hand, and the rejection which this conduct merits on the other. Saul is

> ... an exact portrayal of the monarchy which has made itself independent of the kingdom of God, which is in competition with the latter both in what it does and what it does not do. He is a portrayal of the national kingdom which must be destroyed as such at the very point where God had resolved and was about to inaugurate and reveal the kingdom by His grace and not the grace of man.[49]

Saul's sin of disobedience results in his rejection. But Saul is not first an elect figure who subsequently is rejected. In Barth's view, Saul does not move from one category to another. Rather Saul's election takes the form of rejection in order to embody and express God's judgment:

> The holiness of God requires that the revelation of His grace, victorious over all human sin, should not take place without the revelation of His judgment upon sin; in this case, upon that "great wrong." The instrument of this aspect of God's revelation of His grace is the person of Saul the Benjamite.[50]

Saul is thus primarily a figure who stands in the shadow, but not wholly outside the light. In short, Saul is the elect king whose election consists in his rejection as judgment on disobedience and self-exaltation.

But Saul's election to rejection is also for the purpose of giving

---

[49] *C.D. II*,2:371.
[50] *C.D. II*,2:369.

way to David as the second elect king of Israel. By taking Saul's place, David is the king chosen to be the instrument of God's revelation of mercy. If Saul is the suitable and fit king chosen for the manifestation of judgment in rejection, David is the unsuitable and unfit king chosen for the manifestation of mercy in election. David is chosen in order to embody in his actions the faithfulness and obedience which is intended by God to constitute the life of the elect people on the one hand, and the fact that this election of the unworthy is a divine transformation and exaltation which stands by God's mercy alone and cannot be nullified by human disobedience on the other. In this regard, Barth states:

> But in David, too, we must also see that the divine grace of the monarchy, which took shape in his person, is the grace addressed and given to a sinful nation, which of itself is always ensnared in that great wrong and in itself utterly lost.[51]

David's sin of disobedience does not go unpunished, but neither does it result in his rejection. The reason is that David is first an unworthy sinner who is exalted precisely by God's election, and because the judgment of rejection upon disobedience has already fallen on Saul. David's election takes the form of exaltation in order to express God's constancy and mercy. David is quite simply elect for a different purpose:

> David, then, is elected together with Saul. David represents the Divine Yes where Saul can exhibit only the divine No. David is the bearer of the divine blessing where Saul bears the divine curse. And inevitably there falls on David something of the shadow that lies on Saul.[52]

In the figures of Saul and David, Barth sees evidence of the two sides to God's election: one to humiliation and dismissal, and the other to exaltation and fellowship. Saul is not so much rejected because of his disobedience; rather his disobedience is the sign or outworking of his rejection. Likewise, David is not so much elected because of his obedience; rather his obedience is the sign or outworking of his election. In both its forms, this election "stands or falls with that which *God* purposes and will effect and accomplish with him, and on this very account it can only stand and not fall."[53]

Again, Barth's formal interpretation presupposes a material

---

[51]*C.D. II,*2:377.
[52]*C.D. II,*2:378.
[53]*C.D. II,*2:383.

interpretation which assumes that the subject to which the figures of Saul and David actually refer is unrecognizable in the text as it stands, and that it is only in the light of the revelation of Jesus Christ that this subject is known.[54] It is ultimately the reality of election and rejection executed in the revelation in Jesus Christ that constitutes the basis for the material interpretation and understanding of these figures:

> The elect king of the Books of Samuel ... is, in all his potentialities and in every aspect of his widely divergent appearance, a witness of Jesus Christ. In himself he is never more than His prototype and copy; but in type always He Himself. The fact that this king takes several forms--at least two, or more precisely four in this case too--and that these forms cannot be reduced to any common denominator, and are full of inner contradictions, characterises them as prophetic figures in distinction from the fulfilment actualized in the person of Jesus Christ.... The fulfilment is not to be found in them. The kingship of Jesus Christ is the actuality, the subject which they attest--but which they can only attest.[55]

Materially, the figures of Saul and David together signify the rule of Jesus Christ over the Kingdom of God, and the course which this rule takes in order to establish this kingdom. In the light of the revelation in Jesus Christ, these two figures speak to the promise of a true king for the elect people, one whose reality is seen to consist in his election to rejection for the purpose of the merciful exaltation of others. In this king, the judgment and rejection of Israel is confirmed and executed, as is their ultimate election to restoration. Barth concludes that the elect figure is rejected and humiliated in order to make way for the election and exaltation of the rejected. With this interpretation, Barth brings the election motif to bear on the understanding of the kingly office of Jesus Christ.

The interpretation of I Kings 13 reflects a similar orientation.[56] Barth's concern here is with the manner in which election can be seen to consist in the service of witness on behalf of God's judgment and mercy, i.e., what is involved in serving as a medium of God's self-revelation. As in the Leviticus and Samuel exegesis, the passage in I Kings is interpreted to reflect a symmetry between election and rejection in which one figure gives way to and becomes another.

---

[54]See the discussion at *C.D. II,2*:386-93.
[55]*C.D. II,2*:389.
[56]See *C.D. II,2*:393-409.

The interpretation at this point focuses on the role of the prophet *vis-a-vis* the divided kingdoms of Judah and Israel, and the thrust of the exegesis consists largely in substantiating not the historic development of the interactions between God's prophets and God's people, but rather the interdependence of the divine witness of the elect and the rejected who are now seen facing each other in the person of an elect prophet from Judah and a non-elect prophet from Israel.

Barth contends that the election of the prophet from Judah consists in the fact that he is chosen by God as a representative of true Israel to bring a word of judgment against the false Israel who is rejected because of its disobedience. Upon the completion of his mission, however, this prophet commits an act of disobedience which, like Saul, disqualifies his election and renders him unfit and unusable; he must now be rejected and suffer the death which must inevitably come upon the rejected under God's judgment; he must now be the recipient of the very message he was elected to convey. The one who now serves as the instrument of this message is the rejected prophet of Bethel who represents the false Israel; he is elected and placed in the position vacated by the elect prophet of Judah; he proclaims to Judah the word of God's judgment upon disobedience. It is the once elect but now rejected prophet of Judah who must suffer the divine judgment, while the once rejected but now elect prophet of Bethel lives.

In this exchange of places and functions, Barth sees an indication of the fact that judgment in the form of suffering and death for disobedience which the rejected deserve falls upon the elect, while mercy in the form of reprieve and life is given to the rejected who now stand in the place of the elect. As servants of God, the elect (Judah) suffers the punishment of the rejected, while the rejected (Israel) acts on behalf of the elect. Barth summarizes his interpretation in this way:

> The man of Judah has not ceased to be the elect, nor has the prophet of Bethel ceased to be the rejected. But in their union as elect and rejected they form together the whole Israel from which the grace of God is not turned away. For the rejected acts on behalf of the elect when he takes over the latter's mission. And the elect acts on behalf of the rejected when he suffers the latter's punishment. Similarly, at the end, the rejected acts for the elect by making his own grave a resting-place for the latter. While again the elect acts for the rejected in that the bones of the latter are kept and preserved for his sake, and together with his own bones.[57]

---

[57]*C.D. II,*2:406.

Once again, the formal symmetry of this interpretation presupposes the material interpretation with its two assumptions.[58] Materially, these two prophets, one elected to be rejected and the other rejected to be elected, together signify the one true prophet of God whose mission is to bear the divine revelation of God's judgment and mercy to the world, and whose election takes the form of suffering and death in order that those rejected might move into his place. Barth concludes his exegesis at this point with an affirmation of the election hermeneutic as the key to understanding the significance of the life and ministry of Jesus Christ as well as the Old Testament passages which prefigure him. He says of I Kings 13:

> But this story, too, does point to one real subject if Jesus Christ is also seen in it, if at the exact point where this story of the prophets breaks off a continuation is found in the Easter story. The Word of God, which abides for ever, in our flesh; the man from Bethlehem in Judah who was also the prophet of Nazareth; the Son of David who was also the king of the lost and lawless people of the north; the Elect of God who is also the bearer of the divine rejection; the One who was slain for the sins of others, which He took upon Himself, yet to whom there arose a witness, many witnesses, from the midst of sinners; the One lifted up in whose death all was lost, but who in His death was the consolation and refuge of all the lost--this One truly died and was buried, yet He was not forgotten and finished on the third day, but was raised from the dead by the power of God. In this one prophet the two prophets obviously live.[59]

In this true prophet, the primary witness to the divine act of judgment and mercy is given in the form of rejection and election. Barth is led to the conclusion that the elect is sent as a witness to the rejected, taking the place of the rejected, in order that the rejected might move into the place of the elect. And with this interpretation, Barth brings the election motif to bear on the understanding of the prophetic office of Jesus Christ.

In brief, the formal interpretation of these passages rests on a material interpretation which has its hermeneutical foundation in an electional christology, or in a christological image which is constructed in

---

[58]See *C.D. II,2*:408-9.
[59]*C.D. II,2*:409.

171

terms of the categories of election. The two remaining exegetical sections can be seen as the attempt to substantiate and confirm the implications of this christology for the individual as such.

2. *The Role of the Elect Individual.* Barth now turns to the New Testament in the search of a biblical basis for his view of the elect individual.[60] The material interpretation in the previous section has indicated that the fullest possible understanding of the elect individual cannot come from the Old Testament alone, even though it portrays at certain points a picture of individuals or entities who are manifestly regarded in the categories of election. In the Old Testament exegesis, the primary subject under investigation is always Jesus Christ whose election lends the categories for interpretation and understanding. The same is no less true now when the focus is on a biblical definition of the elect individual. There is, however, a very important paradigmatic shift in the interpretation at this point, a shift which distinguishes the tone and orientation of the present exegesis in comparison to that of the Old Testament, and which can be described in the following ways:

(1) The elect and the rejected are no longer seen together in their relativity and mutual dependence. This is to say that the duality which sheds light on the understanding of both does not figure prominently in the interpretation here.[61]

(2) Certain manifestly elect individuals are identified and singled out as types whose interpretation can give rise to an understanding of what it means to be an elect individual. But overall, such discrete individuals do not constitute the primary subject or object of concern in the course of the interpretation.[62]

(3) The emphasis is not so much on the elect individual as a type who prefigures and signifies the election of Jesus Christ, as in the Old Testament. The New Testament, after all, emerges on this side of the life, death and resurrection of Jesus Christ who therefore needs no additional prophetic signification. Rather the emphasis is on the nature and extent of the active on-going participation of the elect as such in the spatio-temporal execution of Jesus Christ's election.

(4) The exegesis is neither an interpretation of the individual as such, nor an interpretation in which the individual offers the basic categories for understanding. The immediate subject or object of interpretation in the text is the corporate body or gathering constituted by elect individuals, and the concern which informs the exegesis has to do

---

[60]See the exegetical passage at *C.D. II,2*:419-49.

[61]This duality is assumed and acknowledged at the outset (see pp. 419-20), but receives no further definition in the interpretation.

[62]The interpretations of Paul (pp. 428-30) and Peter (pp. 435-42) *et al.* are not to be considered exceptions to this. Rather the context in which they figure in the course of the exegesis removes them from center stage.

with the origin, constitution and purpose of this body. In particular, the interpretation is concerned with the Church in its New Testament form of the apostolate; it is this reality as a post-figuring type of Jesus Christ that is selected by Barth to provide the biblical basis for understanding the elect individual. What this means is that the elect individual is defined not in terms of individuality, but in terms of participation in the mission of the Church. In short, the motif which guides the exegesis is the apostolate as the paradigmatic expression of the function of the Church as one form of the elect community, and therefore as the expression of the function of the elect individual within that community. What Barth attempts to show in his interpretation here is the legitimacy of the functional movement from Jesus Christ through the apostolate to the Church as a whole which is constituted by individuals elected to participation in its mission.

It should be noted that, before entering into the actual interpretation itself, Barth makes it clear that he assumes the validity of the exegetical and dogmatic construct which establishes and reflects the fact that Jesus Christ is the reality and definitive revelation of the one elect human and the one rejected human.[63] This assumption means that the nature and purpose of the individual's election can only be modeled after, and understood in the light of, the election of Jesus Christ. Because his election consists in the execution of the divine self-revelation, the cornerstone to any understanding of the individual must reflect this essential reality. It is fundamentally for this reason that Barth puts aside any attempt to originate or exhaust the understanding of individual election in the traditional categories of personal salvation. On the contrary: "This loving-kindness, which saves and blesses man, is so great and good that it wills to use him. He can serve it. He himself can help to direct and reveal it to others, and therefore to these others. That is what the elect man Jesus Christ did and does."[64] It is just at this point where the hermeneutic of election, or an election-oriented scheme of thought, gives shape to the interpretation. The cornerstone is quite simply expressed: "If only we hold clearly before us the fact that we are to recognise both the electing God and elected man wholly and exclusively in Jesus Christ, we are forced to look in this direction to see the life-content of the elect--that he is elected to be a witness."[65]

Furthermore, when Barth reads the relatively few New Testament passages which impinge upon the question of election, he sees it as

---

[63]See especially *C.D. II,2*:420-23.
[64]*C.D. II,2*:423. See also pp. 443-44.
[65]*C.D. II,2*:424. The New Testament passages cited in support of this contention include Rev. 4:4, 10; 5:9f; 7:9-10, 15-16; 14:2-4; Rom. 8:29; Acts 1:8; John 1:7f, 16; 15:4f; I Cor. 1:26, 30; 2:2; James 2:5.

virtually self-evident that the elect as such are in the Church, having been constituted by their election in Jesus Christ as the visible reality of his community. An elect individual is simply one who is in the Church, so that being a part of the elect community in this form is axiomatic to the definition of individual election.[66]

With this link of election as revelation in Jesus Christ and election as being in the Church, Barth embarks upon the exegesis of the apostolate. At the outset, he indicates the essential trajectory of his interpretation:

> What it means to be in the Church, and even what the Church itself truly is, may be seen typically in what is described in the New Testament as the reality of the apostolate, and particularly in what Paul describes as the reality of his apostolate.... In and with the grace which comes to it, the Church (and therefore the *congregatio electorum*) has its essential direction outwards to mission, to the world, because it is not merely based upon the apostolate but is identical with it. By its very origin and in indissoluble connexion with it, it is the city set on a hill, the light placed upon a candlestick, not hidden but visible. It is of its essence to reveal, to be the bearer of revelation.[67]

Barth's interpretation of the apostolate focuses primarily on the developing relationship between Jesus and his disciples as reflected in the four gospels, and it consists entirely of what he sees to be three distinct, yet overlapping periods of interaction between Jesus and the twelve. Interestingly enough, Barth does not begin at the beginning of this interaction. Rather he begins with the chronologically third period, and works his way back to the beginning. The reason for this is that he sees in the gospels a single picture of the apostolate, and what he intends to portray of this picture is not one that can be understood as or reduced to a mere sequence of spatio-temporal events and interactions. The apostolate is not to be seen as "the picture of a historical development," but rather: "The structure of the apostolate is a material differentiation

---

[66]See especially *C.D.* II,2:426-30. The passages cited in this regard include Matthew 5:14f; John 8:12; Romans 8:28-33; Ephesians 1:3f, 6, 11-12; 3:9-11; Colossians 3:10-12; I Thessalonians 1:2-5; II Timothy 1:9; 2:10; Titus 1:1; I Peter 1:1-2, 9, 16-17; 2:4f, 12; 3:1f, 16; 4:16; 5:13; II Peter 1:10; II John 1, 13; Revelation 17:4, 14. It is in this context that Barth interprets the significance of the figure of Paul, citing Acts 9:15; 22:14f; 26:16f; Romans 1:1; 9:5; I Corinthians 1:4f; 9:27f; 15:10f; II Corinthians 12:9f; Galatians 1:15; Philippians 1:3f; Colossians 1:3f; I Thessalonians 1:2f; II Thessalonians 1:3f; II Timothy 1:15-16.
[67]*C.D.* II,2:430-31.

of one and the same reality."[68] Nevertheless, it is the inter-relatedness of three periods or moments which represents both the reality of the apostolate and the basis for the fact that it gives shape and substance to the understanding of the role of the elect individual. As a whole, the movement is from Jesus Christ to the apostolate to the Church to the individual, and for Barth, it is the movement from Jesus Christ to the apostolate that portrays the meaning and signification of the individual's election. Because the disciples as *individuals* are manifestly the first to be elected *by Jesus Christ*, and to have their lives in this determination, and because it is by means of their election and mission that the Church has its origins, they stand as the embodiment of the content and course of the life of the elect. We can summarize Barth's interpretation of these three periods in the following way:[69]

(1) The apostolate as such begins with the *calling, appointment and sending forth* of the twelve disciples.[70] This period extends generally from the commencement of Jesus' public ministry in Galilee to his withdrawal in preparation for the journey to Jerusalem. This is the manifestly prophetic ministry of Jesus in which the disciples are called, appointed and sent forth to preach the message they have learned from Jesus himself. These twelve are not elect because they are called. Rather they are called because they are already elect, and they are called from their former vocation to be with and follow Jesus, and like him seek and gather the lost sheep of Israel. They are appointed to share in Jesus' prophetic office in which they are to go forth in the freedom of the message, anticipating persecution, but confident that Jesus Christ will remain with them as his emissaries bearing his message. However, the full disclosure of the intended nature, course and outcome of Jesus' own mission is not yet manifest to the disciples.

(2) The apostolate enters a new period with *Jesus' self-disclosure* of the form and significance of his own mission.[71] This period generally corresponds with that time between Jesus' withdrawal with his disciples and his passion and crucifixion. This is the manifestly priestly ministry of Jesus in which the disciples are chosen to hear and observe the course of Jesus' mission of suffering and death on behalf of Israel. In this period, Jesus goes before the disciples, and becomes himself the focus and

---

[68]*C.D. II,2*:432.

[69]Because we believe there is some internal logic to the progression, we will take up these periods in reverse order. In our opinion, the correspondence and continuity between the apostolate as such and the elect individual rests on a spatio-temporal succession in which the third period for one constitutes the activity in and by which the first period for another is precipitated. This does not mean, however, that Barth's sequence is faulty. Rather it simply makes the nature of this correspondence and continuity more explicit *vis-a-vis* the relation between Jesus Christ and the elect individual.

[70]See *C.D. II,2*:442-49.

[71]See *C.D. II,2*:435-42.

content of the emerging mission of the twelve, undertaking an action by means of which he is to become the subject of the message which will constitute their mission. However, the emerging recognition and confession of who Jesus is is not yet complete.

(3) The apostolate reaches its final period with the *re-assembling and empowerment* of the disciples for the discharge of their intended mission.[72] This period encompasses the time between the resurrection and the promulgation of the great commission. This is manifestly the kingly ministry of Jesus in which the disciples are commissioned and empowered to share in his power and glory, and to receive and execute the mission begun by Jesus. The ministry performed by him is now to be transferred to the disciples who are now transformed for this purpose. These disciples are now to do for others what Jesus did for them, namely call and make disciples of others, serving as teachers and preachers of Jesus Christ and his regal lordship.

In Barth's interpretation, therefore, the election of the individual is seen to consist in the advancement toward a quite specific *teleology* which emerges on the basis of, and in fulfillment of, God's election of Jesus Christ to be God's self-revelation to the world. The keynotes to each of these periods are repeated in subsequent fashion with each individual in whom personal election is fulfilled. On the basis of the election of Jesus Christ, in whom the individual's election is included, the fulfillment of that individual's election is to be understood as Jesus Christ's (1) call to mission, (2) self-disclosure as the content of proclamation, and (3) empowerment as a medium for the continuing execution of his own mission. In this sense, the election of the individual is patterned after, and intended to reflect, the election of Jesus Christ. The movement from Jesus Christ to the apostolate to the Church to the individual is expressed in this way:

> To what does God elect a man? The New Testament answers this question with its portrayal of the existence of the apostles; their calling, appointment and mission. It is in them, in their being and their deeds, that the Church can and should recognise itself as the assembly of the elect for all time. It is in them that each individual member of the Church can and should recognise the meaning and purpose of his own election. He who is elect of God is elect in Jesus Christ. For Jesus Christ is the original object of divine election. He is the one Elect, apart from whom there can be no others.... The determination of the apostles is to go into this world with

---

[72]See *C.D.* II,2:432-35.

the task of baptising it. Through the apostles this is the determination of the Church, and in the Church it is the determination of all its members, of the elect. If God elects a man, it is that he may be a witness to Jesus Christ, and therefore a proclaimer of His own glory.[73]

Thus apart from Jesus Christ, it is not to any particular individual that Barth looks for a representation of an elect individual. Rather it is to a functionally defined and manifestly corporate entity, the apostolate, in which the Church is prefigured, and therefore the elect individual.

3. The Role of the Rejected Individual. Barth's exegesis of the biblical view of the rejected individual[74] brings the entire discussion full circle. The essence of this lengthy exegetical passage is to be found in the fact that it stands ultimately as a material interpretation of the election and rejection of Jesus Christ. This is accomplished in the guise of a formal interpretation of the figure of Judas Iscariot and the New Testament concept of "handing over," and the exegesis here necessarily presupposes all the exegetical and dogmatic constructs which have emerged to this point in the doctrine. In comparison to the previous exegetical sections in the discussion of the individual, we once again find a paradigmatic shift which distinguishes the present interpretation and which can be described in this way:

(1) The rejected individual is once more seen in a unity with the elect individual, and the relativity and mutual dependence which characterizes this duality becomes the fundamental ingredient in establishing the reality and execution of election.

(2) One (ambiguously) elect individual is singled out and interpreted as a type, not of what it means to be a rejected individual, but rather of the necessary role played by rejection in effecting the revelation of election in Jesus Christ. In himself, and as reflected in the New Testament, Judas is an enigmatic figure. He is not, however, a type of Jesus Christ's rejection in the same way that an elect individual can be seen as a type of Jesus Christ's election. Rather his action is instrumental in the execution of Jesus Christ's rejection, and in this way he represents one moment of the eternal and temporal *kairos* in which rejection is fulfilled and establishes the possibility and reality of the election of others.

(3) The emphasis is not upon the manner in which the rejected individual actually participates in the rejection of Jesus Christ, for Barth has already established that no other individual participates in or undergoes this rejection. Thus the rejected individual is seen and

---

[73] *C.D. II,*2:449.
[74] See *C.D. II,*2:458-506.

understood only in his/her non-reality, only in the fact that his/her "rejection" is as eternally unreal and temporally disestablished as the "election" of another is eternally real and temporally established. In other words, the emphasis is on establishing not the rejection of the individual *per se*, but rather the ephemeral nature of rejection *vis-a-vis* the individual and the fact that this transient status signifies nothing with regard to human individuality. Rejection is necessary for election, but only to the extent that in the individual, it gives way to election.

Barth begins his exegesis with the unequivocal declaration that, according to the New Testament, Judas Iscariot is an elect individual, elected by Jesus Christ, elected to be with and to follow him, elected to participate in the calling, appointment, sending forth, elected as a recipient of Jesus' self-disclosure in the same way that the other disciples are elect.[75] What Barth does not say, and what the text obviously implies, is that Judas is elected with all the other disciples to be empowered for participation in the third period of the apostolate, the great commission in the post-resurrection period. Neither does Barth say that Judas is elected to be rejected, though in his act, its outcome and his own end are to be seen the supreme manifestation of rejection. Rather Judas is elected to a discipleship which is to end prematurely, to an apostleship which is to be distorted and perverted, but which from the very beginning is intended to be an instrument for the execution of Jesus Christ's election in the form of rejection. Barth's exegesis indicates that there is a singular purpose to Judas' election which differentiates him from all the other disciples. Like them, he is destined to hand Jesus over to sinful men; but unlike them, he is to hand him over in such a way that he is put to death: "The whole significance of the apostolate, of the election of the twelve apostles, depends upon the fact that this happened. And the apostle Judas Iscariot is the special agent and exponent of this handing-over as it was decreed to be necessary in the counsel of God."[76]

It is important to Barth's exegesis that nowhere in the gospels is it said of Judas that he was rejected by Jesus. Quite the contrary, it is implied that he too was the recipient of Jesus' care, concern and ministry. The heinous sin of which Judas is guilty is the fact that he rejected Jesus; he gave him over to the power of persons who would destroy him, and he did so by exercising his freedom to be over against Jesus, usurping power over Jesus and reserving to himself the prerogative of self-determination. But for Barth, the fact remains that Judas acts as an elect individual, and this act does not mitigate or obfuscate his election. However, because his act is itself the act of rejection, the personal attitude and character expressed in this act precipitate and confirm the necessity of rejection as

---

[75] See *C.D. II,2*:458-61.
[76] *C.D. II,2*:461. See also pp. 501-5.

God's act of judgment on sin and disobedience. Judas' act effects Jesus' rejection; it does not effect Judas' rejection. Rather in Judas act, there is acutely represented the ultimate expression of the sin and rebellion of humanity which must be judged and condemned, and has been in the crucifixion of Jesus Christ. In this, Judas is the epitome of Israel and Judah.[77] For Barth, Judas' treacherous act does not bring about his rejection. Rather it confirms the fact that he was elected, like Israel as a whole, to be an instrument for the execution and manifestation of rejection. Judas is a paradoxical figure in this respect, and if the outcome of his life is seen as tantamount to his "rejection," it can be so only in the terms of a self-destruction which points to the real execution of judgment and rejection on Jesus Christ. Barth interprets Judas' rejection in terms of his election when he states:

> His election excels and outshines and controls and directs his rejection: not just partly, but wholly; not just relatively, but absolutely. And this is not because it was not really a serious rejection. It is just because it is so serious. It is just because in this figure if in any biblical figure one perceives nothing at all except divine rejection. This very man, who is wholly rejected, is elect. He is "one of the twelve." And in the decisive situation he more clearly than all the rest must demonstrate and confirm that he is this--that this is the service for which God elects those whom He elects.[78]

Judas' act is viewed by Barth as one which both makes way for, and is the perverse and even opposite expression of, the other divinely intended handing over of Jesus Christ which is seen in the faithful execution of the great commission given to the apostolate. Judas' negative handing over is required in order to make possible the positive handing over of the apostles. In this regard, the faithless act of Judas gives way to the faithful act of Paul. In conformity to the symmetry already described, Barth views Judas as *the elect who is rejected* in order to give way to Paul as *the rejected who is elect*. Paul is the individual who takes the place vacated by Judas and fulfills the apostolic office to which Judas was originally elect, but from which he turned in the pursuit of his own purpose and end. Judas is the elect/rejected figure beside whom the rejected/elect figure of Paul is comprehensible, and for Barth this duality of Judas and Paul means that the negative handing over by Judas is the necessary prerequisite for the fulfillment of the positive handing over of Paul. But even more, it means:

---

[77]See *C.D. II*,2:464-71.
[78]*C.D. II*,2:504.

And in any case, when we consider the question of the determination of the rejected, in view of Judas and Paul we have to bear in mind that the elect always occupies what was originally the place of a rejected, and that the work of the elect can only be the amazing reversal of the work of the rejected.[79]

Judas' overwhelmingly negative act of handing over Jesus to death is transformed by the resurrection into the positive act of handing over exercised by the apostles in their proclamation of Jesus Christ.[80]

Judas and Paul, however, are not the proper subjects of these negative and positive acts of handing over. Rather both acts are considered to have their reality and significance in the fact that they are enabled by, subsequent to, and therefore to be interpreted in terms of, the divine acts of negative and positive handing over. First (and negatively), there is the divine act in which God does to sinners what Judas did to Jesus, namely deprive them of their freedom and hand them over to a destructive power stronger than themselves. "God abandons them to themselves, and therefore to their destruction. This is the operation of His wrath against them."[81] For Barth, this represents the judgment and rejection of humanity by God. This act, however, ultimately gives way to the second (and positive) divine act in which God hands over the divine self in the person of God's Son Jesus Christ to be the bearer of this judgment and rejection. Barth declares:

> Previously it was men that God delivered up, as Judas delivered up Jesus. Now He delivers up Jesus; Jesus hands over Himself. At this point we obviously have to do with the handing-over which takes precedence over all others in value, importance and meaning. Before Judas had handed over Jesus, God had handed Him over, and Jesus had handed over Himself. Before Jesus was the object of the apostolic delivery, God had delivered Him, and He had delivered Himself. Before the wrath of God handed over Jews and Gentiles, abandoning and yielding them to themselves, He had not spared His only Son, but had delivered Him up for us all (Rom. 8:32). Clearly the

---

[79] *C.D. II*,2:480.

[80] See especially *C.D. II*,2:477-84. The course of Barth's interpretation at this point consists in trading on the rich variety of meanings borne by the word *paradounai* (*Überlieferung*) in the New Testament text, a word which, depending on the context, can be translated *handing over, delivery*, or *tradition*.

[81] *C.D. II*,2:485. On the negative divine handing over, see especially pp. 484-88.

necessity and power and meaning of all delivery are established in this first and radical delivery, in which God, in the person of Jesus, or Jesus as the Son of God, made Himself the object of delivery. It is not permissible to understand any other delivery except with reference to this one (without prejudice to its special meaning). All other delivery looks either to or from this. It has its reality in what happened here. It is impossible to interpret it apart from its connexion with this event.[82]

This second divine act is really the one which encompasses and portends the significance of the first act, and thus at the most vital point of comprehending the rejected individual, the "rejection" which is portrayed by the figure of Judas Iscariot, we find once again that Barth appeals to the election and rejection of Jesus Christ as the preeminent reality, the one from whom alone the categories of understanding may emerge, the one whose reality alone qualifies the signification of other figures and matters who appear in the text as illustrations of these categories. The final step in this direction is taken by Barth when he interprets the apostolic handing over as the positive human repetition, reproduction and transmission of this divine handing over, and the act of Judas as the negative instrument through which the divine handing over directly takes place.[83]

We can make the following summary observations about Barth's exegesis of the biblical view of the rejected individual:

(1) In the portrayal and interpretation of the "rejected" individual, the figure of Judas is selected rather than a Cain, Ishmael, Esau, Saul, Jeroboam or Ahab because nowhere in the Bible does Barth find a more substantive picture of a "rejected" individual in direct proximity with an "elect" individual, one with a *telos* so directly related to and qualified by the *telos* of an elect individual. Nowhere is there an unambiguous picture of a rejected individual in the classical, traditional sense either. Barth picks Judas because his proximity to Jesus, the role he played in bringing about Jesus' death and the fact that in him is to be seen the clearest picture of the way taken by all the other "rejected" figures in the Bible: one who turns away from God, despising and rejecting God, and in this act confirming himself as a sinner subject to judgment and destruction. He is one who charts his own course in self-exaltation and disobedience, but whose act is for that reason used by God for his own self-revelation.

(2) The interpretation of Judas takes the form of an interpretation of his action as a medium for the execution and revelation

---

[82]*C.D. II,2*:489. For this second act, see especially pp. 488-97.
[83]See *C.D. II,2*:497-506.

of Jesus Christ's election and rejection. For Barth, it is not a question of trying to make sense of Judas in terms of his rejection. He is not so much attempting to explain Judas in himself in the categories of his own individuality or personal rejection so much as he is trying to understand the mediacy of rejection as a component in God's self-revelation as this is reflected in the figure of Judas. Put in another way, Barth is not so much concerned with Judas himself as a rejected man as he is with what Judas' attitude and actions represent *vis-a-vis* the signification and execution of Jesus Christ's election. Judas in himself is not a "rejected individual" in whom one can see an unambiguous portrayal of rejection or what it means to be rejected. That this is the case for Barth is evident in his emphasizing that Judas is elected to serve, and does in fact serve the self-revelation of God. What he discloses, however, is that precisely as an elect individual, he acts disobediently, perversely, faithlessly and unbelievingly. In the light of the fact that Jesus Christ is the *only* rejected individual, and that rejected individuals are as such the object of God's election, one can only say with Barth that Judas is an elect individual whose particular determination is to manifest the sin and unworthiness which merits rejection and the judgment and destruction which comes as its consequence. Judas' election takes the form of rejection as a result of which he is put aside to make room for another; one also rejected, but who is now elect, will discharge the office originally given to Judas (i.e., Paul). The fact that Judas gives way to Paul does not in itself mean that Judas is eternally rejected. Rather it means that rejection is for the sake of, and ultimately gives way to, election; the story of Judas is continued and fulfilled in the story of Paul. The actual course and outcome of Judas' life is not as important to Barth as what his life signifies for the revelation of election and rejection in Jesus Christ. In Barth's estimation, Judas is an actual figure whose particularity, meaning and *telos* lie not in himself, but rather in the manner in which his life and actions concretely manifest a vital dimension to the execution of election.

(3) Barth does not answer the hypothetical question of whether Judas is eternally lost, or whether there was or may yet be the possibility of his salvation and restoration. The New Testament neither poses nor answers this question. Barth does not answer this question in the terms in which it is posed because, in the light of the revelation of Jesus Christ, he sees the Judas-Paul phenomenon as one which establishes the notion that the elect is rejected precisely in order that the rejected might be elect, i.e., the elect Jesus Christ is rejected (suffers death in the execution of the divine judgment on sin) in order that others who deserve and are rejected might be elect (have life in the execution of the divine mercy of God in fellowship with God). The question of the rejected cannot finally be put and answered apart from their role in the determination of the elect. In the final analysis, we therefore come full circle in the symmetry of election and rejection.

C. Final Observations

We began Chapter Five by calling attention to the questions of whether Barth consistently applies his hermeneutic and whether the exegesis calls for and supports the dogmatic construction of the doctrine of election. In our opinion, Barth's biblical hermeneutic is consistently applied in his exegesis in the doctrine of election. We are brought to this conclusion because we see that his exegesis is constrained throughout by the knowledge of Jesus Christ, the Word of God, as the only true subject matter or referent of the text. It is evident that the reality and knowledge of Jesus Christ as the self-revelation of God is both mediated through the text and brought to bear on the interpretation of the text in such a way that he alone controls its meaning and understanding. We find Barth consistently maintaining the idea that the purpose of Scripture is to present Jesus Christ through its human witness and that it is only through this human witness, as a result of the divine initiative, that he is accessible and knowledge of him possible. Furthermore, we find Barth to be consistent in maintaining a distinction between the language of witness and the reality to which this witness points. Throughout his interpretation, it is clear that it is not possible to separate the human form of witness from the content of the reality which it signifies, and still arrive at a true knowledge and understanding of that reality. At the same time, however, the fact that the reality is bound to and mediated by this witness does not mean that it is wholly reducible to or identical with this witness. There remains a distance between witness and referent which can only be crossed by the execution of revelation, but which is not obscured or removed in that revelation.

We also believe that Barth's exegesis calls for and supports the dogmatic construction of the doctrine. Certainly Barth's exegesis takes a different course in comparison to that of the more traditional formulations, but this fact in itself does not preclude the integrity of his exegesis. Likewise, there is no self-evident or *apriori* reason for denying the validity of Barth's exegetical approach. Consistent with his hermeneutic, Barth begins with the reality of God's self-revelation in Jesus Christ, and at the outset contends that this reality can only be understood in the categories of election and rejection which are given in and with this revelation. The fact that Barth deviates from the traditional doctrines in itself suggests the subordination of human concepts and thoughts to the text; he cannot take the way of the older exponents because he sees their exegesis as determined by an already formulated scheme of thought which is then imposed on the text, and he wills to have the concepts of election and rejection suggested to him by the witness of the text to the self-revelation of God in Jesus Christ. There is no question but that Barth uses a scheme of thought to provide a frame of reference for hearing and understanding the text. In his case, however, this scheme of thought consists in the different and quite unique symmetry of election and rejection as expressed in the reality of God's revelation, and it moves out from this central point to provide the orientation for interpreting the witness of the text to election as a whole. This quite definite, determined and already existent knowledge of Jesus Christ as the subject matter attested in the text is thus the exegetical and epistemological presupposition on the basis of which it becomes possible to elicit the meaning of the text at other places *vis-a-vis* the reality of God's election. Our conclusion at this point, however, is not meant to suggest that Barth's is the only exegesis possible for a doctrine of election. Rather it is simply our contention that the doctrine as Barth has constructed it can be seen to emerge from a realistic and legitimate biblical interpretation which authentically expresses his fundamental hermeneutical principles.

Part IV

The Pervasiveness of Election

Chapter Seven

The Significance of the Doctrine for C.D. III-IV

To this point in the investigation, our attention has been focused on the doctrine of election as it is constructed in *C.D. II,2*. During the course of our analysis to this point, we have had occasion to consider Barth's view of election in relation both to the doctrine of the Word of God in *C.D. I* and the doctrine of God in *C.D. II,1*. We have found that the doctrine of election brings greater clarity and focus to the doctrine of the Word of God to the extent that it represents the objective and subjective basis and substance of the knowledge of God given in God's self-revelation. We have come to discern that, for Barth, God is the revealing God because God is, and always has been, the electing God, and that the execution of revelation in the incarnation of the Word in Jesus Christ is itself the execution of God's election. But we have also found that the doctrine of election brings greater clarity and focus to the doctrine of God to the extent that it represents the original and eternal act of God in which the divine self determines who God is and what God wills to do. With respect to God, the act of election constitutes the ontic self-determination of the divine self, and therefore the beginning of all God's ways and works with respect both to that divine self as well as the reality which is external to God and which has its origin precisely in this self-determining act. Election is thereby established as the means of the knowledge of God because it is itself the primal act in which God determines the divine self and gives this self to an other in revelation.

As we come now to the present chapter, we can complete the inquiry into Barth's view of election by giving careful consideration to the influence of Barth's dogma on the subsequent dogmatic construction in the *C.D.* The fundamental antecedents for the doctrine of creation in *C.D. III* and the doctrine of reconciliation in *C.D. IV* are to be found in the doctrine of election. It will be our task in this concluding chapter to demonstrate the formative role played by Barth's concept of election in the construction of these latter doctrines. In this way we will see clearly the extent to which Barth's view of election is the formal and material key, indeed the fundamental hermeneutic, to the theology articulated in the *C.D.* We will attempt to accomplish this task by regarding the doctrines of creation and reconciliation as the continuing dogmatic interpretation and development of the themes inherent in the doctrine of election, and by exposing the presence and formative role of election in each of the chapters which constitutes those doctrines.[1]

A. The Work of Creation (C.D. III,1)

Barth begins the doctrine of creation with the consideration of the *work* of creation because it is only in and through the work that the Creator can be and is known. The fact that God as Father is Creator, and that creation is the work of this God, is known only because it is revealed in Jesus Christ as the incarnate Son or Word of God.[2] This means that the knowledge of God as Creator and of creation as God's work is a knowledge of faith. Furthermore, this means that election is the act of God which is the presupposition of the being and act of God the Creator, and therefore of the knowledge of God as such. In the knowledge of faith, creation denotes the relationship between God and the world decreed and established in Jesus Christ. "From this revealed fact of the unity of God with man effected in Jesus Christ, the first truth that we learn is the simple one that God is not alone."[3] But there is another side to this truth revealed in Jesus Christ:

> From the same revealed fact of the unity of God with man effected in His Person, we also learn that man is not alone, and that the sphere in which he lives is not the only one.... So man lives as God's creature. That God makes the existence and being of the other reality His own is clearly seen at this point where between God and the reality distinct from God there takes place this absolutely once-for-all and unique relationship; where His eternal Son becomes a creature, and as a creature calls Him Father. Here, then, God confronts the creature as Creator.[4]

The noetic fact that the Creator and creation can be truly known only in Jesus Christ rests on the ontic fact that Jesus Christ is himself the

---

[1]Limitations of space do not allow for an analysis of the doctrines of creation and reconciliation equal in scope to the one undertaken in our discussion of the doctrine of election. More so now than then, our present discussion will (1) assume familiarity with the substance of *C.D. III* and *C.D. IV*, and (2) focus on the major elements which give clear evidence of being determined by the construct of election in *C.D. II,2*.
[2]See the discussions at *C.D. III,1*:11-12, 16, 22-31, 65-67, 229-31, 332-34, 348-50, 363-65, 368-70, 375-78, 380-88.
[3]*C.D. III,1*:25.
[4]*C.D. III,1*:26.

Word by which God made, maintains and rules God's creation.[5] The principle concern at this point has to do with the relation between Jesus Christ and creation, and Barth picks up a major theme of the doctrine of election in order to develop this relation, namely the execution and revelation of the covenant between God and humanity established and confirmed in Jesus Christ.

Creation is the first external work of God, and as such it constitutes the beginning of all things outside of and distinct from God. The discussion in §41, "Creation and Covenant," is intended to answer the question of the origin, purpose and goal of this external creation *vis-a-vis* the divine decision to enter into covenant with humanity. Creation follows from the covenant, and constitutes the beginning of the history of the relation between God and humanity. As Barth states: "The purpose and therefore the meaning of creation is to make possible the history of God's covenant with man which has its beginning, its centre and its culmination in Jesus Christ."[6] Everything outside of God begins with this work of creation, and all the subsequent works of God are designed to implement and fulfill this covenant within the sphere of creation.

Barth's exposition of the creation accounts in Genesis is oriented by the notion of the covenant executed eternally in the God-human Jesus Christ. On the one hand, in the light of the covenant decreed and executed in Jesus Christ, creation is to be viewed as the external basis of the covenant between God and humanity.[7] This is to say that, outside of God, the reality of the covenant stands on the existence of creation and the creature with whom God enters into covenant. Without the externality of creation and creature, there could be no covenant between God and humanity: "Creation took place in order that man's history might commence and take place as the history of the covenant of grace established between God and himself."[8] But one must look to election to discover the internal basis of the covenant, i.e., the being and act of God in which the divine freedom, love and desire to be with and for an other finds its expression in the decision to become a human in Jesus Christ, and thereby execute in history the divine eternal election.[9] Viewed teleologically, the goal of creation is the covenant, and one must therefore understand creation in terms of its participation in and movement toward the eschatological fulfillment of the covenant.

On the other hand, and still in the light of the covenant decreed and executed in Jesus Christ, this means that the covenant is to be

---

[5] See *C.D. III,1*:27-33.
[6] *C.D. III,1*:42.
[7] See *C.D. III,1*:94-228 where Barth discusses Genesis 1:1-2:3.
[8] *C.D. III,1*:219.
[9] See *C.D. III,1*:96-97.

understood as the internal basis of creation.[10] This is to say that, in the inner being and act of God, the reality of creation stands on the fact that it exists only after the purpose, plan and order determined for it by God's free and gracious love in which God elects humanity for fellowship with the divine self. Creation and creature thus become a manifestation of God's election. Without the internality of the covenant, there would be no creation: "Hence what God has created was not just any reality ... but that which is intrinsically determined as the exponent of His glory and for the corresponding service."[11] Thus the covenant decreed and established in Jesus Christ is not only the expression of God's purpose with creation and creature, but it is also the basis for the setting in which this purpose is to be fulfilled. Barth's view is essentially one in which both creation and creature are indissolubly linked to and determined by God's election in which God chooses Godself for covenant fellowship with humanity, and humanity for covenant fellowship with God.

Building on this relation between covenant and creation, Barth proceeds to a discussion of the manner in which the divine election determines the reality of creation and creature. In the light of the revelation of Jesus Christ, creation is seen to express the benevolence of God. Because the purpose of creation lies in the covenant between God and humanity, the whole of creation can be seen only as God's Yes. If the link between covenant and creation is severed or qualified by a divine No directed toward creation, then there is no material basis on which creation can be affirmed. Rather for Barth it is a case wherein that which God elects is consequently created by God. In the election of Jesus Christ, it has been established that the No of God is directed only to that which God does not choose to be and that which God does not will to create. God's Yes to the divine self in election is the basis for God's Yes to that created reality distinct from Godself: "God the Creator did not say No, nor Yes and No, but Yes to what He created.... Creation as such is not rejection, but election and acceptance."[12] This is the contention developed in §42, "The Yes of God the Creator."

God's act of creation is the act of giving reality to that which is other than the divine self, and for Barth it is because of the election executed in Jesus Christ that it is possible to know that this reality is the recipient of the divine Yes; God's affirmation of this reality means its actualization.[13] Creation is affirmed by God as the recipient of the divine love in the covenant because its reality confirms the execution of God's

---

[10]See *C.D. III,1*:228-329. This is the discussion of the second creation account in Genesis 2:4-25.

[11]*C.D. III,1*:231.

[12]*C.D. III,1*:330-31.

[13]See the discussion at *C.D. III,1*:344-65.

eternal election and is constituted as the sphere wherein this election is to be executed. Because of the character of God's election, and because election determines creation and creature, one must see in the creature a being who is elected, created and determined for participation in the covenant:

> Thus even the creature does not merely exist, but does so as the sphere and object of the covenant, as the being to whom God has devoted His good-will and whom He has destined to share in the overflowing of His own fulness of life and love. To be a creature means to be determined to this end, to be affirmed, elected and accepted by God.[14]

It is election that gives creation and creature their unique and characteristic reality; what God elects, God creates solely for the purpose of executing the divine election.

In Barth's view, this actualization of creation implies that creation is good and right in God's eyes, i.e., it is justified. Creation is neither bad nor neutral, but good because it exists for the purpose of rendering service to God. Creation is not without its negativity however. God created the creature in order to exalt him/her to fellowship; this constitutes the positive dimension. In the light of election, however, this exaltation presupposes a human existence which is both incapable and unworthy of fellowship; this constitutes the negative dimension. But because election consists in the incarnation, in the fact that the Creator became a creature in order to effect the covenant, and thus in the divine assumption of this negativity, it can be stated uncategorically that this negativity is overcome in the divine justification of creation. Barth states:

> The self-revelation of God as our Creator consists in the fact that in Jesus Christ He gives Himself to us to be recognised as the One who has made our cause His own before it was or could be ours, who does not stand aloof from the contradiction of our being as a stranger, who has willed to bear it Himself, and has in fact borne it from all eternity.[15]

Thus the election of God means that creation and creature are justified. Because the Creator became a creature who suffered and died for others, the goodness of creation is secured in spite of its apparent imperfection. The goodness of God and the goodness and justification of God's creature are manifest in the fact that in the elect human Jesus Christ,

---

[14]*C.D. III,1*:363-64.
[15]*C.D. III,1*:381.

God has not permitted the contradiction of the creature's existence to go unresolved; the No of the divine non-willing and non-creating is laid upon Jesus Christ precisely in order that the Yes of the divine willing and creating might be given to humanity and the sphere in which humanity has its reality. Because creation is an instrument in the execution of election, creation and all therein are good.

B. The Creature (C.D. III,2)

In this part-volume of the doctrine of creation, Barth takes up the matter of anthropology, or the doctrine of the creature precisely in its determination as the covenant partner of God. This anthropology emerges from, and is therefore determined by, the election executed in Jesus Christ. This is to say that Barth's theological anthropology is grounded in the knowledge of what it means to be the elect of God, and concretely in the knowledge of the elect human Jesus Christ which is given in the execution of election. The dogmatic movement from the *elect* human Jesus Christ to all others is the definition of humanity in terms of the concrete reality of the human Jesus, and this approach represents both a new foundation for anthropology as well as a standpoint from which one can critique all other approaches.[16] The doctrine of creation is not reducible to anthropology for Barth, but the human being is precisely the focal point in the doctrine because creation as such exists for the sake of the relationship between God and humanity, and neither creation nor humanity can be understood apart from this relationship.

Again, the knowledge of what it means to be human is given only in God's divine revelation, and this means that it is a knowledge of faith. God's self-revelation in the elect human Jesus Christ is at the same time the revelation of the origin, nature and goal of humanity. Election executed in revelation means true knowledge of humanity:

> For man is the creature to whom, according to His own Word, God has turned in the work of creation with its centre in the covenant of grace. And it is very man that God Himself has become in the perfect and definitive revelation of this Word of His. Who and what man is, is no less specifically and emphatically declared by the Word of God than who and what God is. The Word of God essentially encloses a specific view of man, an anthropology, and ontology of this particular creature. This being the case, we

---

[16]See Barth's discussion of naturalism, idealism, existentialism and theistic anthropology at *C.D. III,2*:71-132, 198-202.

must accept this view in faith, reflect it in the confession of faith, and develop it as a perception of faith.[17]

The movement from election to anthropology is evident in the notion that it is the eternal election of the human Jesus Christ that determines what human being is, for in him the nature of humanity is established for all others; his is the true and original human nature in which all others share and participate.[18] As articulated in *C.D. II,2*, Jesus' election means that he is a human being in a relationship to God. Here, this relationship between the human and the divine is constitutive for the definition of humanity. In the light of the election and revelation of Jesus Christ, the human being "must be understood as a being which from the very outset stands in some kind of relationship to God."[19] Furthermore, implicit in this election and revelation of humanity in Jesus Christ are the six criteria by which true humanity is to be understood, namely the fact that the human being is (1) conditioned by this relationship, (2) delivered by God, (3) determined for God's glory, (4) under God's sovereign lordship, (5) participation in history with real freedom to decide for God, and (6) an event in which service is rendered to God.[20]

Barth's discussion of "Real Man" can be viewed as the further explication of the discussion of "election in him." The divine decision concerning the human Jesus Christ is at the same time the decision regarding the being and nature of every human as a being deriving from and in relation to God: "The ontological determination of humanity is grounded in the fact that one man among all others is the man Jesus."[21] For all his uniqueness and his unlikeness from others in his reality as the human being whom God became, Jesus Christ is nevertheless the real human in whom humanity participates and is determined. The election of the human Jesus Christ means that to be a human being is to be with God:

As an ontological determination of man in general, the fact that among many others this One is also man means

---

[17]*C.D. III,2*:13. At every crucial juncture in the development of this anthropology, Barth either expressly posits or implicitly refers to the priority and necessity of God's self-revelation in Jesus Christ and the fact that the true knowledge of humanity is strictly a knowledge of faith. See especially *C.D. III,2*:3, 16-19, 25-34, 40-46, 58-71, 122-25, 142-43, 147-52, 174-79, 203-22, 243, 299, 325-32, 346-49, 437-64.

[18]See *C.D. III,2*:47-54.

[19]*C.D. III,2*:72.

[20]See *C.D. III,2*:68-71, 73-74. These elements were first articulated in Barth's discussion of "The Eternal Will of God in the Election of Jesus Christ" in *C.D. II,2*:145-94.

[21]*C.D. III,2*:132.

that we are men as in the person of this One we are confronted by the divine Other.... That this being Jesus can be the divine Counterpart of every man is implicit in the fact that He is among all other men, that He dwells with them as Himself, a man like others, that He belongs to this fellowship and history.[22]

It is precisely at this point that Barth explicitly establishes the fact that God's election constitutes the determination of human being. Jesus' own existence as a human being depends entirely on the fact that he is elected by God, and for this reason there is revealed in him the will of God and the true reality of humanity as created by God. To be a human being is to be with Jesus Christ and to live in the sphere wherein God's merciful and saving will is executed and revealed. Thus to be a human being is to be a witness to and a participant in the election of Jesus Christ which stands as the beginning of all things. In Jesus Christ, the election of humanity means that human being is derived solely from God, resting entirely on God's gracious election; the creature is elected to the extent that precisely as a human being who shares in Jesus' humanity, he/she is the one who is immediately envisioned. Election, creation and creature are indissolubly connected for Barth in the idea that it is by his/her creation that the human being is confirmed as God's covenant partner.[23]

The ontological determination of human being as a being in and with the elect human Jesus Christ implies that humanity is created and determined to hear and respond to God's self-revelation in the Word. As expressed in *C.D. II,2*, election is identical with revelation/incarnation, and this means for Barth that human being has its true reality in the act of hearing this Word and responding in the only way intended. Election places humanity before and in relation to God in the sphere where God's self-revelation is executed; human being is true human being as it is called and placed in a position to respond. Thus for Barth, true human being is one in which there is continuity and congruence of being and act. In particular, and as a consequence of election, human being "is response, being in the act of response to the Word of God."[24] Human being is being in the act of knowing, accepting and affirming the Word of God; willing and choosing to obey and conform to the divine determination; invoking God to sustain and uphold him/her in his/her absolute difference from and dependence upon God; exercising and

---

[22]*C.D. III,2*:134.
[23]On this explicit connection of election and anthropology which issues in the notion of election as analytic to human being, see especially *C.D. III,2*:141-47.
[24]*C.D. III,2*:176.

fulfilling the freedom conferred by the Creator which constitutes him/her as a true human subject in correspondence to the divine Subject. In short, true human being derives from, and is determined to respond to, the self-revelation of God executed in the election of the human Jesus.[25]

On the basis of the twofold fact that the elect human Jesus Christ is the original human being who is for and with God, as well as the human being who is for and with other human beings, Barth moves to the contention that human being in general is a being for and with others. The covenant fellowship and relatedness between the human Jesus and God is the paradigm for the fellowship and relatedness between human beings. Election is participation as a partner in the covenant, and the determination which accompanies this election places the human being not only in a particular relation to God, but to fellow human beings as well. Human being is genuine as it is being in the act of encounter with an other, an act which corresponds subsequently to the encounter of God and human being. The image of God is neither more nor less than this being in encounter with an other.[26]

Barth's discussion of human being as embodied soul and besouled body emerges from the reality of the incarnation in which the Son of God and the Son of Man are together, being and acting in unity.[27] From this reality, Barth postulates the fact that the human being is rooted, constituted and preserved not in and of itself, but by God in God's activity as Spirit. The Holy Spirit as the foundation, constitution and preservation of the intra-divine relationship between Father and Son is also the reality which both gives life to human being and keeps this life in relation to God. Spirit is relation in the Godhead, and relation between God and human being. "Spirit is, in the most general sense, the operation of God upon His creation, and especially the movement of God towards man. Spirit is thus the principle of man's relation to God, of man's fellowship with Him."[28] The Spirit is not something added to human being. Rather it is itself the divine creative reality which grounds, constitutes and preserves the unity and wholeness of the life of human

---

[25] See *C.D. III,2*:147-98. This major discussion of the responsibility of human being has its antecedents in "The Determination of the Elect" in *C.D. II,2*:410-49.

[26] See *C.D. III,2*:222-324. For Barth, the essential form of humanity is fellow-humanity, a form in which human being is not isolated, but together in encounter with an other. This finds its dominant expression in humanity as male and female which for Barth is not so much a sexual or physiological differentiation (though it is this to be sure), but rather a concrete expression of an ontological unity and differentiation within humanity which provides for the encounter and relationship between two who are like and yet unlike each other, and in this way constitute a being together which corresponds to that of the triune God, i.e., the being together of the Father and the Son in the Holy Spirit (see *C.D. III,2*:285-324, and cf., *C.D. III,1*:288-329).

[27] See *C.D. III,2*:325-44.

[28] *C.D. III,2*:356. See also pp. 346-54.

being, and therefore makes this human being a genuine subject; it is God in outward movement and action toward creaturely reality without which the human being cannot exist as such. In correspondence to the intra-divine reality of relationship, the Spirit operative in giving and sustaining life in human being means that human being participates in God's life.[29] As we have seen, for Barth this participation in the divine life is the essence of election as concretely manifest in the elect human Jesus Christ. It is on this basis that Barth can contend that human being, as reflected in Jesus Christ the elect God-human, has its true reality in the fact that it is empowered and sustained by God for the work which God accomplishes in and through humanity.[30]

Barth's doctrine of anthropology does not contain a doctrine of sin as such. Rather, on the basis of the election revealed in Jesus Christ, it presupposes sin as the condition in which humanity finds itself. As we observed in our discussion of election, it is precisely as a sinner that the individual is the object of election. Now, in the doctrine of the creature in *C.D. III,2,* Barth reaffirms this premise with a view of sin which comes directly from the signification of the reality of Jesus Christ's election as articulated in *C.D. II,2.*

The revelation of election in Jesus Christ discloses the fact that the human being lives a perverse and corrupt life, and not the life of wholeness and fellowship intended by the Creator. This revelation indicts the creature for living in contradiction to the God who elected and created him/her. But the fact that this knowledge is given to the creature in revelation implies and confirms that he/she is already elect and the recipient of God's grace as God's covenant partner. The creature does not cease to be creature or the covenant partner because of sin; he/she cannot escape God or cease to be upheld and preserved by God. The demeanor of God with respect to the sinful creature is disclosed in God's relation to the human Jesus, and for Barth this demeanor is evident in Jesus Christ's election, understood as the incarnation of the Son in the human Jesus and the assumption of humanity's sin upon himself. It is always and only in this human being that both the reality of human sin and election of the sinner are manifest.[31]

When election to covenant partnership determines both the sphere of creation and the being of the creature who lives in this sphere as a being with God in Jesus Christ, then the breach between the creature and the Creator can only be described as an *ontological impossibility.* Because

---

[29]See *C.D. III,2:*362-66.
[30]See especially *C.D. III,2:*55-71. This passage, under the title of "Jesus, Man for God," represents the quintessence not only of Barth's theological anthropology, but also (as we have observed) his view of election (cf., *C.D. II,2:*94-145, 306-40).
[31]See the discussion at *C.D. III,2:*26-54. Cf. *C.D. II,2:*103-27, 161-75.

of the divine determination of the creature in the election executed in Jesus Christ, sin as an ontological determination is excluded, and it can therefore be understood only as the creature's groundless affirmation of that which has been negated by God's electing and creating will and action. In the doctrine of the creature, Barth again makes it clear that the ontological impossibility of sin can only be posited on the basis of election. Because the creature is created to be with God, there is no other possibility given to the creature; he/she is and remains a being from and with God, whether or not he/she knows and affirms it. Thus true humanity is that in which human being is fulfilled in the act of conforming to the only ontological determination possible, namely that of participation and service in covenant fellowship with God in Jesus Christ. Any other act, though it may be real for the human, is in fact an ontological contradiction.[32]

C. The Creator and the Creature (C.D. III,3)

In Barth's construction, the doctrine of providence takes up the relation of Creator and creature as it unfolds in the existence of the creature. In particular, providence represents the co-existence and activity of God with the creature which effects the execution of the history of the covenant, and therefore the execution and fulfillment of the divine election. As such, providence is concerned with God as an acting Subject, and with the role of the creature as an acting subject of the concrete history which is given by God to the creature and which constitutes the external basis of covenant history. In its simplest form, the providence of God is understood by Barth as the divine execution in creaturely history of the covenant decreed in the eternal election of Jesus Christ.[33]

It is immediately apparent that the reality of election stands as the presupposition and determination of the divine providence. Election is the eternal predetermination of the relation between Creator and creature, and as such it has to do primarily and originally with the Creator as the electing God. Providence, on the other hand, has to do with the spatio-temporal execution of the decree advanced in God's election, and as such it is concerned with the creature and the actual relation which obtains between the creature and the God who created him/her as distinct from the divine self. As election is the presupposition and basis for creation and the existence of the creature, so it is the presupposition and basis for the providence which guarantees and confirms creation and the co-existence of Creator and creature in the execution of the covenant. As

---

[32]See *C.D. III,2*:134-47, 319-24.

[33]See especially the discussions at *C.D. III,3*:3-14, 33-57, 164-238, 242-47.

creation constitutes the beginning of this relation in covenant history, so providence represents the divine activity in its continuation. Throughout his discussion of providence, Barth constantly appeals to the fact that providence cannot be understood apart from the election of God in which God determines that God will create, enter into a quite specific relation with, and sustain the creature as a subject distinct from Godself.[34]

For Barth, the fact that providence constitutes the divine action of executing the decree of election in the on-going history of the creature has its basis in the reality of election as revelation/incarnation, and this means that the knowledge of the reality of providence is unequivocally a knowledge of faith and belief in God's self-revelation in Jesus Christ. Neither the creature nor creation nor history itself discloses the fact of God's providence. Rather it is disclosed by God's revelation in and through the existence of the creature, its creation and the covenant history established and sustained by God, all of which are grounded in and determined by the election of Jesus Christ. The knowledge of providence is the creature's response to this revelation: "The Christian belief in providence is faith in the strict sense of the term, and this means first that it is a hearing and receiving of the Word of God."[35] Furthermore, this knowledge of providence is itself the sign of the execution of the creature's election, and therefore the creature's inward and outward participation in the reality of the election in which God determines the divine self and the creature for covenant fellowship. In the knowledge effected by the divine self-revelation in Jesus Christ, there is confirmed the particular historical determination of the being and act of the creature: "As the kingdom of Jesus Christ is revealed to men in Jesus Christ, so too is the sway of divine providence, the determination of creaturely occurrence, its function, *telos* and character."[36] Thus the knowledge of providence as God's action *vis-a-vis* the creature in its concrete existence is grounded in and expressive of the reality of divine election as the determination of God and the reality distinct from from the divine self.[37]

---

[34]Barth begins his doctrine with a discussion in which he clarifies the relationship between election, creation and providence in terms of the priority and determination of election (see *C.D. III,3*:3-14). His entire discussion is sustained by this clarification and priority, and perhaps here more than anywhere else in his doctrine of creation the construct of election found in *C.D. II,2* can be seen to inform and determine the doctrinal exposition (see especially pp. 17, 28-29, 35-36, 68-79, 117-23, 130, 167-69, 270-79). It is particularly noteworthy to observe that election explicitly informs the treatment of "Nothingness" (*Das Nichtige*) (see pp. 302-49, 351-53, 360-68), about which we will have more to say below.

[35]*C.D. III,3*:15.

[36]*C.D. III,3*:54.

[37]Because the knowledge of providence is thus grounded in election, it is not an independent theme, idea or conclusion derived from, or in relation to, the general course

In §49, "God the Father as Lord of His Creature," the notion of providence is constructed in terms of the divine preserving, accompanying and ruling of the creature. Barth understands the divine preserving as the conservation and continuity of the creature's existence for the purpose of participation in the covenant of grace. This is an act of God's love and freedom in which God confirms creation and creature, meeting their need to be sustained after being brought into existence. At this point, Barth's thought moves from the origin of the creature in God's election to the preservation of the creature for execution and fulfillment of election. There is no other basis for the fact that the creature is empowered to, and does, endure, and thus there is no other basis for the reality of the creature. This is signified for Barth in God's providence in its action as *conservatio*. As he states:

> On this living and trustworthy basis in God Himself, it is decided, and continually decided, that the creature may have permanence and continuity. Without this living and trustworthy basis in God Himself, without the continuity in which God continually abides by His election, by His free but overflowing goodness, and finally, without the election of His grace which is the basis of His goodness, the creature could not and would not continue. But the living and trustworthy basis in God continues, and therefore the creature continues. Because of God it cannot not continue; it cannot perish.[38]

In the final analysis, the preservation of the creature indicates that election means the origin, actuality and continuity of the creature's being.

For Barth, providence as divine accompanying directs attention to the lordship of God *vis-a-vis* the activity of the creature. The one who elects and therefore creates and preserves the creature does not abandon it to its own activity; rather the Creator surrounds the creature with the divine activity and in this context affirms and attends the autonomous activity of the creature. Prior to, present in and with, and following the creature's activity, there is the divine activity which orients, empowers and brings this activity to its goal. Providence as the divine *concursus* insures that the creature has its being in its particular activity and therefore in its own space and time, but not without the presence of God's being and act:

---

of human existence or world history. Providence is God's co-existence with the creature, and as such it is knowable only in the execution of election in the life of the creature. This fact dominates Barth's discussion at every turn in his discussion of providence (see especially *C.D. III,3*:14-33, 35-36, 54-57, 70-73, 78-80, 161-142, 183-86, 239-48, 271-80), and the related discussion of "Nothingness" (*Das Nichtige*) (see pp. 301-52, 362-68).
[38] *C.D. III,3*:71. See also pp. 58-61, 67-73, 78-85.

> If God the Lord accompanies the creature, what it does mean is that He is so present in the activity of the creature ... that His own action takes place in and with and over the activity of the creature.... But creaturely events take place as God Himself acts. As He Himself enters the creaturely sphere ... His will is accomplished directly and His decisions are made and fulfilled in all creaturely occurrence both great and small.[39]

The fact that this divine accompanying is grounded in and determined by election is evident in Barth's notion that the divine action before, with and following the activity of the creature always takes the objective form of the divine self-revelation and the subjective form of the divinely enabled human response; the divine accompanying is God's activity in the Word and Spirit, i.e., in speaking and hearing, giving and receiving, claim and response, command and obedience.[40]

Providence as the divine ruling is understood by Barth as the divine activity in which God orders, controls, directs and coordinates creaturely being and activity for the purpose of executing the divine will and bringing it to its intended fulfillment and goal. In the final analysis, it is this divine *gubernatio* that guarantees that the divine preserving and accompanying will issue in the realization of the purpose for which God elected and created the reality distinct from Godself. That which God decrees and determines is irrefutably brought to its fulfillment for no other reason than the fact that it is God who so decrees and determines. As Barth contends:

> The rule of God is the operation of God over and with the temporal history of that reality which is distinct from God; the operation by which He arranges the course of that history, maintains and executes His own will within it, and directs it wholly and utterly in accordance with that will. The rule of God is the order of God in this active sense, His ordering of all temporal occurrence.[41]

Because the providence of God is known as such only in the execution of God's revelation, and therefore in the fulfillment of election,

---

[39]*C.D. III,3*:132-33. See also pp. 90-94, 117-23, 130-31.

[40]See *C.D. III,3*:142-54.

[41]*C.D. III,3*:164. See also pp. 154-59, 165-70 (where the relationship, correspondence and compatibility of divine sovereignty/permission and human freedom/responsibility are discussed), 176-78, 183-86.

it is only the believer, the "Christian," who knows and participates ontically *and noetically* in the providential lordship of God. It is the believer alone who can take up the appropriate attitude to the being and activity of God, and the marks of this attitude for Barth come directly from the construct of election, namely (1) faith as hearing and receiving the Word of God, (2) obedience as the response of doing the Word of God, and (3) prayer as the basic form of faith and obedience; as the creature's Yes to the divine Yes; as praise, gratitude, acknowledgement, petition and intercession; as the epitome of the creature's participation in the covenant; and thus as the fulfillment of the creature's existential determination which has its origin and basis in the decree of election.[42]

Barth's discussion of *Das Nichtige* in §50 is to be viewed as an elaboration of the reality and significance of the negative side of God's eternal election as articulated in *C.D. II,2*. In Barth's construction in *C.D. III,3*, providence as the divine preserving, accompanying and ruling of the creature has a twofold presupposition with a positive and negative side. On the one hand, providence clearly presupposes election. The fact that the creature is created, preserved, accompanied and ruled by God has its origin, determination and execution in the eternal decision of God to enter into covenant fellowship with an other outside the divine self; it is the actualization of the Yes which evinces what God wills and chooses for Godself and God's creature. On the other hand, providence no less clearly presupposes what Barth calls *Das Nichtige*, the comprehensive and alien power which opposes and resists God and threatens God's creation and creature. *Das Nichtige* is that from which the creature is preserved, over against which the creature is accompanied, and in opposition to which the creature is ruled. In its totality, it embraces everything which God has not willed and chosen for Godself or God's creature, and therefore not created for participation in the covenant. Providence presupposes *Das Nichtige* as the force which seeks to oppose and contradict the divine purpose in creation, and which therefore must be overcome if this purpose is to be fulfilled. In relation to creation and creature, providence is the divine activity which stands as the barrier to destruction and the absolute consummation of the opposition and contradiction of *Das Nichtige*.

Das Nichtige is neither created by God nor a necessary and inherent element in God's creation.[43] *Das Nichtige* is, and can be known for what it is, only in so far as it has been decisively overcome in the No of God pronounced in the eternal decree of election and executed in the life, death and resurrection of the electing and elect God-human Jesus Christ. *Das Nichtige* "is" only as that which God has rejected, only as the

---

[42] See *C.D. III,3*:239-88, and *C.D. II,2*:145-94, 306-40, 410-49, 552-630.
[43] See *C.D. III,3*:72-79, 289-302.

opposition and resistance which is overruled by the fact that God became a creature, subjecting the divine self to its onslaught, and vanquishing it once for all in the victory that is Jesus Christ. From him, it is known that *Das Nichtige* stands in opposition primarily to God, and that it is God alone who can and does overcome it. As a third factor over against both God and the creature, *Das Nichtige* has its reality only as the antithesis and threat to the execution of God's purpose in election which is nevertheless decisively and absolutely dealt with and overcome precisely in the execution of that election in the creature Jesus Christ.[44]

The concrete form in which *Das Nichtige* is known in Jesus Christ is the creature's personal act of sin, rebellion and opposition to God in the face of God's eternal election. This reality and orientation of the creature is not identical with *Das Nichtige*, but rather its concrete expression. From this point of human sin, *Das Nichtige* is seen also in the form of evil and death, the radical and final destruction of the creature: "It is the comprehensive negation of the creature and its nature. And as such it is a power which, though unsolicited and uninvited, is superior, like evil and death, to all the forces which the creature can oppose to it."[45]

It is clear that for Barth, *Das Nichtige* has its ontic context only in the eternal and temporal reality of God's election. It is only as that which falls under the divine judgment and rejection which constitutes one side of the twofold decree of election, for it is to *Das Nichtige* that God, in the person of the incarnate Son Jesus Christ, submits the divine self solely for the purpose of defeating it and removing its absolute threat from the creature. Only as the object of God's No, as that which God does not elect for the creature, can *Das Nichtige* exist, and because of this decisive judgment and rejection, it can have no permanence. Because it is the defeat and destruction of the creature under the power of *Das Nichtige* that is rejected, there is no basis for contending that the creature is the object of God's rejection; the creature is only in so far as it is elect. It is the creature's rejection that is rejected, negatively in the overcoming of *Das Nichtige* and the judgment executed on human sin, and thus positively in the election of Jesus Christ. And it is also clear that *Das Nichtige* has its noetic context in the execution of God's election in Jesus Christ. At no other point has *Das Nichtige* been *intentionally encountered and overcome*, and the reality of this divine-human action has its origin in, and is itself the execution of, the election of Jesus Christ. The reality of *Das Nichtige*, its opposition to God and the divine purpose, its encroachment upon and manifestation within human being, and its annihilation as the antithesis to God's good will and pleasure for God's

---

[44]See *C.D. III,3*:302-49.
[45]*C.D. III,3*:310.

creature are focused supremely in Jesus Christ because his election for this purpose is also itself incarnation/revelation.[46]

D. The Command of God the Creator (C.D. III,4)

Barth's doctrine of creation concludes with a chapter on the ethics of creation in which he undertakes an investigation of the actions of the true human being as these are determined by and correspond to the true God in God's being and act as Creator. His concern is to describe the nature of theological ethics vis-a-vis creation and human existence in this sphere, and to understand the command of God the Creator as that under which the creature is placed and by which the creature's actions are determined. The leitmotif of the construction is the freedom of the creature, and Barth's exposition emerges formally from the theological anthropology in C.D. III,2. Here in C.D. III,4, the ethical explication of the creature's freedom before God (§53) corresponds to §44, "Man as the Creature of God"; the creature's freedom in fellowship (§54) corresponds to §45, "Man in His Determination as the Covenant-Partner of God"; the creature's freedom for life (§55) corresponds to §46, "Man as Soul and Body"; and the creature's freedom in limitation (§56) corresponds to §47, "Man in His Time." Barth's discussion in the present chapter is thus to be viewed as an effort to render explicit the particular human actions which are commanded and determined by God's act of creation as grounded in election, and which are concretely manifest in Jesus Christ as the elect human who as such is "Man for God," "Man for Other Men," "Whole Man" and "Lord of Time."[47]

It is important to observe that the chapter on the ethics of creation does not constitute a new beginning for theological ethics in Barth's dogmatic program. Rather it represents the beginning of a particularity and concreteness in ethical reflection which is itself grounded in and expressive of the general ethical reflection previously articulated in C.D. II,2. The prevailing orientation to Barth's ethics is determined by the fact that it understands the Word of God as God's command, and in our discussion of the ethics in C.D. II,2, we noted that this Word as command is God's claim, decision and judgment on the actions of humanity in

---

[46]For Barth's discussion of the ontic and noetic context of Das Nichtige, see especially C.D. III,3:302-12, 349-68. For their genesis in the doctrine of election, cf. C.D. II,2:145-94, 205-33, 259-305, 449-506.

[47]These representations of Jesus Christ constitute the point of departure in each of the four major sections in C.D. III,2 as entitled above. As such, these discussions make it clear that, for Barth, the ethical determinations of human existence are correlative to the humanity of Jesus Christ, and therefore to the origin, purpose and goal of God's election.

relation to God's gracious election. In *C.D. III,4*, Barth examines this command as it comes to the creature in his/her concrete existence and situation precisely as a creature, and evokes quite particular actions on his/her part in response. The ethics of creation presuppose the ethics of election not merely in the sense that the particular presupposes the general. Rather the presupposition consists in the fact that the God who commands obedience from the creature in quite specific actions is the God who is *known* in the Word, and therefore as the electing God and the elect human together, the God who as such is both Creator and creature, Reconciler and reconciled, Redeemer and redeemed. For Barth, the one abiding factor in all ethical reflection is the encounter between and history of God and the human in Jesus Christ. What this means in terms of ethics as part of the doctrine of creation is that there are particular spheres, constitutive of human existence, in which it is perceived in faith that God commands, and the creature is thereby placed in a position to respond in obedience or disobedience. As a form of special ethics deriving from and concretizing the ethical dimension of human reality as determined by God's election, the ethics of creation is concerned with the particularity of the creature's relation and response to God, to others and to him/herself.[48] Thus God's election of Jesus Christ is the ontic and noetic origin and determination of creation and the creature as well as the command which renders the creature a response-able human being.[49]

Under the command of God the Creator, human existence is an existence in freedom before God, i.e., existence in responsible relation to God in the covenant. This freedom consists in the creature's readiness for and renewal in the Gospel on the one hand, and his/her liberation for active participation in God's service on the other. It is this freedom that is enjoined in the command to honor the Sabbath, and the creature's response of obedience at this point takes the form of the renunciation of all arbitrary willing and doing which originates in and is determined by the creature's sinful and rebellious disposition.[50] Obedience in the freedom before God is expressed concretely in confession and prayer wherein one acknowledges and affirms God, and attests to others the faith of the community and his/her own participation in it.[51]

Under the command of God the Creator, human existence is an existence of freedom in fellowship, i.e., existence in responsible relation to others, existence as fellow-human. This freedom consists in the creature's being together with an other who is both like and unlike

---

[48]See *C.D. III,4*:3-31, and cf. *C.D. I,2*:782-96, 881-84, *C.D. II,2*:509-51.
[49]See *C.D. III,4*:38-46.
[50]See *C.D. III,4*:49-61.
[51]See *C.D. III,4*:73-115.

him/her in their shared humanity. Man and woman together are the image and likeness of God, and thus within the creaturely sphere they stand as the representation of the divine covenant in which one loves and therefore chooses an other. It is this freedom and participation that is enjoined in the command to be truly and wholly man or woman, and to live together as male and female. The creature's response of obedience takes the form of monogamous marriage in which one loves and therefore chooses an other. The order, structure and determination of this very human relation of marriage is itself reflective of the election of grace and the execution of the covenant. To be a human being is to be elect to participation in the covenant, and this election and covenant are the archetype to which marriage corresponds.[52]

Under the command of God the Creator, human existence is an existence in freedom for life, i.e., existence in responsible relation to self. This freedom consists in the creature's determination to be and to have life as God's gift for a particular purpose, to be a creature distinct from God and therefore to have a life of which the creature is the subject. It is the freedom to live and to be addressed by God that is enjoined in the command to be the subject of one's own life and to accept life as a gift and blessing to oneself and to others. The command to live and to accept life has its origin in the fact that God has become a creature in Jesus Christ, and this alone differentiates human being from the being of everything else. The creature's response of obedience takes the form of respect for life and the acknowledgement that life is an unmerited gift which must be cherished in all; it is obedience to the command which forbids the taking of another's life.[53] More to the point, however, is the fact that the creature's freedom to be is the freedom to have this being in activity. Obedience to the command to be and to honor life is expressed in an action which corresponds to the divine action, an action of service in which the creature places him/herself at God's disposal in and with the service of witness exercised by the Christian community. In the congruity of his/her own being and act, the creature is to reflect and serve the life of Jesus Christ as the elect human, and in this manner participate in the on-going work of God in the world. The creature is given the freedom to live and to continue in existence for the purpose of this active participation in the revealing and reconciling work of God.[54]

Finally, under the command of God the Creator, human existence

---

[52]See C.D. III,4:116-240, but especially pp. 195-99, 213-24, 232. This discussion more fully materializes what Barth stated earlier about man and woman together as the image and likeness of God. There, too, the discussion receives its orientation from the concept of election as participation in the divine covenant (cf. C.D. III,1:228-329 and C.D. III,2:222-324).

[53]See C.D. III,4:324-97.

[54]See especially C.D. III,4:470-86, 502-27. Cf. C.D. II,2:233-59, 410-49.

is an existence of freedom in limitation, i.e. existence in relation to time. This freedom consists in the conduct of life within the limits set by the span between birth and death. Rather than constrict or inhibit human life, the reality of this limit represents the particular opportunity given to the creature to enter into his/her own place and make his/her own choice *vis-a-vis* the election of God. It is this freedom that is enjoined in the command to acquiesce to the divinely willed determination and destiny of the unique human existence of the creature; it is the freedom to accept as right the place provided by the divine election and to live in this place in service; it is the freedom to fulfill one's predetermination within the limits of temporality in a manner which corresponds to that seen in the human existence of Jesus Christ.[55] More concretely, it is the freedom to know and do God's will as one's vocation in fulfillment of one's calling within the limits of what God has chosen for the creature. In the execution of the divine election, God calls the creature to obedience, i.e., to his/her own decision and act in correspondence to the divine decision and act. The vocation of the creature is the particular form taken by his/her life as it is lived in obedient response to his/her calling; it is the whole of the creature's existence, presupposed and engendered by his/her calling, and lived in obedience to, and therefore in fulfillment of, his/her election. The obedience in which this freedom is actualized will then be correlative to the unique place, age, circumstance and relations in which the creature finds him/herself, and will always manifest itself in the continued willingness to receive, accept and obey the choice of God which alone makes him/her free.[56]

E. Jesus Christ, the Lord as Servant (C.D. IV,1)

We turn now to the doctrine of reconciliation, and in its masterful (and unfinished) construction we encounter the pinnacle not only of Barth's dogmatics, but also of his view of election. What we find in *C.D. IV* is not a modest and straightforward doctrine of reconciliation in the usual sense, but rather a taxonomy which ranges across themes and matters not traditionally constitutive of the doctrine of reconciliation. We discover an extraordinary symmetry heretofore unseen in Barth's construction, a symmetry which cannot be dismissed as dogmatic reductionism without doing violence to the pastoral and theological concerns which underlie this part of the *C.D.* Barth's doctrine of reconciliation takes up the themes of election and expands them explicitly into the dogmatic spheres of christology, sin, soteriology and ecclesiology,

---

[55]See *C.D. III,4:565-80.*
[56]See *C.D. III,4:595-647,* especially pp. 595-610.

and the whole sweep and content of the doctrine of reconciliation can be seen to emerge formally and materially from the election executed and revealed in Jesus Christ. Like Barth, we can state at the outset a proposition which both contextualizes his discussion and indicates the course of the exposition: In the unity and differentiation of its moments, reconciliation is nothing less than the execution and fulfillment of God's election, and therefore God's self-revelation in Jesus Christ for humanity. Without Barth's prior construct of election, reconciliation (and creation as its material presupposition) could not and would not be grounded in the being and act of the gracious God who has revealed the divine self in Jesus Christ, for it is election that takes place and is revealed at the very center of reconciliation. To put it in other terms, we can say that Barth's construction of the doctrine of reconciliation emerges formally and materially from the following observations: (1) election is everywhere understood to be the being and act of God in *self-revelation* in Jesus Christ, and thereby *knowledge of God* is effected;[57] (2) as a result, the reality of Jesus Christ is the point of departure in the exposition of reconciliation in that he is himself the *execution and fulfillment of election;*[58] (3) what this means, therefore, is that God's eternal election is the *basis and presupposition* of reconciliation, and reconciliation is the *execution* of election in history.[59] On the basis of these observations, it is not at all a mystery why there is such frequent and explicit reference to election in the discussion of reconciliation in *C.D. IV,1.*[60]

In each of the first three part-volumes of *C.D. IV,* the discussion begins with a christological section in which Barth takes up one side of the incarnation, or the person and work of Jesus Christ, and moves out from there materially to the implications of this reality for our understanding of the reality of human sin, salvation, community and the

---

[57]This axiom which we have encountered over and over again throughout the *C.D.* continues to be woven into the discussion in the first part-volume of the doctrine of reconciliation in a most formative way. See e.g. *C.D. IV,1:*9-10, 34-37, 42, 44-54, 92-95, 117, 122-23, 170-71, 219, 240, 304-5, 344-45, 348-50, 354-57, 358-59, 389-91, 397-413, 478-79, 514-15, 548-49, 569, 650-51, 656.

[58]The centrality of Jesus Christ in Barth's discussion of reconciliation is indissolubly linked to the fact that his reality consists in the execution and fulfillment of election. See especially *C.D. IV,1:*18-21, 34-35, 44-45, 50, 67-78, 114-18, 122-28, 136-37, 158, 222-24, 228-59, 348-51, 358, 418, 432, 445, 458, 514-15, 549-50, 630, 635-37.

[59]For Barth at this point, it is manifestly a case in which the *terminus ad quo* of reconciliation is election, and the *terminus ad quem* of election is reconciliation. See the discussions at *C.D. IV,1:*3, 22-66, 92-95, 128-54, 177-210, 514-16, 528-68, 650-51.

[60]The emphasis here must be placed on the *explicit* reference to the themes and contours of election. The fact that the doctrine of election as a whole so thoroughly determines the doctrine of reconciliation is most evident at *C.D. IV,1:*9-10, 19, 34-35, 45, 50, 54-66, 95, 170-71, 174-75, 220-21, 235-38, 309, 350, 354-55, 408-10, 414-15, 489, 515-16, 532, 540-41, 563, 568, 594-95, 651, 669-71, 747.

individual. An examination of this movement exposes both the breadth of Barth's agenda as well as the substantive influence of his view of election.

In *C.D. IV,1*, the discussion of reconciliation as the divine being and act of Jesus Christ emerges from, and therefore corresponds to, the discussion in *C.D. II,2* concerning Jesus Christ as the electing God, i.e., God's election and self-determination for fellowship with humanity, God's becoming a human being in the human Jesus Christ and his submission to the divine judgment and rejection which the sin and disobedience of humanity merits. This is the act of election executed in Jesus Christ, and this is now understood as one moment in the act of reconciliation, namely the priestly work of Jesus Christ in the history of God with humanity and humanity with God. "Noetically, reconciliation is the history about Jesus Christ; ontically, it is Jesus Christ's own history."[61] In the light of election, God's act of reconciliation executed in the incarnation means the obedience of the Son of God to the Father, the condescension of the Son in becoming a human being, and the self-humiliation of Son in subjecting the divine self to the sinful condition of humanity and its consequences. "That God as God is able and willing and ready to condescend, to humble Himself in this way is the mystery of the 'deity of Christ'..."[62] The acting Subject in the human Jesus is thus God in the person of the Son,[63] and the purpose for which the Son became a human being in Jesus Christ is here the execution of divine judgment upon the sin of humanity. In Jesus Christ, God takes the place of sinful humanity in the event of judgment, taking the merited condemnation and rejection upon Godself and away from humanity. "And for this reason the incarnation of the Word means the judgment, the judgment of rejection and condemnation, which is passed on all flesh."[64] Reconciliation is thus God's making the human situation God's own in order to effect salvation; the electing God (Judge) in the elect human (judged) takes humanity's merited rejection (judgment) upon the divine self in order that humanity might be restored to fellowship with God in fulfillment of the covenantal decree (reconciliation).[65] The very heart of election viewed from this angle, and

---

[61]*C.D. IV,1*:158. Translation mine. It is unfortunate that the English translators of *C.D. IV* have taken the liberty of rather uniformly translating *Versöhnung* as "atonement." This has conjured an inappropriately narrow understanding of Barth's rich and complex notion of reconciliation and resulted merely in exposing the theological prejudice of the translators.

[62]*C.D. IV,1*:177. See also pp. 164, 170-75, 183-86, 192-207.

[63]The preeminence of God as the acting Subject in the reconciliation accomplished in the God-human Jesus Christ is decisive for Barth's construction of both christology and reconciliation as such. See especially *C.D. IV,1*:12, 18-21, 183, 197-99, 207-10, 222-23, 552, 555, 560-61, 564.

[64]*C.D. IV,1*:220.

[65]See *C.D. IV,1*:211-17. The discussion of "The Judge Judged in Our Place" (pp. 228-

therefore the very heart of reconciliation in its christological form, is God's victory over sin in the death of Jesus Christ on behalf of all humanity.

A particular anthropology emerges from this christology, and the transition to the former is signaled ontically and noetically by the resurrection of Jesus Christ which Barth understands as the divine acceptance and acknowledgement of the obedience of Jesus Christ. In the resurrection as a new and separate act of God, there is actualized first and foremost the self-justification of God, i.e., the establishment and confirmation of God's love, grace, righteousness and honor in God's self-determination to be and act as the electing God who chooses Godself for fellowship with humanity. But as a result, there is also actualized the justification of the human Jesus Christ who in obedience subjected himself to divine rejection and judgment of the cross, satisfying the righteousness of that judgment merited by humanity. The fact that he is raised from the dead to a new life means that the passing and death of the old humanity and the coming and life of the new humanity are the manifestation of the two sides of the one event of election, and therefore the accomplishment of reconciliation for all in this one human being. The resurrection, therefore, is the disclosure of the justification of sinful humanity. The crucifixion and resurrection of the human Jesus mean that in this One and at this place, the fundamental determination of humanity by the election of God is realized and disclosed: "This verdict is therefore both the ontic and also the noetic--first the ontic and then the noetic--basis of our being--not outside but in Jesus Christ as the elected Head of the whole race--but of our own being and to that extent of our being with Him and side by side with Him."[66] Ontically, and therefore noetically, this one human being is the prototype of all human being, and his history (living, dying under the judgment on sin, and rising in justification to new life) is the prototype of human history determined in God's eternal decree of election.

From the exposition of his electional christology, Barth moves to the consideration of the sin from which humanity is saved in the reconciliation accomplished in Jesus Christ. As a result of the resurrection of Jesus Christ, it is the obedience of the Son in the Son's humiliation and condescension that exposes a form of human sinfulness and its consequences, a form which takes a contradistinctive shape *vis-a-vis* the humanity of Jesus Christ. It is only in the knowledge of the election and therefore the reconciliation accomplished in him that there

---

73 emphasizes the *Deus pro nobis* which in this context corresponds to the "in him" of the doctrine of election.

[66]*C.D. IV,1:355.* See also pp. 304-17, 348-57.

is knowledge of sin.[67] The obedience of the Son in the human Jesus exhibits the fact that human sin is pride in the form of disobedience and unbelief in which the human being rejects God as the source and determination of his/her life. Humanity exalts itself over against God, denying God as it attempts to be its own judge and seeking to help, support and define itself on its own self-serving terms. The self-exalting and lordly action of humanity in this form of sin is the opposite of the humble and servant action of the human Jesus.[68] The fact is, however, that this sinful attempt at self-determination results in humanity's fall, and therefore its coming under the judgment and rejection of God: "It is the threat of divine rejection into the shadow of which man moves when he sins and becomes guilty, which he evokes when in his misery and pride he sets himself in contradiction to the good will of God."[69] Nevertheless, the execution and fulfillment of reconciliation in Jesus Christ signifies that it is precisely this humanity which is chosen by God for fellowship in the fact that it is this humanity which God takes upon Godself in the incarnation. Election means that no one falls so far as to be outside the will and reach of God's decision to have humanity as God's covenant partner.[70]

With this understanding of the sin and sinner who have come under the divine judgment in the human Jesus Christ, Barth moves to the doctrine of justification in which he considers the implications of this particular divine action, and the peculiar form taken by reconciliation with respect to humanity. Justification is the right of God which sets aside the wrong of humanity and places humanity in the right. In relation to humanity's wrong, this divine right is judgment. But the goal of this judgment is the overthrow of humanity's sin and its restoration to fellowship. In the judgment executed in Jesus Christ, God affirms and maintains Godself as the One who has elected the divine self for humanity and humanity for the divine self by putting to death the old humanity and raising up the new humanity to life; God severs the creature from its sin, and restores it to its divine determination. Thus it is election, and not rejection, that stands as the *telos* of judgment.[71] Because this constitutes the direction of God's judgment executed in Jesus Christ, it means the forgiveness and pardon of sinful humanity, i.e., its justification in the positive will of God. There is now the one and only real future, for a transition has been made by God in the life of the human being as he/she hears and receives God's self-revelation in Jesus

---

[67]See the discussions at *C.D. IV,1*:358-59, 389-413.
[68]See *C.D. IV,1*:413-78.
[69]*C.D. IV,1*:489. See also pp. 492-513.
[70]See especially *C.D. IV,1*:478-89.
[71]See *C.D. IV,1*:528-68.

Christ.[72] This justification is by faith alone, and what Barth means by this is that it is a divinely-enabled human action in which there is achieved a correspondence to the human action of Jesus Christ; it is a genuine *imitatio Christi* in which the human being and act of Jesus Christ is reflected. Faith is the determined response to Jesus Christ, the unequivocal response of humility and obedience, submitting wholly to the election of God revealed in him, and therefore an absolute dependence on and bondage to his life as a human being. Faith is one form of the human response in which the election executed *in him* is fulfilled in the individual.[73]

To this point in his exposition, Barth has been dealing with the objective reality of reconciliation. This is followed by the final two sections in which he takes up the matter of the subjective realization of reconciliation, and therefore election, first in the community as such and then in the life of the individual, a pattern in keeping with his progression in the doctrine of election. The subjectivity of reconciliation is the point where the active participation of humanity in the divine being and act comes to the front. For Barth, reconciliation is realized subjectively in the work of the Holy Spirit as the presence of the risen Jesus Christ and therefore the eternal fellowship between the Father and the Son. The Holy Spirit is the self-communication and self-attestation of Jesus Christ whose role it is to effect in the human being the response of obedience. In the execution of election, the awakening by the Holy Spirit is the divine effect on proud and fallen humanity whose rejection and judgment were taken on and away by the Son of God in the human Jesus of Nazareth. It is the Holy Spirit who gathers the community in history, infuses it with the eternal life decreed by God and constitutes it as the earthly-historical form of Jesus Christ's existence. In its corporate correspondence to Jesus Christ and as the community who is gathered by and participates in him, the Church in the world is (1) a unity, and therefore singular even as Jesus Christ is a unity in his divinity and humanity, and God is a unity as Father, Son and Holy Spirit; (2) holy, and thus particular in its differentiation from the world which surrounds it, deriving its holiness from its Head in whose life it participates; (3) catholic, and therefore steadfast, comprehensive and universal, always and everywhere the same in its essence in spite of its changing temporal forms; and (4) apostolic, and therefore in continuity with the reception and passing on of the original and determinative witness to the reality of God's being and act in Jesus Christ.[74] The fact that the being of the Church can be described in this way rests upon the premise that it exists

---

[72]See *C.D. IV,1*:568-608.
[73]See *C.D. IV,1*:609-42.
[74]See *C.D. IV,1*:643-725.

on this side of the crucifixion and resurrection of Jesus Christ as both the environment of the elect human and as the medium in and through which his self-revelation and election are extended out into the world.

The subjective realization of reconciliation in the individual is described by Barth in this first part of the doctrine in terms deriving from the fulfillment of election in the individual articulated in *C.D. II,2*. He speaks here of faith as an ontic and noetic determination of the individual in relation to the reconciliation accomplished objectively in Jesus Christ. As noted earlier, faith is belief and obedience in which the action of the individual is an *imitatio Christi*. Here, in relation to the deity of the obedient Son incarnate in the human Jesus who takes humanity's merited rejection upon himself, thus effecting the divine and human justification, the corresponding human response is that of faith, understood as an orientation of the human subject to Jesus Christ as the object of faith who awakens the individual and constitutes him/her as a subject in conformity with his eternal election.[75] More importantly in Barth's estimation, however, is the fact that faith is a human act which is noetically determined by the election of God to be that act in which the individual perceives, confirms and repeats in his/her own life the decision of God by which God's justification and reconciliation are accomplished. Barth therefore speaks of faith as the human act of knowledge which consists in (1) acknowledgement as the response to the encounter with the witness of the community, and therein as an obedient confirmation of his/her divine determination; (2) recognition as the awareness that the object of the witness and proclamation of the community is in fact the authentic humanity of Jesus Christ who is and acts for the individual; and (3) confession as the individual's own witness, as the human act in which God's reconciliation (and therefore God's election) is continually proclaimed in human language in order to effect an encounter with the One who now lives in and through the spatio-temporal reality of the community.[76] In short, faith is the knowledge of God actualized in and determined by the fulfillment of the individual's election, a knowledge which has as its *telos* the witness of the individual to the election decreed and executed in Jesus Christ.

F. Jesus Christ, The Servant as Lord (C.D. IV,2)

Barth now takes up the second moment in reconciliation from the standpoint of the work of Jesus Christ as very human, the Son of Man. Here again we find this reality grounded in the being and act of God in

---

[75]See *C.D. IV,1*:740-57.
[76]See *C.D. IV,1*:757-79.

the execution of the election which constitutes the center of reconciliation. And again, the discussion emerges formally and materially from three key dimensions articulated in the doctrine of election, namely (1) election is God's self-revelation which effects the knowledge of God,[77] (2) Jesus Christ is the execution and fulfillment of election,[78] and therefore (3) election is the basis and presupposition of reconciliation, and reconciliation is the execution of election.[79] At every turn in Barth's discussion in *C.D. IV,2*, there is explicit reference to the fact that election is the essential determination of what is to be said regarding reconciliation.[80]

In *C.D. IV,2*, Barth's discussion emerges from and corresponds to the discussion of Jesus Christ as the elect human in *C.D. II,2*, i.e., the humanity of Jesus Christ as the other partner in the covenant, the one who is the other object in God's election, determined for fellowship with God. This moment in reconciliation is understood as the kingly work of the human Jesus Christ, and Barth takes up this moment as it is executed in the incarnation in which human nature is taken up by and to God. Viewed from the humanity of Jesus Christ, the incarnation can be seen to be grounded in God's election which has determined humanity for upward movement to God. Jesus' humanity, therefore, has its basis in the divine election, and it consists in his exaltation as a human being. In Barth's view, this exaltation is the human reality accomplished in reconciliation.[81]

As God's act, election has its historical fulfillment in the incarnation. It is the divine act in which the being and act of the human Jesus are grounded, and as such it speaks to the determination of all humanity. Incarnation means that God the Son took human being and essence upon the divine self, exalting the *humanum* of all to unity and fellowship with Godself, and thereby effecting the determination of what it means to be human. In the concrete life of Jesus of Nazareth, the Son became a human being without ceasing to be God, so that the Son has reality in the union and mutual participation of the divine and human natures. That which the Son has in common with the Father and the Spirit is united with that which Jesus has in common with humanness,

---

[77] For the manner in which this revelation and knowledge determines the discussion, see *C.D. IV,2*:26, 31-32, 36-40, 101, 116-54, 294-300, 318-19, 331, 340-41, 345, 379-84, 397-400, 403, 409, 415, 499, 518-19, 522, 534, 570, 579-82, 620, 651, 654, 729-30, 756-61.

[78] See especially *C.D. IV,2*:19, 21, 28-29, 96, 117, 292, 318, 345, 380-81, 409-10, 432-33, 452, 467-68, 483-85, 490-97, 499-502, 507, 514, 518-19, 523, 553, 581-82, 598-600, 620.

[79] See especially *C.D. IV,2*:20-21, 31-36, 505, 511-33, 766-71.

[80] See *C.D. IV,2*:6, 31-36, 47-49, 84, 87-91, 96, 117, 241-42, 300, 318, 345-46, 381-82, 410, 452, 494-95, 515-16, 579, 588, 593, 600, 604-5, 642-43, 727-31, 759-60, 766-71, 777, 789-95.

[81] See the discussion on the presupposition of election at *C.D. IV,2*:31-36.

and this union means both the condescension of God the Son and the exaltation of human being. This union is not static, but active and dynamic, for it has as its origin, execution and goal the restoration and exaltation of human being to fellowship with God. In this human Jesus, this exalted human being, this object chosen by God for union, it is God the Son who has this being, and who therefore stands as the acting Subject in the life of this individual.[82] The reality of this God-human is thus the manifestation of the fact that human being is determined in and by God's election to be and act in union with God.[83]

The fact that this divine and human being and act is, and is known as such, is based on the contention that election is identical with incarnation/revelation. Barth states that "the only source of the knowledge of the eternal will of God is the knowledge of His act fulfilled in time, and therefore the fact of the existence of Jesus Christ as the Son of God and Son of Man."[84] Election (and therefore reconciliation) has a subjective character in that it establishes itself noetically in the knowing subject. This element of the incarnation addresses the resurrection in which is revealed the divinity and humanity of Jesus Christ on the one hand, and therefore the humiliation of the Son and the exaltation of humanity on the other:

> His death on the cross was and is the fulfilment of the incarnation of the Word and therefore the humiliation of the Son of God and exaltation of the Son of Man.... The resurrection and ascension of Jesus Christ are the completed revelation of Jesus Christ which corresponds to His completed work.[85]

In his spatio-temporal reality as the new and true human being, Jesus Christ is the One who encounters others and demands from them the decision which he himself is and has made. In this activity, he exists as a reflection of the divine work in the execution of the purpose of election, i.e., he is with and for others. Jesus' life as a human being is therefore to be understood as his history in which his peculiar human

---

[82]For Barth's contention that, even from the 'very human' side of the incarnation, the Son of God is and always remains the acting Subject in the human essence of the human Jesus, see especially *C.D. IV*,2:28, 44-51, 61-63, 69-71, 84, 90.

[83]See Barth's discussion of the fulfillment of reconciliation in the incarnation at *C.D. IV*,2:36-116.

[84]*C.D. IV*,2:119.

[85]*C.D. IV*,2:140-41. This passage appears within Barth's discussion of the resurrection/ascension as the single reality which both confirms and reveals the deity and humanity of Jesus Christ in accordance with its eternal pre-determination (pp. 117-54).

being is expressed and confirmed in his act. Furthermore, this human being-in-act is characterized as a self-actualization and self-impartation which consists in the movement from his origin to the fulfillment of his destiny. In Jesus Christ, it is manifest that humanity is destined for this same movement.[86]

Again, a particular anthropology is implicit in this christology, and Barth extricates it by examining the transition which moves from the One in whom humanity is exalted to the humanity which is exalted in him. Jesus' human being is an ontological reality in which human being as such is included, and therefore exalted in him. As his death is the goal of his existence, the reality and signification of the passing of the old sinful humanity, so his resurrection is the accomplishment and revelation of the new determination and beginning which is decreed in election. In Jesus' resurrection there is disclosed the royal human in whom is actualized the reality of divine-human communion, and therefore the authentic expression of the divinely enabled transition from his being and act to the being and act of others. In Jesus' own history, there is to be seen the will of the Father executed in the life and history of the Son of Man, and thus the presence of God in human history, actualizing the purpose of the divine election. The application of this reality to the life of others is the particular work of God the Holy Spirit, and it consists in the ordering of human being by giving it direction to the place where it can begin to live authentically in its divinely determined freedom, correction in the differentiation between real freedom and the ostentatious freedom of the old humanity, and instruction in which the use of this freedom for the will of God issues in obedience and positive action.[87]

Barth moves from this electional christology to the consideration of the form of sin from which humanity is saved in the execution of reconciliation in Jesus Christ. Here it is the exaltation and lordship of the Son of Man which exposes human sin in its inevitability and universality.[88] In the light of the exaltation of the true and royal human who hears and receives God, lives with and for others, is at peace with himself in the unity of his soul and body, and gives up himself to God and humanity, human sin is understood as disobedience and unbelief in the form of sloth, i.e., foolishness in the rejection of God's gracious gift, inhumanity in the hostility toward and isolation from others, dissipation in the waste and neglect of one's self, and apprehension in the futile attempt to secure and protect one's life.[89] This form of self-determination is false and

---

[86]See *C.D.* *IV*,2:154-247 in Barth's discussion of "The Royal Man."
[87]See the section on "The Direction of the Son" at *C.D.* *IV*,2:264-377.
[88]See "The Man of Sin in the Light of the Lordship of the Son of Man" at *C.D.* *IV*,2:378-403.
[89]See "The Sloth of Man," *C.D.* *IV*,2:403-83.

results in the misery of an inauthentic existence in exile. It is a diseased life from which humanity cannot cure itself, and its grievous and mortal outcome is certain. The activity of such a miserable life expresses the old being effectively displaced by the new and royal human Jesus Christ, and in this old life, human will is bound in the non-freedom of inability to do otherwise.[90] As a result of sin in the form of sloth, misery marks the discontinuity with and contradiction to the being and act of the one who lives in Jesus Christ and therefore in the fulfillment of election.

With this view of the sin and sinner set aside by the exalted Son of Man, Barth turns to sanctification as the divine effect upon the humanity exalted in and with Jesus Christ. In relation to justification, sanctification is the effect of conversion and transformation, the real transition from the old to the new, the fulfillment of election. Because of Jesus Christ, justification and sanctification have taken place *de jure* for all, i.e., each and every human being is elect. But this *de jure* reconciliation is *de facto* only in the event in which particular human beings actually have been and are converted and transformed by the Holy Spirit, i.e., all do not live in the knowledge and fulfillment of their election. "*De facto*, however, it is not known by all men, just as justification has not *de facto* been grasped and acknowledged and known and confessed by all men, but only by those who are awakened to faith."[91] The difference between the two is the difference between *not yet* and *no longer*, and those who are transformed and liberated to conformity to Jesus Christ in the new life of obedience and faith are the once rejected who now live in the fulfillment of their eternal election. They are the saints who now actively participate in the accomplished election of Jesus Christ. Reconciliation in its moment of sanctification is the *participatio Christi*.[92] This sanctification places one under a new determination, and it is effected as awakening and conversion by the Holy Spirit in the call in which the exalted royal human Jesus Christ is revealed, a call which commands and enables obedience to discipleship and bondage to the person of Jesus Christ. Sanctification is the determination of human existence in which it continually is and acts in the transformation and transition from the old to the new.[93] In the power and determination of the Spirit, the activity of the sanctified conforms to and participates in the revealing and reconciling activity of God, thereby confirming and expressing both the electing being and act of God as well as the elected being and act of

---

[90]See "The Misery of Man," *C.D. IV,2*:483-98.
[91]*C.D. IV,2*:511.
[92]This *participatio* is the essential motif developed in the section "The Holy One and the Saints" at *C.D. IV,2*:511-33.
[93]Here we view synoptically the subsection "The Call to Discipleship" and "The Awakening to Conversion" at *C.D. IV,2*:533-84.

humanity.[94]

In the last two sections of *C.D. IV,2*, Barth considers the subjective realization of reconciliation as sanctification in the community and the individual. In its corporate expression, sanctification is the upbuilding of the Christian community, i.e., its extensive and intensive enlargement, its preservation from external and internal threat, and its order of life in worship, service, discipline and interrelations. The community is the true Church to the extent that it consists of those who are awakened, transformed and empowered by the Spirit in its service and attestation to the reconciliation accomplished in Jesus Christ from whom it derives its life. It exists authentically as the earthly-historical form of his existence in the event of the fellowship of divine service, and therefore as the provisional representation *de facto* of the *de jure* sanctification of all humanity in Jesus Christ.[95] In short, the community participates in the election of Jesus Christ in so far as it has its being and activity in the fulfillment of its election, serving in the power of his Spirit as the extended medium of the revelation and actualization of his election.

The subjective realization of sanctification in the individual is described by Barth in terms which derive from the fulfillment of individual election described in *C.D. II,2*. In the present context, the execution of election means that the individual's life consists in a definite action, namely the decision to follow the direction prescribed by Jesus Christ's election. On the basis of the reception of faith in justification, the individual now lives and acts in the confirmation of election, and the particular form which this new act takes is love, i.e., the giving of one's self in correspondence to the divine self-giving. It is the act in which the individual freely turns away from him/herself toward an other purely for the sake of the other, and gives to the other that on which there is no claim. Barth states: "As this self-giving, the Christian love which is from God is man's response to God's own love. It is in this way that God loves man. He does not seek Himself, let alone anything for Himself, but simply man, man as he is and as such, man himself."[96] The free action of love is based in, and therefore a participation in, the being and act of God as the One who loves in freedom. God's love is electing, purifying and creating love which in grace evokes in the individual the response of love directed toward God, others and self. As response in which the electing God and one's election are confirmed, love is a genuine action of the human subject, a quite specific and determined action which is radically new, freely volitional, self-giving and exalting. As a divinely

---

[94] See *C.D. IV,2*:584-98 for Barth's discussion of "The Praise or Works."

[95] See §67, "The Holy Spirit and the Upbuilding of the Christian Community" at *C.D. IV,2*:614-726.

[96] *C.D. IV,2*:750.

enabled human action, grounded in the election of God in Jesus Christ, love is the determination which corresponds to the sanctification of the individual.[97]

G. Jesus Christ, The True Witness (C.D. IV,3)

The form and progression of the construction in *C.D. IV,3* corresponds to that found in the first two parts of the doctrine of reconciliation which dealt with the material dimension of the reconciling work accomplished in Jesus Christ. The agenda in *C.D. IV,3* brings this material work to its final zenith by taking up directly the manner in which the objective reality of the justification and sanctification accomplished in Jesus Christ is revealed to and fulfilled in human existence. This revelation and fulfillment is identical with reconciliation, and for this reason the discussion in *C.D. IV,3* can be viewed as the answer to the question regarding how it comes about that God is known in Jesus Christ and what this knowledge entails for human being and act. Or to put it in other words, how it is that election comes to be fulfilled in human life and what this means for human being and action. The discussion is directly concerned with the actualization of the knowledge of, transition to and participation in the being and act of Jesus Christ as the electing God and the elect human. As in the case of the first two parts, so it is also a case here that the construction emerges from and is determined by the doctrine of election. This is evident in the three postulates which here too inform the discussion, namely (1) election is God's self-revelation and therefore the actualization of the knowledge of God,[98] (2) the point of departure for the doctrine of reconciliation is the reality of Jesus Christ as the execution and fulfillment of election,[99] and for this reason (3) election is the basis and presupposition of reconciliation and reconciliation is the execution of election.[100] The development of these postulates in *C.D. IV,3* requires the constant and explicit reference to election, and in particular to its ontic and noetic determination.[101]

---

[97]See §68, "The Holy Spirit amd Christian Love" at *C.D. IV,2*:727-840.

[98]See especially *C.D. IV,3.1*:8-9, 38-39, 45-49, 52, 71, 81-85, 96-113, 154-63, 165, 180-97, 211-31, 261-74, 279-84, 290-91, 296-301, 314-22, 368-71, 376-97, 410-12, *C.D. IV,3.2*:497-520, 536-37, 650-51, 658-62, 710-12, 751-52, 769-70, 784-95, 802-12, 852, 903, 915.

[99]See *C.D. IV,3.1*:3-5, 8, 11, 38-86, 105-10, 165, 173, 183, 211, 213-14, 216-17, 221, 239, 274-75, 278-79, 282, 297, 314-15, 378-79, 388, 411-12, 440, 475, *C.D. IV,3.2*:497, 605-6, 634, 642, 724, 728, 797, 831, 903, 915.

[100]See especially *C.D. IV,3.1*:3-4, 227, *C.D. IV,3.2*:483-90.

[101]See *C.D. IV,3.1*:3-4, 49, 69-70, 81-82, 105-6, 227, 278, 282, 302, 315-16, 354-55, 372-73, 390-91, 413, 442, 447, 464, *C.D. IV,3.2*:534-37, 638, 647-48, 665, 712, 724, 727-29, 737-38, 743, 751-54, 777-78, 809, 826, 932-33.

The christological discussion which opens this third part emerges from the discussion in *C.D. II,2* wherein the being together of this electing God and this elect human in Jesus Christ is the execution and revelation of the covenant fellowship of mutual relatedness between God and an other. "In Him God is the One who graciously elects man and man is the one who is graciously elected by God. He is the actualisation of the covenant between God and man, both on the side of God and also on that of man."[102] This is reconciliation in its third moment. And furthermore: "Revelation takes place in and with reconciliation. Indeed, the latter is also revelation. As God acts in it, He also speaks."[103] This means that God is the acting Subject in this event of reconciliation and revelation executed in Jesus Christ,[104] and therefore his divine-human life is the disclosure of being in act, i.e., in personal self-actualization which is at the same time self-manifestation.[105] This is what Barth means by the statement that, as the God-human, Jesus lives for humanity as the preeminent Subject of salvation history, and on this basis speaks of and for himself as his own Witness. His very eternal and spatio-temporal reality is thus the reality of his *Light, Name, Revelation, Truth* and *Life-act*.[106] The identity of reconciliation and revelation, and therefore the identity of election and revelation/incarnation, is the self-authenticating reality of Jesus Christ in which is perceived God's own presence and action in the establishment of the covenant. This event constitutes the prophetic work of Jesus Christ: "His prophecy is the direct self-declaration of His life of grace and salvation, of the life of the God who has condescended to man and of the man exalted to God. It is the revelation of His life in the fulfillment of the act of reconciliation."[107] Jesus Christ alone is the one true, full and definitive Word of God who reveals God to humanity; this is who he is and what he does in the prophetic aspect of his threefold work in the execution of reconciliation, i.e., in the execution of election.[108]

As revelation, the life of Jesus Christ is a history which has its own beginning, direction and goal, a history which encounters and overcomes the opposition of ignorance by mediating a knowledge of himself, thereby effecting an event which impinges on all of history and advances toward

---

[102] *C.D. IV,3.1*:4.
[103] *C.D. IV,3.1*:8.
[104] See especially *C.D. IV,3.1*:40-41, 79, 160-61, *C.D. IV,3.2*:501-5, 791.
[105] On the identity of Jesus Christ's divine-human being and act in the event of revelation and reconciliation, see especially *C.D. IV,3.1*:40-41, 46-47, 216-17, 274-75, 376-77.
[106] See *C.D. IV,3.1*:39-49.
[107] *C.D. IV,3.1*:52.
[108] See *C.D. IV,3.1*:96-113, 154-64.

the victory and fulfillment of God's purpose in election. The noetic aspect of this reality is grounded in the *prius* of its ontic aspect; reconciliation here implies the knowledge of its origin and goal as a consequence in the execution and movement of election from the *illic et tunc* of Jesus Christ's history to the *hic et nunc* of present human history. The course of this event of revelation sets the world in a new light wherein it is seen as having been reconciled to God. Though the world may oppose this reality and knowledge, it cannot finally succeed because it is the unconditional reality and knowledge of the Word of God, i.e., of Jesus Christ who is himself the being and act of God in self-giving to humanity.[109]

The transition from the person and work of Jesus Christ to the being and action of humanity effected in his prophetic work is again the movement to a particular anthropology implicit in this christology. Once again it is the resurrection that marks this transition. In the present context, the Easter event is the single and irrevocable self-revelation of God in which God demonstrates God's union and commitment to humanity, and as such it stands as the total, universal and definitive determination of humanity as God's covenant partner. Jesus' resurrection is the beginning of his coming again, as the age of the Church is its continuation and the final appearing is its concrete consummation. What is encountered in the resurrection is "a divine noetic which has all the force of a divine ontic. He has spoken in acting. Hence He has spoken unequivocally, once for all and irrevocably."[110] Human time following this event is the time of the advance and fulfillment of reconciliation, now actualized in and through the power of the Holy Spirit as the contemporary presence and action of Jesus Christ. It is the work of the Holy Spirit to effect in human beings the subjective realization which corresponds to the objective reality of reconciliation accomplished in the God-human Jesus Christ. The promise of the Spirit is that the final appearing of Jesus Christ and the consummation of reconciliation is certain for those who know him. For those who do not yet know him but have been so determined, it is to be expected that this promise holds true for them and that the present reality of reconciliation is their determination as well. In short, the determination of humanity in the election of Jesus Christ is to *know and experience* the fulfillment of election.[111]

This electional christology gives rise to the knowledge and

---

[109]See "Jesus is Victor", *C.D.* *IV,3.1*:165-274.
[110]*C.D.* *IV,3.1*:297.
[111]See the transition discussion "The Promise of The Spirit" at *C.D.* *IV,3.1*:274-367. For Barth's discussion of the universality of this ontic and noetic determination (election *de jure*, or the "not yet" of fulfillment) and the transition therefrom to its actualization in the Spirit (election *de facto*, or the "already" of fulfillment), see especially *C.D.* *IV,3.1*:278, 283-84, 353-54, 477-78, *C.D.* *IV,3.2*:493-94, 534-37, 604-5, 658, 801-12, 850-52.

understanding of a particular form of human sin as well as the human sinner on whose behalf the prophetic work of Jesus Christ is undertaken. In this regard, Jesus Christ is the true witness who exposes the falsehood and untruth embraced by humanity. As a first and basic response to his/her encounter of God's self-revelation in Jesus Christ, the human being attempts to evade, obstruct and otherwise reject the divine truth by offering a fraudulent and contradictory truth in its place. He/she opposes the truth that Jesus Christ is the one authentic and free human being who exists in true relationship to God, and for this reason may accuse and condemn inauthentic humanity. He/she denies that the form of Jesus Christ's true witness is his reality as the suffering and crucified servant who is himself the Son of God for humanity. He/she closes his/her ears to the word of reconciliation spoken by Jesus Christ in the victory of his resurrection, and refuses to acknowledge that Jesus Christ is himself the truth in his being and action. This sinful action calls only for the condemnation of the sinner, a condemnation which is held up only by the grace and love of God. In short, the sin of humanity is that it does not and will not know the full reality of its election accomplished in Jesus Christ, and for this reason, it stands under the threat of rejection. The knowledge and the removal of this threat is what is realized in the fulfillment of election.[112]

Barth now moves to the discussion of vocation as the implication of the divine action in Jesus Christ. The one who lives in falsehood and condemnation is now the one who lives in the execution of the calling given in election. Barth describes vocation as

> ... the event in which man is set and instituted in actual fellowship with Jesus Christ, namely, in the service of His prophecy, in the *ministerium Verbi divini*, of the Word of reconciliation, and therefore in the service of God and his fellow-man.[113]

The event of vocation is nothing less than the execution of revelation which effects the knowledge of God. As such, it indicates the historic, spiritual and personal conversion of the sinner. As the encounter with Jesus Christ, it is the noetic illumination, new creation and awakening of the individual on the basis of the ontic determination of election.[114] The goal of this encounter, effected in its event, is the actuality of the knowledge of and fellowship with Jesus Christ, i.e., Christian existence as one who belongs to and lives obediently with Jesus Christ. It is human

---

[112]See "The Falsehood and Condemnation of Man" at *C.D. IV,3.1*:368–478.
[113]*C.D. IV,3.2*:482.
[114]See "The Event of Vocation" at *C.D. IV,3.2*:497-520.

existence lived in the union of Jesus Christ with the human being, and the human being with Jesus Christ, a union in which Jesus Christ speaks, acts and rules and the human being accepts and affirms this speaking, acting and ruling.[115] In particular, vocation is human existence lived in the execution of the task of witness laid upon the Christian by the election of God; it is his/her being and act in participation with the prophetic being and act of Jesus Christ in salvation history. Vocation is the transition to the service of attesting to others the divine self-revelation executed in reconciliation, and therefore in the fulfillment of election.[116] Thus the vocation of the Christian is the liberation of being for action, the transition from the old and passing life to the new and coming life in and with Jesus Christ.[117]

In the final two sections of *C.D. IV,3* Barth returns to the community and the individual, and both in the light of the subjective realization of reconciliation in its distinctive noetic dimension. To the Christian community is given the task of mission to the world, and for this purpose it is commissioned and sent out into the world. As such, this community is part of the world, having its own history in the world's history. On the basis of the revelation executed in reconciliation, the Christian community knows and can interpret the world as the object and recipient of its witness. Corresponding to Jesus Christ, the community is visible and invisible, dependent and independent, weak and strong, in its worldly reality and the execution of its service. This community is called into existence by Jesus Christ in the power of the Holy Spirit, and it therefore lives as he lives, i.e., in the discharge of its task of witness.[118] It exists to the extent that it knows the world as God's, and knows it in both its present and intended character as the object of God's creation and reconciliation. As those sent, the community therefore stands in solidarity with and under obligation to the world as those who are elect, but do not yet live in its fulfillment.[119] As it exists in the world, and yet is a new and radically distinct reality which does not emerge from the world, the Christian community has its being and action in the obligation to confess

---

[115]See "The Goal of Vocation" at *C.D. IV,3.2*:520-54.

[116]See "The Christian as Witness" at *C.D. IV,3.2*:554-614. Barth's discussion of "The Christian in Affliction" (pp. 614-47) bears upon the extent to which the Christian as such participates in the suffering and rejection of Jesus Christ. This participation takes the form of Christian suffering as the reflection of and likeness to his passion, and results from the compulsion to be and act as a witness to the election of God realized in Jesus Christ. As such, it is genuine human suffering, but not an existential reality which effects the transformation of reconciliation or cancels its fulfillment, i.e., it is not rejection (cf. *C.D. IV,2*:598-613).

[117]See "The Liberation of the Christian" at *C.D. IV,3.2*:647-80.

[118]See "The People of God in World-Occurence" at *C.D. IV,3.2*:681-762.

[119]See "The Community for the World" at *C.D. IV,3.2*:762-95.

and proclaim the person and work of Jesus Christ to those for whom this Gospel is intended, to those who are yet ignorant, disobedient and disbelieving. Their task is to witness to the election executed and revealed in Jesus Christ, and fulfilled in their own lives.[120]

In the last section of the doctrine, Barth speaks of the individual in terms of hope as the effect of the prophetic work of Jesus Christ. In the fulfillment of reconciliation as the knowledge of God, hope marks the awareness that the work of Jesus Christ is not yet completed and that his *parousia* has not yet taken place in its fullness. Hope is the secure and inescapable knowledge and expectation that the work of election will be consummated; as surely as faith knows and is bound to the *already* of his resurrection, as surely as love marks the *even now* of his presence, just as surely does hope hold to and live in the knowledge of the *not yet* of the final manifestation of Jesus Christ. He and he alone is the object of the Christian's hope, and therefore the basis, content and goal of the subjective appropriation of hope as the human determination of life in the service of witness. Hope therefore is the quite particular and forward-looking determination of the individual as a member of the Christian community who encounters others as recipients of the Gospel message. In this hope which has its origin in God, there is freedom from worldly optimism and pessimism in an action which is oriented toward participating in God's election and reconciliation here and now, in spite of the obfuscation which characterizes the world's own articulated future and the dubious and contradictory determination it gives to itself. Life in this hope results from the work of the Holy Spirit who awakens the Christian to freedom, and thrusts him/her into a speaking and acting existence in the space and time between Jesus Christ as the finally coming One and those to whom it has not yet been given to know him.[121]

H. Final Observations

The way from *C.D. II,2* to *C.D. IV,3* is far more sumptuous and extraordinary in both its expanse and detail than what can be represented here in the space of several dozen pages.[122] Nevertheless, for those who

---

[120]See "The Task of the Community" at *C.D. IV,3.2:795-830*. In the discussion of "The Ministry of the Community" which follows (pp. 830-901), Barth enumerates the various forms of the community's ministry of speaking and acting as the proclamation, interpretation and application of the reality of Jesus Christ to itself and to the world. As such, these forms are quite definite and limited by the specific nature of the witnessing task given in the execution of its election.

[121]See the two short sub-sections in §73, "The Holy Spirit and Christian Hope" at *C.D. IV,3.2:902-42*.

[122]The expected volume on ethics which would have completed the doctrine of

wish to take up this journey, the one single reality which they can expect to encounter at every step along the way is, as we have seen, the reality of the gracious election of God as the basis, determination and goal of both God's self-determination as well as *all* that constitutes the reality external to God. What we have chronicled in our examination of Barth's dogmatic construction following his doctrine of election is the fact that everything that is, and everything that can be known about God and God's dealings with the reality outside the divine self, consists in its origin in and determination by the singular act of God's gracious eternal and spatio-temporal election of, and therefore revelation in and through, Jesus Christ, so much so that now truly substantive breadth and depth is added to Barth's thesis that:

> The election of grace is the eternal beginning of all the ways and works of God in Jesus Christ. In Jesus Christ God in His free grace determines Himself for sinful man and sinful man for Himself. He therefore takes upon Himself the rejection of man with all its consequences, and elects man to participation in His own glory.[123]

---

reconciliation was never written. In its place, and only as a fragment, Barth published one of the sections which would have constituted the whole chapter under the title "The Christian Life," and it deals with the baptism of the Holy Spirit and water baptism. We will not address this volume here, but there are passages there which reflect the continuing influence of election on his thought (see e.g. *C.D. IV,4*:6-7, 13-14, 17, 20-21, 29, 31-38, 54, 58-61, 65, 72-73, 81, 84-86, 89-90, 98-99, 128, 131-32, 134, 143, 150, 158-63, 203).

Thirteen years after Barth's death, an english translation of his unpublished lecture notes on the ethics of reconciliation appeared (see Bromiley, *Chr. Life*). The sections in this work took the form of (1) a special ethics under the rubric of reconciliation and (2) an exposition of the first three petitions in the Lord's Prayer. It also reflects the influence of election (see e.g. pp. 4, 6-7, 13, 19-22, 29-30, 70, 74-76, 95, 111-12, 124-25, 142-44, 149).

When these two works are added to the 1928-29 lectures on ethics given at the University of Münster (see Barth, *Ethics*, which deals not only with ethics as a component of dogmatics, but with ethics as the command of God the Creator, Reconciler *and Redeemer* as well), it becomes possible to gauge both the development and magnitude of Barth's ethical thinking, and obtain some concrete insight into what Barth may have said had the God he knew and loved allowed him to live long enough to complete the *C.D.*

[123]*C.D. II,2*:94.

Afterthought

It is evident that a formal and material inquiry into Barth's dogmatic theology is a most formidable task indeed, one which has frightened away many an otherwise energetic and well-intentioned seeker of theological insight. The road he himself has taken is one which few others have traveled in the history of Christian thought, and perhaps the reason why is that its length and breadth do not lend themselves to the faint of heart. If one attempts to enter the sphere of Barth's theology, it must be with the acknowledgement that it stands, in all its architectonic sophistication and penetrating insight, as a witness to the one true God who has revealed the divine self in the God-human Jesus Christ. And this means that when one inquires into Barth, one must do so with great humility, awe and respect, indeed with *fear and trembling*, not so much directed at Barth himself, but rather at the holiness, sovereignty and majesty of the Lord and Master to whom he sought to give witness. If, in reading and wrestling with Barth, one cannot and does not hear this witness to Jesus Christ, then one has not really read and wrestled with Barth, for he claimed nothing for himself and everything for him.

For this reason, one cannot remain in the school of Barth and at the same time do justice to the task of theological struggle and construction which is mandated to the Christian community. We must learn from Barth, but we must not repristinate either his own theological agenda or its formulation. Contemporary scholarship in Barth's theology is justified if it genuinely seeks to discover and expand upon the gains won by his work, and move onward to ever new and penetrating reflection for the sake of the mission of the Church in the present world situation.[1] There are yet many suggestive insights to be won from Barth's theology (as is the case with the formative theologians of the past), but

---

[1] One particularly fruitful area of advance in this regard can be seen in the development of Barth's insights and influences in North American and Third World liberation theologies (see e.g., J. Deotis Roberts, James Cone, Rosemary Radford Reuther, Jose Miguez-Bonino, Juan Luis Segunda, Alan Boesak, Charles Villa-Vicencio et al.). To a great extent, one can find in these theologies both a premium on the role of human subjectivity in theological construction as well as a constraining of that subjectivity born from an emphasis on the hermeneutics of socio-political liberation derived from the earthly ministry of Jesus Christ.

if such progress is to be successful, time must first be spent in the *C.D.* in order truly to hear and understand Barth himself. Whether Barth has anything to say to the present generation of theologians, and whether his program is endurable and suggestive for contemporary and future theological construction is finally answerable only after one has engaged the whole of Barth's theology. The magnitude and influence of his contribution preclude giving serious plausibility to any engagement with Barth which depends upon second-hand analysis and critique for its insights. One must struggle to understand Barth's theology on its own terms and within the bounds of its own infrastructure. Only then is it possible to press on to programmatic and methodological suggestions implicit in Barth's theology for present and future theological construction.[2]

It is in this spirit that the present investigation has been undertaken. Having come this far, it would be unnecessarily tautological to rehearse the argument. It is sufficient merely to state here that the essence of the contribution which this study seeks to make to Barth scholarship lies in its attempt to demonstrate that the structural and hermeneutical determinant in the *C.D.* is to be found not in Barth's doctrine of the Word of God or his doctrine of the person and work of Jesus Christ *per se*, but rather in the category of election, which precedes hermeneutically, and therefore formally and materially the seeming centrality of his view of revelation or his formulation of christology. If this contribution advances both the discussion of Barth's theology as well as the reconsideration of the significance of election for theological reflection and the life of faith in the Christian community, then the time spent in the school of Barth will have been profitable and worth all "the agony and the ecstasy."

---

[2]One contemporary scholar has even argued that Barth's theology is the only modern theology which has both preserved the integrity of Reformed theology at the same time that it has taken seriously the radically new intellectual and theological milieu resulting from the Enlightenment, and that as a result, Barth's theological program represents the only viable and consistent paradigm for contemporary "evangelical" theology (see Ramm, *After*).

Abbreviations

Complete information on the following sources may be found in the bibliography.

Adam	Karl Barth, *Christ and Adam: Man and Humanity In Romans 5.*
After	Bernard L. Ramm, *After Fundamentalism.*
Alpha	Robert W. Jenson, *Alpha and Omega: A Study in the Theology of Karl Barth.*
Anselm	Karl Barth, *Anselm: Fides Quaerens Intellectum Anselm's Proof of the Existence of God in the Context of His Theological Scheme.*
Barth	A.D.R. Polman, *Barth.*
C.D.	Karl Barth, *Church Dogmatics*, 4 vols.
C. & T.	Oscar Cullman, *Christ and Time.*
Changed	Donald K. McKim, ed., *How Karl Barth Changed My Mind.*
Chr. Doc.	Emil Brunner, *The Christian Doctrine of God.*
Christ.	Oscar Cullman, *The Christology of the New Testament.*
Christian.	Cornelius Van Til, *Christianity and Barthianism.*
Christol.	Ernst-Heinz Amberg, *Christologie und Dogmatik.*
Chr. Life	Karl Barth, *The Christian Life.*
Conflict	Gustaf Wingren, *Theology in Conflict.*
Credo	Karl Barth, *Credo: A Presentation of the Chief Problems of Dogmatics with Reference to the Apostles' Creed.*
Crisis	Peter Y. De Jong, ed., *Crisis in the Reformed Churches.*

Decree	Richard A. Muller, *Christ and the Decree: Christology and Predestination in Reformed Theology from Calvin to Perkins.*
Decrees	J.G. Riddell, "God's Eternal Decrees."
Determ.	Dan L. Deegan, "The Christological Determinant in Barth's Doctrine of Creation."
Div. Elec.	G.C. Berkouwer, *Divine Election.*
Doct.	Colin Gunton, "Karl Barth's Doctrine of Election as Part of His Doctrine of God."
Doctrine	Frank H. Woyke, "The Doctrine of Predestination in the Theology of Karl Barth."
Early	Thomas F. Torrance, *Karl Barth: An Introduction to His Early Theology, 1910-1931.*
El. & Pr.	Paul K. Jewett, *Election and Predestination.*
Election	H.H. Rowley, *The Biblical Doctrine of Election.*
Enc.	Emil Brunner, *The Divine-Human Encounter.*
Erwähl.	Pierre Maury, "Erwählung und Glaube."
Ethics	Karl Barth, *Ethics.*
Evang.	Karl Barth, *Evangelical Theology: An Introduction.*
Fate	Karl Barth, "Fate and Idea in Theology."
Form	George S. Hendry, "The Dogmatic Form of Barth's Theology."
Found.	Otto Weber, *Foundations of Dogmatics*, 2 vols.
Freedom	James Daane, *The Freedom of God: A Study of Election and Pulpit.*
G.G.	Karl Barth, "Gottes Gnadenwahl."

Abbreviations

Gemina	Heinrich Vogel, *"Praedestinatio Gemina*: Die Lehre von der Ewigen Gnadenwahl."
Glauben	Regin Prenter, "Glauben und Erkennen bei Karl Barth."
Hum.	Karl Barth, *The Humanity of God.*
Humanity	Stuart D. McLean, *Humanity in the Thought of Karl Barth.*
Intro.	Geoffrey W. Bromiley, *Introduction to the Theology of Karl Barth.*
Just.	Hans Küng, *Justification: The Doctrine of Karl Barth and a Catholic Reflection.*
KB	Henri Bouillard, *Karl Barth*, 3 vols.
K. Barth	David L. Mueller, *Karl Barth.*
Karl Barth	T.H.L. Parker, *Karl Barth.*
KB Christ.	Charles T. Waldrop, *Karl Barth's Christology: Its Basic Alexandrian Character.*
KB Doct.	William John Hausmann, *Karl Barth's Doctrine of Election.*
KB Elec.	Anthony C. Yu, "Karl Barth's Doctrine of Election."
KB & Evang.	Gregory G. Bolich, *Karl Barth & Evangelicalism.*
Kierk.	James Brown, *Kierkegaard, Heidegger, Buber and Barth.*
Kingdom	Jürgen Moltmann, *The Trinity and the Kingdom.*
Know.	Karl Barth, *The Knowledge of God and the Service of God According to the Teaching of the Reformation.*
Knowledge	Henri Bouillard, *The Knowledge of God.*
Legacy	Eberhard Jüngel, *Karl Barth, A Theological Legacy.*
Life	Eberhard Busch, *Karl Barth: His Life from Letters and*

Autobiographical Texts.

Man	Soon Kyung Park, "Man in Karl Barth's Doctrine of Election."
Message	Karl Barth, "The Proclamation of God's Free Grace."
Mind	Karl Barth, *How I Changed My Mind.*
Modernism	Cornelius Van Til, *The New Modernism: An Appraisal of the Theology of Barth and Brunner.*
Office	J.K.S. Reid, "The Office of Christ in Predestination."
One	Peter Toon and James D. Spiceland, ed., *One God in Trinity.*
Outline	Karl Barth, *Dogmatics in Outline.*
Perspect.	John Thompson, *Christ in Perspective: Christological Perspectives in the Theology of Karl Barth.*
Portrait	Georges Casalis, *Portrait of Karl Barth.*
Prädest.	Gerhard Gloege, "Zur Prädestinationslehre Karl Barths."
Preach.	Arnold B. Come, *An Introduction to Barth's "Dogmatics" for Preachers.*
Pred. & FW	David Basinger and Randall Basinger, eds., *Predestination and Free Will.*
Pred. & Ot.	Pierre Maury, *Predestination and Other Papers.*
Proslog.	M.J. Charlesworth, *Introduction to St. Anselm's Proslogion, by Anselm of Canterbury.*
Ref.	F.W. Camfield, *Reformation Old and New.*
Ref. Dog.	Heinrich Heppe, *Reformed Dogmatics.*
Report	Otto Weber, *Karl Barth's Church Dogmatics: An Introductory Report on Volumes I:1 to III:4.*
Review	George S. Hendry, Review of *Church Dogmatics.*

Abbreviations

Revision	Walter Sparn, "'Extra Internum'. Die christologische Revision der Prädestinationslehre in Karl Barths Erwählungslehre."
Romans	Karl Barth, *The Epistle to the Romans*.
Signif.	Fred H. Klooster, *The Significance of Barth's Theology. An Appraisal: With Special Reference to Election and Reconciliation*.
Sov.	Karl Barth, "The Souvereignty of God's Word and the Decision of Faith."
Spirit	Philip J. Rosato, *The Spirit as Lord: The Pneumatology of Karl Barth*.
Studies	S.W. Sykes, ed., *Karl Barth: Studies in His Theological Method*.
Theo. Elec.	Jakob Jocz, *A Theology of Election: Israel and the Church*.
Theo. KB	Hans Urs von Balthasar, *The Theology of Karl Barth*.
Theology	Herbert Hartwell, *The Theology of Karl Barth*.
Trinity	Eberhard Jüngel, *The Doctrine of the Trinity: God's Being is in Becoming*.
Triumph	G.C. Berkouwer, *The Triumph of Grace in the Theology of Karl Barth*.
Types	Hugh Ross Mackintosh, *Types of Modern Theology: Schleiermacher to Barth*.
Ult. Tri.	Charles S. Duthie, "Ultimate Triumph."
Univ.	Joseph D. Bettis, "Is Karl Barth a Universalist?"
Victor	Donald G. Bloesch, *Jesus is Victor! Karl Barth's Doctrine of Salvation*.
Word	Karl Barth, *The Word of God and the Word of Man*.
Zur Präd.	Eduard Buess, "Zur Prädestinationslehre Karl Barth."

Selected Bibliography

A. Primary Sources

Barth, Karl. *Anselm: Fides Quaerens Intellectum: Anselm's Proof of the Existence of God in the Context of his Theological Scheme.* Translated by Ian W. Robertson. London: SCM Press Ltd., 1960; reprint ed., Pittsburgh Reprint Series, No. 2. N.p.: The Pickwick Press, 1975. Ger: *Fides Quaerens Intellectum: Anselms Beweis der Existenz Gottes im Zusammenhang seines theologischen Programms.* Zweite Auflage. Zollikon: Evangelischer Verlag AG., 1958.

_____. "Christ and Adam: Man and Humanity in Romans 5." *Scottish Journal of Theology Occasional Papers* No. 5 (1956): 1-45. Translated by T.A. Smail. Ger: "Christus und Adam nach Röm. 5." *Theologische Studien* Heft 35 (1952): 5-55.

_____. *The Christian Life (Church Dogmatics IV,4: Lecture Fragments).* Translated from unpublished lectures by Geoffrey W. Bromiley. Grand Rapids: William B. Eerdmans Publishing Co., 1981.

_____. *Church Dogmatics.* Vol. I,1: *The Doctrine of the Word of God.* Edited by G.W. Bromiley and T.F. Torrance. Translated by G.W. Bromiley. 2nd ed. Edinburgh: T. & T. Clark, 1975. Ger: *Die Kirchliche Dogmatik.* Bd. I,1: *Die Lehre vom Wort Gottes. Prolegomena zur kirchlichen Dogmatik.* Siebente Auflage. Zollikon-Zurich: Evangelischer Verlag AG., 1955.

_____. *Church Dogmatics.* Vol. I,2: *The Doctrine of the Word of God.* Edited by G.W. Bromiley and T.F. Torrance. Translated by G.T. Thomson and Harold Knight. Edinburgh: T. & T. Clark, 1956. Ger: *Die Kirchliche Dogmatik.* Bd. I,2: *Die Lehre vom Wort Gottes. Prolegomena zur kirchlichen Dogmatik.* Vierte Auflage. Zollikon-Zurich: Evangelischer Verlag AG., 1948.

_____. *Church Dogmatics.* Vol, II,1: *The Doctrine of God.* Edited by G.W. Bromiley and T.F. Torrance. Translated by T.H.L. Parker, W.B. Johnston, Harold Knight, and J.L.M. Haire. Edinburgh: T. & T. Clark, 1957. Ger: *Die Kirchliche Dogmatik.* Bd. II,1: *Die Lehre von Gott.* Dritte Auflage. Zollikon-Zurich: Evangelischer Verlag AG., 1948.

_____. *Church Dogmatics*. Vol. II,2: *The Doctrine of God*. Edited by G.W. Bromiley and T.F. Torrance. Translated by G.W. Bromiley, J.C. Campbell, Iain Wilson, J. Strathearn McNab, Harold Knight, and R.A. Stewart. Edinburgh: T. & T. Clark, 1957. Ger: *Die Kirchliche Dogmatik*. Bd. II,2: *Die Lehre von Gott*. Dritte Auflage. Zollikon-Zurich: Evangelischer Verlag AG., 1948.

_____. *Church Dogmatics*. Vol. III,1: *The Doctrine of Creation*. Edited by G.W. Bromiley and T.F. Torrance. Translated by J.W. Edwards, O. Bussey, and Harold Knight. Edinburgh: T. & T. Clark, 1958. Ger: *Die Kirchliche Dogmatik*. Bd. III,1: *Die Lehre von der Schöpfung*. Zweite Auflage. Zollikon-Zurich: Evangelischer Verlag A.G., 1947.

_____. *Church Dogmatics*. Vol. III,2: *The Doctrine of Creation*. Edited by G.W. Bromiley and T.F. Torrance. Translated by Harold Knight, G.W. Bromiley, J.K.S. Reid, and R.H. Fuller. Edinburgh: T. & T. Clark, 1960. Ger: *Die Kirchliche Dogmatik*. Bd. III,2: *Die Lehre von der Schöpfung*. Zollikon-Zurich: Evangelischer Verlag AG., 1948.

_____. *Church Dogmatics*. Vol. III,3: *The Doctrine of Creation*. Edited by G.W. Bromiley and T.F. Torrance. Translated by G.W. Bromiley and R.J. Ehrlich. Edinburgh: T. & T. Clark, 1961. Ger: *Die Kirchliche Dogmatik*. Bd. III,3: *Die Lehre von der Schöpfung*. Zollikon-Zurich: Evangelischer Verlag AG., 1950.

_____. *Church Dogmatics*. Vol. III,4: *The Doctrine of Creation*. Edited by G.W. Bromiley and T.F. Torrance. Translated by A.T. Mackay, T.H.L. Parker, Harold Knight, Henry A. Kennedy, and John Marks. Edinburgh: T. & T. Clark, 1961. Ger: *Die Kirchliche Dogmatik*. Bd. III,4: *Die Lehre von der Schöpfung*. Zweite Auflage. Zollikon-Zurich: Evangelischer Verlag AG., 1957.

_____. *Church Dogmatics*. Vol. IV,1: *The Doctrine of Reconciliation*. Edited by G.W. Bromiley and T.F. Torrance. Translated by G.W. Bromiley. Edinburgh: T. & T. Clark, 1956. Ger: *Die Kirchliche Dogmatik*. Bd. IV,1: *Die Lehre von der Versöhnung*. Zollikon-Zurich: Evangelischer Verlag AG., 1953.

_____. *Church Dogmatics*. Vol. IV,2: *The Doctrine of Reconciliation*. Edited by G.W. Bromiley and T.F. Torrance. Translated by G.W. Bromiley. Edinburgh: T. & T. Clark, 1958. Ger: *Die Kirchliche Dogmatik*. Bd. IV,2: *Die Lehre von der Versöhnung*. Zollikon-Zurich: Evangelischer Verlag AG., 1955.

_____. *Church Dogmatics*. Vol. IV,3, First Half: *The Doctrine of Reconciliation*. Edited by G.W. Bromiley and T.F. Torrance. Translated by G.W. Bromiley. Edinburgh: T. & T. Clark, 1961. Ger: *Die Kirchliche Dogmatik*. Bd. IV,3, Erste Hälfte: *Die Lehre von der Versöhnung*. Zollikon-Zurich: Evangelischer Verlag AG., 1959.

_____. *Church Dogmatics*. Vol. IV,3, Second Half: *The Doctrine of Reconciliation*. Edited by G.W. Bromiley and T.F. Torrance. Translated by G.W. Bromiley. Edinburgh: T. & T. Clark, 1962. Ger: *Die Kirchliche Dogmatik*. Bd. IV,3, Zweite Hälfte. *Die Lehre von der Versöhnung*. Zollikon-Zurich: Evangel- ischer Verlag AG., 1959.

_____. *Church Dogmatics*. Vol. IV,4: *The Doctrine of Reconciliation*. [*The Christian Life. (Fragment) Baptism as the Foundation of the Christian Life*]. Edited by G.W. Bromiley and T.F. Torrance. Translated by G.W. Bromiley. Edinburgh: T. & T. Clark, 1969. Ger: *Die Kirchliche Dogmatik*. Bd. IV,4: *Die Lehre von der Versöhnung*. [*Das Christliche Leben. (Fragment) Die Taufe als Begründung des christlichen Lebens.*] Zurich: EVZ-Verlag, 1967.

_____. *Credo: A Presentation of the Chief Problems of Dogmatics with Reference to the Apostles' Creed*. Translated by J. Strathearn McNab. London: Hodder & Stoughton, 1936. Ger: *Credo: Die Hauptprobleme der Dogmatik dargestellt im Anschluss an das Apostolische Glaubensbekenntnis*. Zollikon-Zurich: Evangelischer Verlag A.G., 1948.

_____. *Dogmatics in Outline*. Translated by G.T. Thomson. London: Student Christian Movement Press, 1949; reprint ed., Harper Torchbook. New York: Harper & Row, 1959. Ger: *Dogmatik im Grundriss*. Zollikon-Zurich: Evangelischer Verlag A.G., 1947.

_____. *The Epistle to the Romans*. Translated from the Sixth Edition by Edwyn C. Hoskyns. London: Oxford University Press, 1933; reprint ed., New York: Oxford University Press paperback, 1968. Ger: *Der Römerbrief*. Sechster Auflage. München: Chr. Kaiser Verlag, 1933.

_____. *Ethics*. Edited by Dietrich Braun. Translated by Geoffrey W. Bromiley. New York: Seabury Press, 1981. Ger: *Ethik I (1928)*. Zurich: Theologischer Verlag, 1973, and *Ethik II (1928-29)*. Zurich: Theologischer Verlag, 1978.

_____. *Evangelical Theology: An Introduction*. Translated by Grover Foley. New York: Holt, Rinehart and Winston, 1963. Ger: *Einführung in die evangelische Theologie*. Zurich: EVZ Verlag, 1962; reprint ed., Siebenstern-Taschenbuch 110. München und Hamburg: Siebenstern Taschenbuch Verlag, 1968.

_____. "Fate and Idea in Theology" in *The Way of Theology in Karl Barth. Essays and Comments*. Edited by H. Martin Rumscheidt. Translated with an Introduction by Stephen W. Sykes. Princeton Theological Monograph Series. General Editor, Dikran Y. Hadidian. Allison Park: Pickwick Publications, 1966. Ger: "Schicksal und Idee in der Theology." *Zwischen den Zeiten* 7. Jahrgang (1929): 309-48.

_____. "Gottes Gnadenwahl." *Theologische Existenz Heute* Heft 47 (1936): 3-56.

_____. *How I Changed My Mind*. Introduction and Epilogue by John D. Godsey. Richmond: John Knox Press, 1966.

_____. "The Humanity of God" in *The Humanity of God*. Translated by John Newton Thomas. Richmond: John Knox Press, 1960. Ger: "Die Menschlichkeit Gottes." *Theologische Studien* Heft 48 (1956): 3-35.

_____. *The Knowledge of God and the Service of God According to the Teaching of the Reformation*. Translated by J.L.M. Haire and Ian Henderson. London: Hodder and Stoughton, 1938. Ger: *Gotteserkenntnis und Gottesdienst nach reformatorischer Lehre*. Zollikon: Verlag der Evangelischen Buchhandlung, 1938.

_____. "The Proclamation of God's Free Grace" in *God Here and Now*. Translated by Paul M. van Buren. New York and Evanston: Harper & Row, 1964. Ger: "Die Botschaft von der freien Gnade Gottes." *Kirche für die Welt* Heft 14 (1948): 5-35.

_____. "The Souvereignty of God's Word and the Decision of Faith" in *God Here and Now*. Translated by Paul M. van Buren. New York and Evanston: Harper & Row, 1964. Ger: "Die Souveränität des Wortes Gottes und die Entscheidung des Glaubens." *Theologische Studien* Heft 5 (1939): 3-22.

_____. *The Word of God and the Word of Man*. Translated by Douglas Horton. Forward by Douglas Horton. New York: Harper & Row, 1957; reprint ed., Gloucester, Mass.: Peter Smith, 1978. Ger: *Das Wort Gottes und die Theologie*. München: Chr. Kaiser Verlag, 1924.

B. Secondary Sources

Amberg, Ernst-Heinz. *Christologie und Dogmatik*. Gottingen: Vandenhoeck & Ruprecht, 1966.

Augustine, Aurelius. *Concerning the City of God Against the Pagans*. Translated by Henry Bettenson with Introduction by David Knowles. London: Penguin Books Ltd, 1972.

_____, "The Free Choice of the Will" in *The Fathers of the Church*. Edited by Bernard M. Peeples. Translated by Robert P. Russell. Washington D.C.: Catholic University of America Press, 1968. Volume 59.

_____. "Grace and Free Will" in *The Fathers of the Church*. Edited by Bernard M. Peeples. Translated by Robert P. Russell. Washington D.C.: Catholic University of America Press, 1968. Volume 59.

_____. "On the Gift of Perseverance" in *A Select Library of the Nicene and Post-Nicene Fathers of the Christian Church*. Volume V. Edited by Philip Schaff. New York: The Christian Literature Company, 1887; reprint ed., Grand Rapids: Wm. B. Eerdmans Publishing Company, 1971.

_____. "On Nature and Grace" in *A Select Library of the Nicene and Post-Nicene Fathers of the Christian Church*. Volume V. Edited by Philip Schaff. New York: The Christian Literature Company, 1887; reprint ed., Grand Rapids: Wm. B. Eerdmans Publishing Company, 1971.

_____. "On the Predestination of the Saints" in *A Select Library of the Nicene and Post-Nicene Fathers of the Christian Church*. Volume V. Edited by Philip Schaff. New York: The Christian Literature Company, 1887; reprint ed., Grand Rapids: Wm. B. Eerdmans Publishing Company, 1971.

Balthasar, Hans Urs von. *The Theology of Karl Barth*. Translated by John Drury. New York: Holt, Rinehart and Winston, 1971.

Basinger, David and Basinger, Randall, eds. *Predestination and Free Will*. Downers Grove: Inter-Varsity Press, 1986.

Battenhouse, Roy W., ed. *A Companion to the Study of St. Augustine*. London: Oxford University Press, 1955; reprint ed., Grand Rapids:

Baker Book House, 1979.

Bentley-Taylor, David. Augustine: *Wayward Genius*. London: Hodder and Stoughton, 1980; reprint ed., Grand Rapids: Baker Book House, 1981.

Berkouwer, G.C. *Divine Election*. Translated by Hugo Bekker. Grand Rapids: Wm. B. Eerdmans Publishing Co., 1960.

_____. *A Half Century of Theology*. Translated and Edited by Lewis B. Smedes. Grand Rapids: William B. Eerdmans Publishing Co., 1977.

_____. *The Triumph of Grace in the Theology of Karl Barth*. Translated by Harry R. Boer. Grand Rapids: Wm. B. Eerdmans Publishing Company, 1956.

Bettis, Joseph D. "Is Karl Barth a Universalist?" *Scottish Journal of Theology* 20 (December 1967):423-36

Bloesch, Donald G. *Jesus is Victor! Karl Barth's Doctrine of Salvation*. Nashville: Abingdon Press, 1976.

Bockmuehl, Klaus. *The Unreal God of Modern Theology. Bultmann, Barth, and the Theology of Atheism: A Call to Recovering the Truth of God's Reality*. Translated by Geoffrey W. Bromiley. Colorado Springs: Helmers & Howard, Publishers, Inc., 1988.

Boettner, Loraine. *The Reformed Doctrine of Predestination*. Philadelphia: Presbyterian and Reformed Publishing Co., 1932.

Bolich, Gregory G. *Karl Barth & Evangelicalism*. Downers Grove: InterVarsity Press, 1980.

Bouillard, Henri. *Karl Barth*. Vol. 1: *Genese et Evolution de La Theology Dialectique*; Vols. 2-3: *Parole de Dieu et Existence Humaine*. Paris: Aubier, 1957.

_____. *The Knowledge of God*. Translated by Samuel D. Femiano. New York: Herder and Herder, 1968.

Bromiley, Geoffrey W. *Introduction to the Theology of Karl Barth*. Grand Rapids: William B. Eerdmans Publishing Company, 1979.

Brown, James. *Subject and Object in Modern Theology*. New York: The Macmillan Company, 1955. Also published as *Kierkegaard, Heidegger,*

Selected Bibliography

Buber and Barth. New York: Collier Books, 1962.

Brunner, Emil. *The Christian Doctrine of God*. Translated by Olive Wyon. Philadelphia: The Westminster Press, 1950.

_____. *The Divine-Human Encounter*. Translated by Amandus W. Loos. Philadelphia: The Westminster Press, 1943; reprint ed. Westport, Conn.: Greenwood Press, 1980.

Buess, Eduard. "Zur Prädestinationslehre Karl Barth." *Theologische Studien* Heft 43 (1955): 5-64.

Busch, Eberhard. *Karl Barth: His Life from Letters and Autobiographical Texts*. Translated by John Bowden. Philadelphia: Fortress Press, 1976.

Calvin, John. *Concerning the Eternal Predestination of God*. Translated with an Introduction by J.K.S. Reid. London: James Clarke & Co. Ltd, 1961.

_____. *Institutes of the Christian Religion, 1536 Edition*. Translated and annotated by Ford Lewis Battles. Revised ed. Grand Rapids: Wm. B. Eerdmans Publishing Co., 1986.

_____. *Institutes of the Christian Religion (1559 edition)*. *The Library of Christian Classics*. Volumes XX and XXI. Edited by John T. McNeill. Translated by Ford Lewis Battles. Philadelphia: The Westminster Press, 1960.

Camfield, F.W. *Reformation Old and New*. London: Lutterworth Press, 1947.

Casalis, Georges. *Portrait of Karl Barth*. Translated by Robert McAfee Brown. Introduction by Robert McAfee Brown. Garden City: Doubleday & Company, Inc., 1963.

Charlesworth, M.J. Introduction to *St. Anselm's Proslogion*, by Anselm of Canterbury. London: Oxford University Press, 1965; reprint ed., N.p.: University of Notre Dame Press, 1979.

Clark, Gordon H. *Biblical Predestination*. Nutley, N.J.: Presbyterian and Reformed Publishing Co., 1969.

Come, Arnold B. *An Introduction to Barth's "Dogmatics" for Preachers*. Philadelphia: Westminster Press, 1963.

Cullman, Oscar. *Christ and Time: The Primitive Christian Conception of Time and History.* Translated by Floyd V. Filson. London: SCM Press Ltd., 1951.

_____. *The Christology of the New Testament.* Translated by Shirley C. Guthrie and Charles A.M. Hall. Revised Edition. Philadelphia: The Westminster Press, 1963.

Daane, James. *The Freedom of God: A Study of Election and Pulpit.* Grand Rapids: William B. Eerdmans Publishing Company, 1973.

Deegan, Dan L. "The Christological Determinant in Barth's Doctrine of Creation." *Scottish Journal of Theology* Vol. 14, No. 2 (June 1961): 119-35.

De Jong, Peter Y., ed. *Crisis in the Reformed Churches.* Grand Rapids: Reformed Fellowship, Inc., 1968.

Duke, James O. and Streetman, Robert F., eds. *Barth and Schleiermacher: Beyond the Impasse?* Philadelphia: Fortress Press, 1988.

Duthie, Charles S. "Ultimate Triumph." *Scottish Journal of Theology* Vol. 14, No. 2 (June 1961): 156-71.

Frei, Hans W. "The Doctrine of Revelation in the Thought of Karl Barth, 1909 to 1922: The Nature of Barth's Break with Liberalism." Ph.D. dissertation, Yale University, 1956.

Garrigou-Lagrange, Reginald. *Predestination.* Translated by Dom Bede Rose. St. Louis and London: B. Herder Book Co., 1953.

Gloege, Gerhard. "Zur Prädestinationslehre Karl Barths." *Kerygma und Dogma* 2. Yahrgang, Heft 3 (July 1956): 193-217; and 2. Jahrgang, Heft 4 (October 1956): 233-55.

Gunton, Colin. "Karl Barth's Doctrine of Election as Part of His Doctrine of God." *Journal of Theological Studies* XXV (October 1974):381-92.

Hamer, Jerome. *Karl Barth.* Translated by Dominic M. Maruca. Westminster: The Newman Press, 1962.

Hartwell, Herbert. *The Theology of Karl Barth.* London: Gerald Duckworth & Co. Ltd., 1964.

Selected Bibliography

Harvey, Van. *The Historian and the Believer*. New York: Macmillan Co., 1966.

Hausmann, William John. *Karl Barth's Doctrine of Election*. New York: Philosophical Library, 1969.

Hendry, George S. "The Dogmatic Form of Barth's Theology." *Theology Today* Vol. 13, No. 3 (October 1956): 300-14.

_____. Review of *Church Dogmatics*, Vol. II, Part 2 in *Theology Today* Vol. 15, No. 3 (October 1958): 396-404.

Heppe, Heinrich. *Reformed Dogmatics*. Translated by G.T. Thomson. Revised and Edited by Ernst Bizer. Foreword by Karl Barth. N.p.: n.p., 1950; reprint ed., Grand Rapids: Baker Book House, 1978.

Hoyle, R. Birch. *The Teaching of Karl Barth: An Exposition*. New York: Charles Scribner's Sons, 1930.

Jenson, Robert W. *Alpha and Omega: A Study in the Theology of Karl Barth*. New York: Thomas Nelson & Sons, 1963.

Jewett, Paul K. *Election and Predestination*. Grand Rapids: William B. Eerdmans Publishing Company, 1985.

Jocz, Jakob. *A Theology of Election: Israel and the Church*. Preface by F.D. Coggan. London: S.P.C.K., 1958.

Jüngel, Eberhard. *The Doctrine of the Trinity: God's Being is in Becoming*. Translator unnamed. Grand Rapids: William B. Eerdmans Publishing Co., 1976.

_____. *Karl Barth, A Theological Legacy*. Translated by Garrett E. Paul. Philadelphia: Westminster Press, 1986.

Kelsey, David. *The Uses of Scripture in Recent Theology*. Philadelphia: Fortress Press, 1975.

Klooster, Fred H. *Calvin's Doctrine of Predestination*. 2nd ed. Grand Rapids: Baker Book House, 1977.

_____. *The Significance of Barth's Theology. An Appraisal: With Special Reference to Election and Reconciliation*. Grand Rapids: Baker Book House, 1961.

241

Küng, Hans. *Justification: The Doctrine of Karl Barth and a Catholic Reflection*. Translated by Thomas Collins, Edmund E. Tolk, David Granskou, and Edward Quinn. Philadelphia: The Westminster Press, 1964.

Mackintosh, Hugh Ross. *Types of Modern Theology: Schleiermacher to Barth*. London: Nisbet and Co. Ltd., 1937.

Matczak, Sebastian A. *Karl Barth on God*. New York: St. Paul Publications, 1962.

Maury, Pierre. "Erwählung und Glaube." *Theologische Studien* Heft 8 (1940): 4-24.

_____. *Predestination and Other Papers*. Memoir by Robert C. Mackie. Foreword by Karl Barth. Translated by Edwin Hudson. London: SCM Press Ltd., 1960.

McGrath, Alister E. "Karl Barth als Aufklärer?" *Kerygma und Dogma* 30 (October-December 1984):273-83.

McKim, Donald K., ed. *How Karl Barth Changed My Mind*. Grand Rapids: William B. Eerdmans Publishing Co., 1986.

McLean, Stuart D. *Humanity in the Thought of Karl Barth*. Edinburgh: T. & T. Clark, 1981.

Moltmann, Jürgen. *The Trinity and the Kingdom*. Translated by Margeret Kohl. San Francisco: Harper & Row, Publishers, 1981.

Mueller, David L. *Karl Barth*. Waco: Word Books, 1972.

Muller, Richard A. *Christ and the Decree: Christology and Predestination in Reformed Theology from Calvin to Perkins*. Studies in Historical Theology 2, David C. Steinmetz, ed. Durham: The Labyrinth Press, 1986.

Niesel, Wilhelm. *The Theology of Calvin*. Translated by Harold Knight. London: Lutterworth Press, 1956; reprint ed., Grand Rapids: Baker Book House, 1980.

O'Grady, Colm. *The Church in Catholic Theology. Dialogue with Karl Barth*. Washington: Corpus Publications, 1969.

Selected Bibliography

Pannenberg, Wolfhart. *Human Nature, Election and History*. Philadelphia: The Westminster Press, 1977.

Park, Soon Kyung. "Man in Karl Barth's Doctrine of Election." Ph.D. dissertation, Drew University, 1966.

Parker, T.H.L. *Karl Barth*. Grand Rapids: William B. Eerdmans Publishing Company, 1970.

Polman, A.D.R. *Barth*. Translated by Calvin D. Freeman. Grand Rapids: Baker Book House, 1960.

Prenter, Regin. "Glauben und Erkennen bei Karl Barth." *Kerygma und Dogma* 2. Jahrgang, Heft 3 (July 1956): 176-92.

Ramm, Bernard L. *After Fundamentalism*. San Francisco: Harper & Row, 1983.

_____. *An Evangelical Christology: Ecumenic & Historic*. Nashville: Thomas Nelson Publishers, 1985.

Reagan, Charles E. and Stewart, David. *The Philosophy of Paul Ricoeur: An Anthology of His Work*. Boston: Beacon Press, 1978.

Reid, J.K.S. "The Office of Christ in Predestination." *Scottish Journal of Theology* Vol. 1, No. 1 (June 1948): 5-19; and Vol. 1, No. 2 (September 1948): 166-83.

Riddell, J.G. "God's Eternal Decrees." *Scottish Journal of Theology* Vol. 2, No. 4 (June 1949): 352-63.

Robinson, James M., ed. *The Beginnings of Dialectic Theology*, Vol. I. Richmond: John Knox Press, 1968.

Robinson, James M. and Cobb, Jr., John B., eds. *The New Hermeneutic*. New Frontiers in Theology, Vol. II. New York: Harper & Row, 1964.

Rosato, Philip J. *The Spirit as Lord: The Pneumatology of Karl Barth*. Edinburgh: T. & T. Clark, 1981.

Rowley, H.H. *The Biblical Doctrine of Election*. London: Lutterworth Press, 1950.

Runia, Klaas. *Karl Barth's Doctrine of Holy Scripture*. Grand Rapids: William B. Eerdmans Publishing Co., 1962.

243

Smart, James D. *The Divided Mind of Modern Theology: Karl Barth and Rudolf Bultmann 1908-33*. Philadelphia: Westminster Press, 1964.

Smart, James D., ed. *Revolutionary Theology in the Making: Barth-Thurneysen Correspondence, 1914-1925*. Richmond: John Knox Press, 1964.

Sparn, Walter. "'Extra Internum'. Die christologische Revision der Prädestinationslehre in Karl Barths Erwählungslehre." In *Die Realisierung der Freiheit*, pp. 44-75. Edited by Trutz Rendtorff. Gutersloh: Gutersloher Verlagshaus Gerd Mohn, 1975.

Sykes, S.W., ed. *Karl Barth: Studies in His Theological Method*. Oxford: Clarendon Press, 1979.

Thompson, John. *Christ in Perspective: Christological Perspectives in the Theology of Karl Barth*. Grand Rapids: William B. Eerdmans Publishing Company, 1978.

Toon, Peter and Spiceland, James D., eds. *One God in Trinity*. Westchester: Cornerstone Books, 1980.

Torrance, Thomas F. *Karl Barth: An Introduction to His Early Theology, 1910-1931*. London: SCM Press Ltd., 1962.

Van Til, Cornelius. *Christianity and Barthianism*. Philadelphia: Presbyterian and Reformed Publishing Company, 1962.

_____. *The New Modernism: An Appraisal of the Theology of Barth and Brunner*. 3rd ed. Philadelphia: Presbyterian and Reformed Publishing Company, 1972.

Villa-Vicencio, Charles, ed. *On Reading Karl Barth in South Africa*. Foreword by Allan Boesak. Grand Rapids: William B. Eerdmans Publishing Company, 1988.

Vogel, Heinrich. "Praedestinatio Gemina: Die Lehre von der Ewigen Gnadenwahl." In *Theologische Aufsätze*, pp. 222-42. Edited by E. Wolf. München: Chr. Kaiser Verlag, 1936.

Waldrop, Charles T. *Karl Barth's Christology: Its Basic Alexandrian Character*. Berlin: Mouton Publishers, 1984.

Weber, Otto. *Karl Barth's Church Dogmatics: An Introductory Report on*

Selected Bibliography

Volumes I:1 to III:4. Translated by Arthur C. Cochrane. Philadelphia: Westminster Press, 1953.

_____. *Foundations of Dogmatics.* 2 vols. Translated by Darrell L. Guder. Grand Rapids: William B. Eerdmans Publishing Co., 1981-83.

Weber, Otto; Kreck, Walter; and Wolf, Ernst. "Die Predigt von der Gnadenwahl." *Theologische Existenze Heute* Nr. 28 (May 1951): 3-94.

Welch, Claude. *In This Name. The Doctrine of the Trinity in Contemporary Theology.* New York: Charles Scribner's Sons, 1952.

Wingren, Gustaf. *Theology in Conflict.* Translated by Eric H. Wahlstrom. Philadelphia: Muhlenberg Press, 1958.

Woyke, Frank H. "The Doctrine of Predestination in the Theology of Karl Barth." Ph.D. dissertation, Yale University, 1952.

Yu, Anthony C. "Karl Barth's Doctrine of Election." *Foundations* XIII (July-September 1970):248-61.

About the Author

Douglas R. Sharp is Associate Professor of Christian Theology at Northern Baptist Theological Seminary in Lombard Illinois. A native of Colorado, Dr. Sharp took the B.A. degree from William Jewell College in Liberty Missouri, the M.Div. degree from the American Baptist Seminary of the West, and the Ph.D. from the Graduate Theological Union, both in Berkeley California. He is an ordained minister in the American Baptist Churches, U.S.A., and he and his wife Linda presently live in Downers Grove Illinois.

DATE DUE